Practitioner Series

Springer
London
Berlin
Heidelberg
New York
Barcelona
Budapest
Hong Kong
Milan
Paris
Santa Clara
Singapore
Tokyo

Other titles in this series:

The Politics of Usability
L. Trenner and J. Bawa
3-540-76181-0

Electronic Commerce and Business Communications
M. Chesher and R. Kaura
3-540-19930-6

Key Java
J. Hunt and A. McManus
3-540-76259-0

Distributed Applications Engineering
I. Wijegunaratne and G. Fernandez
3-540-76210-8
Publication due Autumn, 1998

Finance for IT Decision Makers
M. Blackstaff
3-540-76232-9
Publication due Autumn, 1998

Using Interface Design: Conceptual Modelling using ERMIA
D. Benyon, D. Bental and T. Green
1-85233-009-0
Publication due Autumn, 1998

Middleware
D. Serain
1-85233-011-2
Publication due Autumn, 1998

Ken Burnett

The Project Management Paradigm

With 118 figures

 Springer

Ken Burnett, BComm
8-2-2A Tivoli Villas
Jalan Medang Tanduk
Bukit Bandaraya
59100 Kuala Lumpur
Malaysia

HD
69
.P75
B873
1998

ISBN 3-540-76238-8 Springer-Verlag Berlin Heidelberg New York

British Library Cataloguing in Publication Data
Burnett, Ken
   The project management paradigm. - (Practitioner series)
   1.Industrial project management
   I.Title
   658.4'04
   ISBN 3540762388

Library of Congress Cataloging-in-Publication Data
Burnett, Ken,1930-
      The project management paradigm / Ken Burnett.
      p.cm. -- (Practitioner series)
      Includes index.
      ISBN 3-540-76238-8 (paperback : alk. paper)
      1. Industrial project management.I. Title.II. Series:
   Practitioner series (Springer-Verlag)
   HD69.P75B8731998
   658.4'04--dc21

© Springer-Verlag London Limited 1998
Printed in Great Britain

Typesetting: Ian Kingston Editorial Services, Nottingham
Printed and bound at the Athenæum Press Ltd, Gateshead, Tyne and Wear
34/3830-543210 Printed on acid-free paper

Dedication

To family, friends and colleagues, who gave continual encouragement. To Mr Sam Ho, Ms Julie Lavigne, Encik Afandi Hj Dollah and Professor Dato' Anuar, who practice and encourage loyalty, empowerment, team building and commitment to both the organization and the project.

To Encik Wan Mhd Saleh, Encik Akbar Yasin, Encik Rahmanudin Shamsudin and Encik Shabudin Md Saman, who helped me adapt to a multicultural environment.

To Mohamad Noor Hussain who follows the practices and principles in this book and has found them to be practical and useful in his capacity as a project manager.

Thanks also to Sandra Garrison, whose patience, love, support and commitment were essential.

Contents

Preface

Introduction

The changing business environment, of global operations, mergers, decentralization, increased competition, pressure on budgets etc., has contributed to a positive change in the workplace. As this change continues, we must keep up to date and follow good standards, principles and practices. To help, we present the 'Paradigm of Project Management', which is based on a simple practical approach to managing projects. The method is flexible and may be applied to any project, although in this book we concentrate on the development of systems. However, it also illustrates that the formation and management of project teams are changing in line with technology. As Dr Tom Peters says: 'Stability and predictability are gone forever...'. For example, project teams may work from home (telework), using email and groupware along 'electronic highways'. Therefore, instead of going through a pyramid of people to reach an executive, one can use the Internet, an intranet or an extranet and go direct. Another change is represented by the transient teams and Get-it-Done working approaches. An example of how a global project was managed is one in which Malaysia's International Shipping Corporation (MISC) implemented MISC*Net, a networking project to link online all of its shipping agents worldwide to its HQ in Malaysia. Project management was a key component in the solution prior to awarding the contract. IBM and MISC worked on the International Project Management System. Project specialists got feedback daily, and if a partner from the other side of the world did something, all that was required was to update the work status on one terminal for all to be aware of it being actioned.

Computer-based communication systems have brought project teams together in unprecedented ways, and McLuhan's global village is becoming more of a reality every day. Computer-mediated communication systems are being deployed widely and are having a significant impact upon geographically dispersed multicultural project teams.

The book is about project management and how projects should be managed and controlled, including people and tools. Its format consists of two major components. The first concentrates on principles and the human aspects of project management, because, as stated by Dr Nik Mohammad Zain Haj Omar[1] 'Good Management would comprise having a team of dedicated

---

1 *New Straits Times - Management Times*, 22 September 1995

and able employees who can work together in achieving the company's goals'. The second component of the book specifies a structured, practical, formal process to managing projects and ensuring their success. A *project*, according to the *Oxford Advanced Learning Dictionary*, means a plan for a scheme or undertaking a course of action; while *management* means control and organization. Hence project management refers to the organization of a course of action, or in short *to manage a project*.

The principles and approaches in this book lend themselves to project managing the paradigm of technological, management, and organizational changes. To use the methodology effectively, it is necessary first to understand and appreciate the aspects of the people behind a project, such as their multicultural diversities and the roles and responsibilities of each project player. Combining human aspects and methodological principles is the basic purpose throughout this book; and our objective is to disseminate a better understanding of a project management methodology and illustrate its universality.

Who Should be Reading this Book?

All individuals involved in the management, delivery and acceptance of projects should read this book. It can add another dimension to any formal project management methodology that an organization might already have adopted. Large organizations tend to have sophisticated methodologies that may be intimidating to an inexperienced user. Following this book may assist a junior project member to understand some ideas and principles that may not be clear in a multi-volume, formal, sophisticated process. Smaller organizations may not even have a methodology, in which case the ideas, principles and guidelines in this book could be followed. Practitioners will find the book useful by providing the basic information for implementing a project management methodology in an organization.

Too often staff are promoted to greater responsibility on a 'sink or swim' basis. Although this book cannot make experienced project managers out of inexperienced ones, it does provide explicit instructions for using some simple tools that enable a project manager to deal with executives, managers, peers, clients, users and project team members. Collectively these people impose innumerable constraints on the project manager.

Development projects considered to be mostly technical are generally approached with a set of technical solutions. Experience has shown, however, that overall success requires much more than merely a technical solution. Therefore, applying good management principles is necessary to all aspects of project deliverables. A project management process is therefore necessary and is independent of the tools used for systems analysis, design and development. Any approach must not, however, be followed blindly.

As the approach to project management is changing, as the great philosopher Spinoza said: 'One should learn to collaborate with the inevitable'. There is a new technological paradigm changing the world of work that is so fundamental that it cannot be stopped and is therefore inevitable. It is embracing technology and affecting the way in which work is being conducted, causing the road ahead to be full of twists and turns and rapid change. Therefore it is crucial that project managers realize that to manage projects successfully it is necessary to follow standards and maximize communication among the members of their project team. Managers will be managing project teams under different organizational and technical environments. More attention will need to be focused on planning, education and training, and team empowerment. Empowerment means allowing teams to work directly with users, attacking a problem that has been defined; allowing them to make decisions quickly; and implementing the decision without having to seek approval from a higher authority. Of course, these actions are done within prescribed policies and procedures.

The Get-it-Done school of thought is not going to be paralyzed by a methodology. However, coupled with this approach is the fact that people may also work as a transient team. Although they may work in a very dynamic environment, the principles in this book are still valid. What may not be valid is the completion of all of the paper forms that a methodology may require. The team may be simply empowered to solve a certain problem, so the problem is put on a whiteboard (or someone may sit at a terminal), and as the ideas flow the problem is solved iteratively. This does not need a formal project management methodology. However, the project manager who understands the principles in this book may well do a better job than the one who uses a seat-of-the-pants approach.

In the new environment we will see the end of the autocratic manager, who will be replaced by one who is more in tune with managing diversity in people and flexibility in the work process. Gone are the days when one worked between 7:00 a.m. and 6:00 p.m. daily. With the arrival of teleworking and flexible hours, the approach to managing project teams will need to change.

It is immaterial whether the project is managed or coordinated by a professional project manager, a user or a subject matter specialist. One does not have to be a computer specialist to follow the principles promoted. Therefore this book is of interest to a cross-section of readers, including:

- General readers who would like to obtain an appreciation of what is happening in the area of project management and how projects are managed.
- Line and staff management who have an interest in or need to understand the principles and functions behind successful project management.
- Project monitors, coordinators and users who have an interest in knowing what activities should be going on during a project life cycle.
- Subject matter specialists (specialists in a field of expertise) or technical staff given a 'sink or swim' project to manage.
- Educators, who should ensure that they teach a methodology before giving instruction in tools that serve to complement a methodology.

- Students who are taking courses in business, computer science or engineering.

Managers are realizing that speed in producing something by itself in the development process is not always desirable and that using a formal structured process provides long-term benefits. Time to pause, reflect and decide a strategy can be more important than speed. Although the complex legacy systems of the past are still required, whether they are on a personal computer, server or mainframe, they should all be developed using a methodology. To decide how to approach a task, methodologies can be checklists used to decide consciously what components are to be followed and those that are to be rejected or modified to suit one's own environment.

Editorial note

Wherever possible, words with a sexist connotation have been avoided. Rather than make sentences clumsy, wherever 'he', 'his', 'she', 'her' etc. appears alone you should assume that the word means 'he or she', 'his or her' etc.

The author is a self-reliant working, international, management consultant and project manager well versed in the informatics profession. This practical book will be a valuable tool in successful project management and consequently the production of quality deliverables.

Acknowledgments

Sincere thanks go to many individuals for their stimulating and fresh viewpoints. However, this book would not have been started were it not for Dr B. Welland of the University of Glasgow, who recognized the value of practical books. It has been completed with the support of the publisher and its reviewers, who supplied constructive criticism and provocative comments. Thanks go also to Mike Howe, who taught me a practical methodology and sparked my initial interest; Jon Pearkins and Guy Boyd who were always available for input; and Julie Lavigne, Clive Burnett, Bill Taggart, Rick Morris, Roger Burlton, Bill Maddison, and Peter Wheaton, who contributed ideas and material and have used many of the principles in their extensive management and consulting activities. Many thanks go to my Malaysian colleagues, with whom I have worked with for many years. They showed their willingness to adopt a methodology, but only in the context of how they function harmoniously.

Many times this book was close to being abandoned, but tenacity and the encouragement of colleagues prevailed. It is hoped that the effort will provide readers, as it continues to do for the author, with a handy reference checklist when a proposal has to be written or a project undertaken.

1. The Philosophy of Project Management

1.1 Introduction

Project management continues to grow and improve as an area of professionalism. We are now seeing a resurgence of methodologies applied to the management of projects. This applies to a range of professions, such as construction, engineering and informatics. As technology changes we see a continuing growth in the need for professional project managers in such areas as managing application systems development, software development, multidimensional databases, logical and physical design of local and wide area networks, multimedia, office automation, systems, generic office and common operating environments, integration and re-engineering the workflow of an office. This latter type of project is similar to paperwork simplification, which was popular before the proliferation of computers but is now a requisite for document image-processing systems and workflow analysis. The paradigm is that, whereas in the past project teams were captive audiences, this is no longer the case. Project managers must now manage in a variety of ways.

1.2 Components of a Project Environment

Implementing the quality management processes and methodologies outlined in this practical book is a management challenge. Many managers fail to recognize that applying and following a methodology is important to success. In the rush to get something done, standards are often ignored in order to meet impossible deadlines. Inexperience leads to seat-of-the-pants management and disregarding tried and proven methods. Emphasis is therefore placed in this book on the fact that the process, if followed, is performed to accomplish desired results.

All too often technical staff, consultants and subject matter specialists do things their own way without consideration of standards etc. The results can be disastrous. Managers must take some blame for this when it happens, as they invariably believe that action is progress.

Also often overlooked by management is the resistance to change. Management, before a project is initiated, should ensure that the system to be developed has the support of line management. When change fails, it is invariably not because of lack of effort but because of a lack of understanding. Project managers should always be on

1

their guard against resistance and, when detected, should measure its strength. Thus an essential component in being successful is in understanding the mind-set, i.e. the way employees think and act about a change. This resistance may be observed at any point of the systems development life cycle. Developing a new system or changing an existing one implies positive change to the environment in which it is to be implemented. It is wrong to think that it is always welcome. Some of the strongest resistance in making changes may come in response to 'positive' changes – the ones everybody said they wanted, i.e. their mind-set is not conducive to change. Managers complain about major positive change because they fear losing control and are comfortable with the *status quo*. In fact, it is a common complaint of managers that staff gives negative responses to change. The reality is that reorganizing, re-engineering and total quality management (TQM) do not fully deliver the promised results.

Managers, before starting a project, should appreciate that people and, by extension, organizations, can only take so much change. Therefore it is essential to ensure that any change proposed is imperative, else people could be overwhelmed, even if the changes are all positive. Thus it is imperative to ensure that there is a change-positive climate, i.e. the environment must be conducive to change. Beware, though, that even the changes that take off can wane after the publicity has subsided.

For illustrative purposes, to decide how much change can be assimilated imagine that each person has a number x of assimilation points to use in absorbing change over a one-year period. There are three types of change that make simultaneous demands on those points, namely: macro (political for example); organizational; and micro (ones close to home, such as a new baby or divorce). As changes are assimilated, decrement the number of points assigned each time until there are no more points left or very few are available. At this point any additional change(s) could be considered risky and no more should be contemplated unless a risk factor is measured.

Micro changes use up most points. This is not because managers are not concerned with macro changes (e.g. war), but because these cannot be stopped. Micro changes, on the other hand, are generally manageable. You get to work to find that the boss has reorganized and your power base has gone. You come home and find the children in trouble or that incompatible individuals have moved into the house for a prolonged stay. These have an immediate effect, but can be managed.

Poor planning, ignorance of how people change or inept communication use up these assimilation points needlessly. On the other hand, helping employees to prepare for change by anticipating why they might resist and by planning the best way to deal with the resistance will use up fewer points and the organization will be less likely to face change overload. As a result the change is more likely to be successful. Furthermore, to encourage a change-positive attitude among employees management should consider *preparing a reason for the change*. For example, suppose that a company wants to implement a data warehouse primarily for marketing; it could be illustrated that having such a tool available would help the company in its marketing efforts to get an edge over the competition. The change would improve customer service, increase profits and consequently allow the company to pay salary increases or a bonus. These reasons could be compelling enough to smooth introduction of the change and motivate employees to accept it, even if a comfortable *status quo* is affected. Other considerations could be the use of credible leaders in selling or managing the change. Of course, empowerment of the staff in implementing the change can be a key factor in its success. In this case employees should be encouraged to act as a cohesive team in making collective on-the-spot decisions without getting the approval of management. This collective responsibility allows the team to be accountable for the outcome and allows the project manager to measure commitment.

A project manager who detects resistance to change should consider using a situation analysis methodology (SAM) such as that outlined in Appendix A at the end of this chapter. This will help resolve a resistant situation or at least lead to the conclusion that implementation of the change is inappropriate. The three-part methodology illustrated covers examination, evaluation and action. Preventing resistance to change by getting the players to buy into it up-front is better than having to take corrective action after the resistance has been detected. If corrective action is necessary, it is usually because the problem is visible, and the project manager may be seen as having failed or not being suitable for the job. Therefore, whenever confronted with resistance, immediately put into action the SAM methodology to *examine*, *evaluate* and *act*.

Although the methodology concerns resistance to change, the reader may find it useful to review the action component to ensure success in implementing change. If we accept that the results of a project can be assimilated and implemented satisfactorily, it is important to create a project environment that is conducive to ensuring success. That is, we should ensure that the project resistance has been minimized or subdued. To do this, follow the underlying philosophy and approach to project management by understanding the whys and hows of a project management methodology, a systems development life cycle and quality management. Furthermore, by focusing on gradual implementation, i.e. taking one step at a time, it is possible to bring about change in a positive way.

In any systems project environment, there are four components (systems development, project management, quality management and resource management) that should be kept distinct. These are summarized below.

1.2.1 Systems Development

The project manager is responsible for managing systems development using a Project Management Methodology based upon principles that follow traditional guidelines, in a disciplined order, resulting in a set of deliverables. The manager also follows a Systems Development Life Cycle (SDLC); see Fig. 1.1.

There are numerous other models, but the events that need to be managed are basically the same, albeit with different names; for example: Initiation, Feasibility (Concept Definition); Analysis; Design; Development; Acceptance Testing; and Conversion and Implementation, i.e. the end of the project. After implementation, support (maintenance) would either be provided as an ongoing function by an in-house operations unit or would be outsourced.

A post-implementation review (new project) is done after a period of operations to verify that the original product meets or exceeds original specifications. The

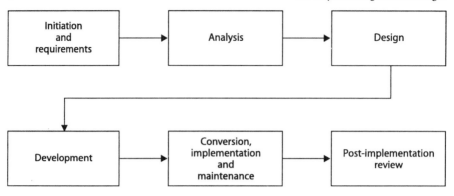

Fig. 1.1 Systems development life-cycle.

original project manager is not normally assigned this project as the manager's report might be biased.

Other systems development life cycle models can be related to specific CASE (computer-aided systems engineering) tools or a prototyping methodology. The different models may use an iterative approach with prototyping rather than a linear approach, but they all cover events that need to be managed. It is one of the functions of the project manager to determine what approach is best and to manage accordingly. For example, in a new system data may not need to be converted from a previous one, such as in a financial system that is to be installed at the beginning of a new year. It may be decided that all old data will be archived and the new system will start from scratch. Therefore, the project manager would not plan conversion as something to be completed.

1.2.2 Project Management Methodology (PMM)

The tools and techniques of a PMM, if used, encourage the monitoring of project team members' personal commitments and their responsibilities through all the phases of a project, i.e. from initial project identification to project completion. In this book's methodology we cover project identification and its planning, control and completion. It will also be realized that quality management supports the SDLC and must be part of any project plan. The methodology therefore supports all phases of the systems development life cycle (SDLC).

1.2.3 Quality Management (QM)

Project managers must realize the importance of QM. It is useless having a project management methodology and a systems development life cycle in place without giving some thought to the quality of their deliverables. Project managers should ensure that time and resources are assigned to this function. Quality management can be defined as a program of planned and systematic activities to determine, achieve and maintain required deliverable quality, or, as in ISO 8402: 'Quality is defined as the Quality characteristics of an entity that bear on its **ability** to **satisfy** an implied need'. What is needed therefore is 'Conformance to requirements'. Project managers in innumerable instances give quality a low priority or even overlook it within the development process.

1.2.4 Resource Management (RM)

A fourth component is resource management. Functions in this discipline deal with skilled resource planning and scheduling, cost accounting and performance measurement. Finance, for example, is responsible for ensuring that costs are recorded correctly, that they are compared with budgets and that the information is fed back to the project manager promptly.

Many of a project manager's difficulties can be attributed to a careless mixing of the above components. Therefore our project management methodology concentrates on the personal commitment to delivering a quality product, while clearly defining the nature of interfaces with the other components. Undoubtedly managing the components is difficult, but it is necessary and must be done in an integrated fashion.

1.3 Project Management

Most organizations experience difficulties managing projects, but following a good project management methodology would help alleviate many of these without encumbering the project manager's flexibility. The methodology is a process independent of any automated (computer-aided systems engineering) or manual tools used for analysis, design and development. It rests on a set of management principles applicable to all sizes and types of systems projects in any context.

Complementary to the use of a methodology is the appointment of a skilled and competent project manager, an important individual who is essential to the success of any project. To keep good project managers, executives in an organization cannot leave the entrepreneurship ways of their project managers to the stifling hierarchies of their autocratic or stale managers. If it is perceived that a line manager's performance has atrophied, or that the manager is burnt out (as evidenced by an impression that he or she is too bureaucratic and only interested in the process), then this manager is unlikely to be a good supervisor or client. A project manager wanting to achieve quality deliverables on time and within budget could be constrained by working for such a person.

Traditionally, project management has been assisted by a set of technical tools, such as PERT or CPM. These are not project management methodologies, but are excellent planning, control and scheduling tools to assist a manager. However, in researching such project management tools it is important to determine whether an industry-specific (e.g. construction) or general tool is appropriate. Research and experience have shown, however, that the problem is less of a technical nature than one of human nature. That is, the tools are available, but project managers must manage team members appropriately through the consultation process and empower them to make decisions regarding their tasks.

When considering the use of tools, such aspects as whether the plan will be event- or activity-driven must be understood. Generally an executive would only need to be concerned with the completion of an event. A project manager, however, needs to be concerned with the completion of activities. Many project managers have lost the idea that PERT is event-driven and CPM activity- (task-) driven, and the two are now considered by many as synonymous. The reader who explores them more fully will come to understand that there is a difference. If events and activities are used as intended, they can help improve the planning of projects. The reader who is interested may obtain publications and other information from the following:

- Diploma in Project Management, a professional qualification issued by the British Computer Society (BCS). For information point your Web browser at the URL `http://www.bcs.org.uk/`.
- Boston University Center for Project Management, 72 Tyng Road, Boston, Massachusetts 01879, USA. Membership includes access to research studies and *CPM Bulletin*, the centre's newsletter. It also runs a Certificate Program in Project Management.
- Center for Project Management, 1 Annabel Lane, San Ramon, California 94583, USA. Publishes a quarterly newsletter that includes interviews and articles from leaders in the project management field.
- Project Management Consortium. Sponsored by the Center for Project Management. This is an industry-wide effort to share and refine a professional knowledge base. International memberships are available.
- Project Management Institute. A professional organization dedicated to raising the level of excellence in project management.

A sound Project Management Methodology helps to solve the human problems that occur in any project and results in project team members:

- understanding their roles in the project;
- being motivated and willing to accept personal commitments; and
- knowing how to delegate effectively and how to share responsibility when appropriate.

The way in which a project team is managed will reflect the values of the project manager and establish the attitudes of the team. The manager's attitude is probably also that of the company's management. Therefore, if the attitude is one of arrogance, autocracy, *laisser-faire* or similar negative traits, this will permeate throughout the team. However, assuming you have selected a competent, experienced manager, to ensure that the team provides good service the manager must introduce empowerment and welcome new ideas and constructive criticism in order to obtain quality of work and loyalty from them. The manager must therefore lead by example. With a positive approach the team will learn to care and reinforce their commitment to the project. The reverse of allowing new ideas is to wrench the maximum effort from the team for the least amount of reward. This approach will ensure that the project manager is repaid in kind, i.e. team players will do exactly as told: no more and no less. Thus that intangible quality 'leadership' is mandatory in good project managers. General Eisenhower demonstrated leadership with a piece of string. By laying it on a flat surface he illustrated that by gently pulling it it would follow wherever you wished. On the other hand, if you pushed it it would not go anywhere. The principle is that people must want to follow and cannot be forced. While on the subject of 'leadership' we will explore this in a little more detail.

The everyday use of the term 'leadership' supports the fact that humans at work or at play are successful leaders to the degree in which they are effective in influencing the thoughts and actions of others.

1.3.1 Leadership

We can define a leader as one who has followers. Therefore we are all leaders, because we exert influence over our friends, families and colleagues. Exceptions of course are hermits or sole survivors, who have no followers or dependants. Leadership can be considered a key quality that every manager needs; combined with good project management skills it will go a long way in ensuring success. We mention the need for project managers to function in a borderless environment where a captive project staff does not exist. We have a better-educated workforce – to get things done from these *individuals* following the principles in this book will be invaluable.

We can conclude that leadership influences the thought process of people and stimulates their actions. There is no one leadership style that will suit all situations; teamwork and participative management are replacing the 'personality theory' of leadership. However, we must not lose sight of the fact that through participation we could lose some positive traits, such as imagination, creativity, innovation and vision. Much has been written about leadership styles, and it is in the reader's interest to understand the subject fully.

Four types of leadership and their characteristics are summarized in Table 1.1. Thus readers should determine what their position is, study their own style to see if they fit the model, and, if not, decide whether they should change. It is also suggested that, as jobs change, the incumbent changes his or her style.

1.3.2 Other Aspects of Project Management

Some other positive aspects of good project management are to:

- allow team members to follow their intuitions. With proper planning and control a failure will be noticed before it becomes a disaster.
- realize that it is not necessary to wait for perfect information. As soon as information is available it is usually dated. Decisiveness is a necessity. Liken a project to a river: it will always keep running, and urgency is important if one does not want to be a casualty of the rapids.
- understand the importance of keeping things simple. Generally it is said that committees usually provide needless complexity, and this has been accepted as a truism. Remember the cliché: 'search the parks and you will see plenty of statues to leaders and not one of a committee'. The author does not subscribe

Table 1.1 Reponsibility profile matrix

	Manager – executive	Middle management
Responsibilities	Defines strategic plans (goals) and organizes to achieve the goals	Coaches by motivating and rewarding staff
Focus	Endeavours to be cost-effective with the best mix of staff, machines, material and money	Tries to motivate staff and minimizes issues so that they can concentrate on the job at hand
Motivation	Stability and maturity in the organization, i.e. fail-safe systems, standards, policies and procedures	Driven by a need for motivated staff who work as a team
Environment	Creates an environment where the risk is low and predictable	Creates conditions for staff that satisfy his or her motivation
Approach	Influenced by past experiences and attitude, e.g. conservative would say 'we've always done it this way' or ' we've never done this before'	Approaches task with a 'Let's get it done now' approach in order to meet goals.
Action affects	Follows bureaucratic style, perhaps following a 'paralysis by analysis' approach. May also implement unnecessary rules and paperwork	Under pressure may not delegate
Statement	Let's work smarter not harder	Let's get things done together
Orientation	Holistic view	Outward-looking to produce deliverables according to predetermined levels
Values	Conformity, procedures, accountability and harmony.	A loyal staff who work as a team
Proactive/reactive	Proactive and reactive as appropriate. Mind-set may be complacency.	Reactive is a continuous achiever and inspires employees.

	Entrepreneur	Technical
Responsibilities	Provides a vision of the future	Leads by example, which is based upon experience
Focus	Opportunities	Applies energies to work
Motivation	Driven by ideas and change.	Empowerment so that talent can be applied
Environment	Likes high risk and challenge	Job satisfaction and control of own destiny
Schedule	Immediate exploration of ideas. Future is moulded by the imperfect present	Get the job done and stop dreaming
Action affects	Threatens stability of others	Becomes an indispensable employee
Statement	Get the right things done	Do it yourself because you cannot rely on others

Table 1.1 *(continued)*

	Entrepreneur	Technical
Orientation	Focused on client satisfaction and satisfying their needs	Looks to self as supplying the capability for success
Values	Self-realization and striving for change	Personal ability and individuality
Proactive/reactive	Proactive	Active

wholeheartedly to this. With a leader who is also a senior executive in charge of a committee, concepts can be sold to management much more easily than by a sole project manager. The project review committee mentioned in this book goes a long way towards ensuring a project's success. In fact, why not view a project team as a working committee, led by the project manager?

1.4 A Project

Project management methodologies differ from systems development methodologies, which identify *what* has to be done and the relationship of the required skilled tasks. This book's practical project management methodology emphasizes the importance of people, i.e. *who is concerned* and *who should be concerned* about what does and does not get done. It does this by emphasizing a clear understanding of the roles and responsibilities of all project players, and also by providing project managers with explicit instructions for using the simple tools provided to deal with their managers, the clients (users) and the project team. Quality management is an integral part of all three components mentioned earlier. This aspect reassures everyone involved that deliverables meet specifications.

What constitutes a project? A project is defined as the process of an individual delivering to a second person a product that satisfies the needs of that second person. Whenever anyone says 'Will *you* do *this* for *me*?' and it is accepted, a project is created and a contract formed. Projects come in all sizes and shapes. For example: getting people to the Moon was a large project with hundreds of sub-projects; to change the wheel on a car is a small self-contained project. System development, system maintenance and system enhancements are all projects. Therefore the principles of a project management methodology, coupled with an SDLC, resource management and quality management, apply to all of them.

Project management is the process that deals with elements of the unknown and uses the personal commitment of project team members to ensure the project is successfully terminated when agreed upon objectives have been met. Simply put, it is the process of administering a project, from its initiation through to its completion, by offering and soliciting personal commitments. These personal commitments are both the driving force and the controlling component of all project work. Therefore an essential element in successful project management is maintenance of each responsible individual's feeling of commitment towards the project.

1.5 Summary

In summary, the prescribed philosophy of project management methodology is a process that includes leadership used to gain the involvement and the commitment of individuals to the tasks required in completing a deliverable or producing a product for a client. During the process, of course, it is also essential to complete tasks that make up a quality deliverable, i.e. an event. The result from following the process is that activities are managed at the correct time, within the project cycle and budget. The emphasis here is not of a technical nature but on the human element. Everyone must embrace the principles if they want to achieve success in team arrangements. Evangelical as this may sound it is a truism.

Another important aspect mentioned is change. We live in an era in which radical, fast and constant changes are taking place. Project managers must change and be able to cope with the paradigm change for project management, which includes globalization, client satisfaction, educated employees, informed staff and clients, and a global outlook. One of the laments of corporate leaders is the negative response to change. As explained, change must be managed, but too much change can be negative. Therefore it is important to understand how, if a situation (real or perceived) were to occur that might be detrimental to a successful project, a situation analysis should be undertaken. It has been pointed out that personnel issues are generally more difficult to resolve than deciding technical issues such as whether to buy a single or multi-processor client–server system or to upgrade software. The next chapter deals with the organization of projects and the characteristics of individuals involved in meeting requirements.

Appendix A: Situation Analysis Methodology (SAM)

Here we cover a practical situation analysis methodology (examination, evaluation and action) that can be used as a guide if it is perceived that there is resistance to change.

A.1 Examination

In an examination it is necessary to conduct a minimum of five steps, as follows:

1 *Understand the situation.* Under this point write out the situation in as precise a way as possible. For example, if you are to migrate from one email system to another more functional one, and you personally do not think that it will be easy to get the cooperation of regional managers, record the pertinent points.

2 *It should be decided how the situation was determined.* For example, it might be that while a manager was at a coffee or tea break individuals were talking about the inappropriateness of implementing a certain change because in their opinion it was too complex.

3 *If the situation is not corrected, the impact should be described.* For example, if the change in item 1 is perceived as too expensive or the result would not be accepted by the majority of managers, say so.

4 *Ask oneself whether the concern is serious and what its priority for resolution should be.* If significant time, effort and money are about to be expended, then specify 'Critical'. This may be particularly true if there are no back-out procedures, i.e. once the change has been started there is no way to stop it.

5 *A timetable should be decided upon as to the latest date any corrective action can be completed.* If contracts are ready to be signed then there is minimal time. If there is significant time available before the decision has to be made to start the project then there is time to do more analysis.

A.2 Evaluation

To evaluate the situation, real or perceived, properly, complete the following seven steps:

1 *Collect the facts.* These are sometimes difficult to obtain. Besides the project manager's own experience, call on that of the parties who will be involved in the change. The pride of managers and any individual involved in the change will often allow them to provide information (which under normal conditions might be difficult to obtain) to prevent a potential failure.

2 *Determine the source of the facts (rumours).* If the change is a corporate initiative and is (say) to be implemented on a region-by-region basis, it may be observed that nobody has asked to participate voluntarily. Thus it might be concluded that, since nobody has asked any questions or shown any interest whatsoever, the change would not be welcome. This conclusion might be reinforced by the fact that resentment has always been obvious for corporate initiatives.

3 *Consider whether the facts are factual or hearsay.* This will need investigation. A trip to regional offices to put managers on the spot is a way to elicit support, learn that there is no support for the change or determine that there is actually no resistance to the change.

4 *When determining whether the facts are real or not, analyze what created the situation.* Some pointers to look for are: arrogance of central managers; using a generic solution without modification that has worked in a different environment; lack of communication to the front line people; and the diversity of the environment, which might make a single standard inappropriate.

5 *It is important to know whose negative attitudes or opinions must be changed to obtain positive support for the change.* Looking to the creators of the situation in item 2 could make a start.

6 *What is the mind-set of the individual(s) involved?* It could be that the individuals involved are happy with the *status quo* and do not want to improve the situation because the *status quo* is satisfactory.

7 *You must decide how it will be known that the problem has been solved.* This will be known when acceptors have signed off on the project and managers are happy.

Consider suggesting a six-month pilot, or limited implementation, to give the managers a chance to try the new approach without full commitment.

A.3 Action

It is important having examined and evaluated the situation that some form of action be planned. The following six steps will help to conclude successfully the problem.

1 *Relate the key individuals to the main issues.* If regional managers do not see the need for the change, a way must be found to persuade them to implement it. Developing a compelling reason for the change may do this. The objective would be to capture their imagination and provide a dynamic driving force that is persuasive. For example, a change could be to re-engineer the current marketing process by implementing a data warehouse so that information can be retrieved that enables the marketing department to capture a larger market share. This would be a challenge and should appeal to marketing staff. Such a vision should capture their imagination and motivate them to accept the change.

2 *Determine why the key individuals believe the issues.* Some of the reasons might be parochial thinking; the 'not invented here' syndrome; or simply that the individuals cannot see any need to change. If it is a corporate initiative, are the macro issues on which the change was approved different from regional reality? To move forward, the confidence of staff is necessary.

3 *Ascertain, if possible, how to separate the important individuals from their beliefs.* One way might be to get them to discuss the issues among themselves and with some champions of the change. The hope is that they will form a positive consensus. However, a negative consensus might save the project from being a disaster. In such an instance, recommend putting it on hold until a more suitable climate materializes.

4 *Consider an approach such as forming a focus group and holding a meeting to separate dissenters from their beliefs.* It is essential that the feeling of trust be nurtured. This would begin with openness, requiring people to communicate openly among themselves. Change should be seen as a friend and not as an enemy. Dissenters should be able to speak without fear of being victimized. At a group meeting, leaders should communicate the rationale and the benefits of the change.

5 *How should the approach be implemented?* Using a facilitator to run a group meeting where the pros and cons could be described might be an appropriate way. Each organization must understand its own culture to determine what approach would or would not work, e.g. is it authoritarian (military)?

6 *Having decided upon a solution, record what can be done to prevent a reoccurrence.* Some pointers can be gleaned from looking at the analysis: determining what caused the situation and ensuring it cannot happen again would be a good starting point. Realize that the effectiveness of any program is reliant on the participation and commitment of individuals. To obtain commitment it is usually worth considering rewarding people for a successful change. The rewards can come in many ways: internal, external or intrinsic.

2. Elements of the Project Management Methodology

2.1 Introduction

Chapter 1 introduced the philosophy of a project management methodology and the components of a project environment, namely: development, project management and resource management. It was also pointed out that quality management (QM) is an integral part of the systems development life cycle (SDLC). The importance of this aspect is to reassure everyone involved that deliverables will meet specifications. Collectively, the QM and SDLC, together with resource management, fit into the overall scheme of the project management process. It was explained that the SDLC, project management, quality management and resource management should each be treated as separate components, albeit complementary to each other. It was also explained that even if the completed project deliverable promises positive change to the organization, it might not be possible to implement the project. Therefore a situation analysis was described that, if used, could help change a negative situation into a positive one; or by alerting management to the resistance, a disaster might be prevented from occurring.

A project is much easier to manage well in theory than in practice. Managing projects is difficult, with the diversity of organizational elements (autocratic management, crossing organizational boundaries, *laisser-faire* attitudes, multicultural mix) that must be considered, together with rapid technological change, and the diverse mix of individuals that make up project teams. The secret to successful project management is to find and keep competent project managers, i.e. capable, confident individuals who will dedicate themselves to delivering a quality end product (deliverable). Good project managers know when, and how, to share responsibility with their managers; users or clients; and project team members. They know how to motivate the team based upon their own training or experience and use this in mentoring their team; this aspect is outlined in the paragraphs that follow. Furthermore, they also know what tools to use in project planning and control.

2.2 Traits of Good Project Managers

Some common traits of a good project manager are based upon suitable training, diverse management experience (business and technical), good interpersonal skills, integrity, candour, patience, an understanding of what is required of a manager and a knowledge of processes with a quality orientation. These traits, as will be shown later, are those that should also be developed in team members in order to keep them motivated. The manager should be a visionary who knows what is wanted and focuses on its achievement. To be effective the manager must be enthusiastic and decisive, thus connoting self-confidence and a willingness to lead by taking a stand. To do this he or she needs to have a broad range of skills and tools to deal effectively with the complexities of project management.

A project manager must have the willingness to teach or mentor team members through role modelling and providing on-the-job training ('I hear, I forget; I see, I remember; I experience, I understand' – Chinese proverb) and not by being a know-it-all. The project manager must also be unwilling to accept the *status quo* if it is wrong; the *status quo* should be accepted only with an open mind. The manager should also be fully committed to the organization. Good managers are people who are not worried about their own careers but rather about the careers of those who work for them.

Industry puts great value on the ability of individuals to work in teams. Therefore competitiveness should not be centred on individuals. This means that it is import-ant for project managers to have maturity of judgement, be strong and steady, and not be swayed by the whims or aggressiveness of individual team players. They must have the skill and intention to build and nurture a team. It is also important to let go the leadership role when another person's skill is more appropriate to the team's needs. As project management is an ongoing process that spans a project life cycle, it is important to accept that the aptitudes, characteristics and abilities outlined above are crucial. A cautionary note is inserted here to alert the reader to the principle of self-destruction as a trait of some smart people. The exceptional brain seems to function beneath the curious level and bypasses logic through recklessness, isolation and deafness to feedback. An exceptional project manager may become a risk junkie. 'Smart guys and gals get used to knowing more than anybody else', says Brendan Sexton, Vice President of the Rockefeller Group. 'It's all too short a step from knowing more than anybody else to thinking that you know everything.' To ensure that self-destructive traits are not allowed to propagate, a sound structure and methodology must be in place with checks and balances. Working in isolation, groups or individuals may rely on brilliance to the exclusion of experience and therefore create many of their own problems. Many of us know that the scars of ex-perience may be, in some instances, worth more than being smart. It may be relatively difficult to (say) get a diploma in engineering, but it needs practical experi-ence for the diploma to be recognized as having real value.

Recognizing feedback deafness is important. In a team setting, the team collec-tively and individually needs to be heard and taken seriously. Members of the team must be allowed to be innovative and submit new ideas. If this is practised, situations will not become troublesome. This is where the skill of the manager in problem res-olution needs to be continually honed, together with the skill to dispose of problems immediately when they occur. Questions often asked are: 'Who is competent to be a project manager? 'Are technical skills important? Are interpersonal skills important? How about conceptual skills? As an individual's management level increases, the need for technical competence decreases and the importance of taking a holistic

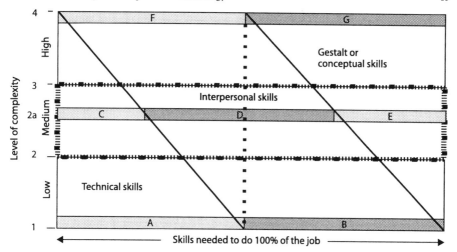

Fig. 2.1 (Reprinted (modified) from *Information Strategy – The Executives Journal* (New York - Auerbach Publications), 1991. Used with permission.)

view increases (Fig. 2.1). What is this view? It is the ability to see the whole rather than a part and to be able to explain in simple terms the subject. All areas are important, interrelated and necessary for a project to be completed successfully. These changing skills are illustrated in Fig. 2.1.

Assume that you have a requirement to program a change to a report format and consider that this job has the Lowest Level of complexity possible. If we draw a line A from the lowest level (1) of complexity to the point where it joins the interpersonal skills slope and then draw another line B to the end, i.e. 100% of the skills needed to do 100% of the job, you can see that the requirement would be for an individual with about equal technical (writing programs) and interpersonal (dealing with client) skills.

Let us now assume that you have a new job such that the complexity increases from 1 to about halfway between 2 and 3, i.e. to 2a. Draw a line C to the first intersection of the sloping line, then another D to the next intersection and a third one E to the end where the three lines represent the skills needed to do 100% of the job. You can easily see that there is a need for an individual with approximately 25% technical, 50% interpersonal and 25% conceptual skills.

At the highest level (4) of complexity, i.e. where interpersonal and conceptual skills join, importance is given to the grasping of new ideas quickly and the ability to view the project as a sum of many interrelated areas. These aspects, coupled with the ability to relate to people, are required more than technical skills. If we draw a line F from the vertical to the first slope and another line G to the end, it can be seen that a person with approximately 50% interpersonal skills and 50% conceptual skills is needed.

At the low level of complexity, one individual could be the project manager, designer, developer and implementer, with the client being the acceptor and champion of the project, i.e. a technical person may be assigned all roles. In some organizations this might be the way things are always done. However, for big or small organizations, as projects become larger and perhaps need to be integrated with other projects the manager would need less technical knowledge but would need to increase interpersonal and theoretical skills. This is where the decision to select a project manager is important. It is also where a technical person might have trouble making the transition from one skill or mind-set to a mix of all three.

It must be appreciated that the perfect technical solution to a problem may not be warranted. This is why talented technical staff who want to become superior managers must move along to the highest managerial level attainable. This is hard for many to understand. A technical individual may say: 'This is the only opportunity I will get to build this so it must be the best I can do irrespective of whether there is a simpler but maybe less complex way of doing it'. Such a person may lack experience in 'soft' skills. These are such skills as interpersonal relations (ability to work harmoniously in any environment); creative insight (consider all angles of an issue/solution); sensitivity (ensure project members' needs are met); vision (seeing the invisible and anticipating solutions); versatility (accept project change in a positive manner); keeping focused (during a project keep to the current activities and not wander to activities that need not be addressed until later); patience (project managers will face many frustrating situations and it is important not to lose one's control; and communication (practice makes perfect whether it be written or verbal). On the other hand, a successful project manager will be able to balance technical excellence with the need to support the business and deliver the project deliverable. This person must have the right hard skills (statistics, estimating, budgeting and computing) coupled with the right soft skills. This balancing act between soft and hard skills is usually a trial and error exercise. It is therefore important to match the right team to the right type of problem. Good executives generally deal best with conceptual and strategic issues. Others, such as project managers, analysts and programmers, deal best with aspects such as analysis and planning based upon their practical experience and knowledge.

As technical staff progress along the spectrum of management they must also become aware of such elements as strategic planning, informal organizations, enterprise-wide characteristics and the culture practised (e.g. benevolent or autocratic). This is not to say that maintaining a level of technical competence is not important, but to realize that to develop as managers other attributes must be continually honed.

To reiterate, the process of project management is a simple approach designed to encourage good work habits in the project manager, who it is assumed fits the foregoing model. Applying the methodology requires a common understanding of the simple principles for using the communication tools. These principles, which hold together the project management cycle, are:

- Observation of the rules for delegating, accepting and sharing responsibility.
- Conforming to the project model, consisting of the three entities that represent the identity of any project, i.e.
  - the individual responsible for acceptance, i.e. the acceptor
  - the individual responsible for delivery of the end product, namely the project manager
  - the deliverable

- Establishing an effective project management organization.
- Acknowledging the importance of visibility to encourage responsible behaviour by all project team players.

2.3 The Theme of Personal Commitment

The underlying theme of the project management cycle is personal commitment. It is important for the users of the methodology to have a common understanding of its psychology. The interactions of people on a project team produce relationships. Peter F. Drucker states that: 'For work to be productive, it has to be organized into a team that is appropriate to the work itself'. In individual sports, such as swimming, individuals delegate to themselves the task of winning for the team. The same can be said for baseball or cricket, where individuals have fixed tasks and *play on the team*. For systems projects, we can liken a project team to a soccer or football team where each individual knows his or her job and coordinates with the rest of the team. The team captain would be the project manager. In this scenario, *members play as a team*. They support each other and therefore simply do not play as a *member on the team*. Players should realize that the environment in which they play has not been created specifically for them. Therefore they must continually adjust to make it purposeful and pleasant. This is the same in a multicultural project team, where all members must appreciate and understand each other's differences and adjust accordingly. For example, in the USA people are direct in giving constructive criticism because it is seen as helping the individual. On the other hand, people from Mexico, Malaysia and other places would see this as hurting their self-esteem, which they place great emphasis on keeping (saving face).

When tasks are assigned to team members, to which they personally commit themselves, the result is an integration of activities toward goal attainment, and members play as a team. It is imperative, however, to match the tasks to the skills required. Accordingly, the people available for a project team must be selected taking into account many facets, some of which are described below. Of course, most organizations have more than one project, so it is obvious that the 'best' players cannot be assigned to every project. Although pulling the *best available* people away from other jobs can be disruptive, it may be necessary. This is very important: just putting an extra body on the project is not conducive to successful project harmonization. It is also necessary to replace anybody on the team who is unable to contribute effectively to the team effort. Experiment with team sizes. With many members on the team, communication problems may arise. With a small number of people that have not been matched harmoniously, the results may be based on the strongest person's (an 'intimidator') ideas in that that person's will is imposed on the team. This is less true of a large team because it is unlikely that one individual can monopolize the process.

Of concern to many executives is the growth in the size of project teams. Many executives will throw money and people at a project to get the project completed either earlier or within the planned time frame. The reason for this is that benefits accrue to an organization as soon as the end product is delivered. Nevertheless, as large projects get larger their complexity increases exponentially. Also, as teams increase in size, so does the proportion of non-productive time due to communication between team members. This is caused by the need for increased interactions among team members. The answer to the problem of countering non-productive time and complexity is to structure large projects into smaller sub-projects.

It is becoming harder to maintain working relationships effectively in an increasingly complex environment. This is the effect of the world's peoples becoming participants in all lifestyles, forming multi-faceted mosaics that are now being reflected in the make-up of project teams. Therefore project managers who are expected to manage across cultures must be comfortable with themselves. To do this will require a global mind-set so that they can handle the paradoxes and differences that will present themselves. One approach is through the project teams themselves, by enabling and helping the team members to work with others from different countries or backgrounds.

Another difficulty often encountered is the mixing of internal and external staff. This can be compounded if the different team members are not cognizant of the need to experience and appreciate egalitarianism in any inter-group or gender relationship. Thus it is important to develop an environment that fosters harmony among these diverse peoples when they work together. Management often takes the view that external consultants are better or more motivated. In the author's experience there is room for all types to work harmoniously together, but it depends on a project manager's skill, knowledge and background. If, however, consultants are the senior members of the team, then it is incumbent on the project manager to keep a close watch on the attitudes of everyone and to nip in the bud any attempt by any person or group to become elitist or obstructionist.

A major factor in misunderstanding is in the interpersonal communication among team members, which may lead to inadequate communication and consultation about the importance of changes. This is compounded in a multicultural environment where, if practised, stereotyping of different ethnic groups can be harmful, although we must recognize and accept that there are differences. For example, to Asians 'hard work' is more important than 'freedom of expression', which is important to North American managers. Thus difficulties can be encountered through unfounded, negative and inaccurate judgements about individuals on the team that can result in inappropriate thoughts or behaviour of project team members although, as Stephen Covey warns, 'Asians as they grow richer risk losing their fundamental value systems' (*Asian Wall Street Journal*, 5 March 1996). Tom Peters also commented on cultural customs during a preview interview for a satellite broadcast[1]. One question asked was 'how are we going to deal with diversity in cultural customs in different environments?'. He replied that there is a Dutch management consultant by the name of Fon Trompenaars, who wrote a fabulous book called *Riding the Waves of Culture*. The first paragraph of this says, 'For gosh sake, don't ever listen to Peter Drucker or Tom Peters because they purely talk

---

1 On 13 September 1996, a satellite broadcast was beamed from Lexington, Kentucky, in the USA, where three renowned minds, namely Dr Stephen Covey, Dr Tom Peters and Dr Peter Senge got together for the first time. The three thinkers shared the stage to talk about 'How to Make Your Team Unstoppable'.

Americanism. Nothing that they say makes sense if you're outside the United States'. Peters went on to explain that respect for the fundamental dignity of the individual person makes a lot of sense; there may be many differences among us all, but there is also a lot of commonality.

To illustrate some differences, Wirthlin Worldwide did a study and derived the following tables that illustrate the differences between Asian and North American executives, ranked by importance:

Asia	North America
Hard work	Freedom of expression
Respect for learning	Personal freedom
Honesty	Self-reliance
Openness to new ideas	Individual rights
Accountability	Hard work
Self-discipline	Personal achievement
Self-reliance	Thinking for oneself

The importance of freedom of expression for North Americans can be seen in their everyday speech: 'Speak your mind or forever hold your peace'; 'Don't mince words, or beat around the bush, or sugar-coat the bad news'. However, freedom of speech does not imply freedom of action.

Wirthlin Worldwide also published some important country differences of which project managers should be cognizant, namely:

Country	Importance
Japan	Harmony
Hong Kong	Orderly society, personal freedom
Singapore	Orderly society
Thailand	Achieving financial success
South Korea	Thinking for oneself
Taiwan	Self-reliance

Managers must realize that when working in a project environment there could be a difference in interpretation of values. Therefore regularly discuss options with subordinates, peers and management before making a final decision; i.e. practice participative management. However, don't get misled into thinking that harmonious agreement implies an intention to follow through to its completion. The agreement may simply be done to avoid conflict by disagreeing.

A project management methodology instils a formal process that, if followed, will minimize the risk of individual practices adversely affecting a schedule. This is because the interaction necessary (status reports, project control etc.) will minimize the possibility of members holding beliefs that are too rigid and building walls against change. A project manager must ensure that team members do not get into the frame of mind of saying: 'This is what you asked for and this is what you have got'. We usually have a mix of individuals from whom to choose, and it is the primary goal of management to gain the greatest return possible while assuming the least risk. Therefore, *the goal is to fit the right peg (person) in the right hole (position)*, as illustrated in Fig. 2.2, i.e. the person must be able to 'do' the job and 'fit' the position.

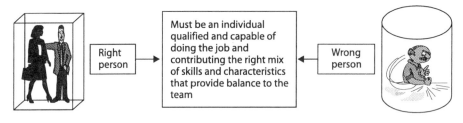

Fig. 2.2 Putting the right person in the right job.

2.4 Selecting the Right People for Project Teams

A model that may help in the selection of project team members is illustrated in Fig. 2.3. Readers should develop their own models to suit their environment because in some countries the asking of certain questions, such as enquiring about a person's religion, would be illegal. However, bear in mind that the objective is to obtain the best person for the job, and certain questions, such as age or marital status, are

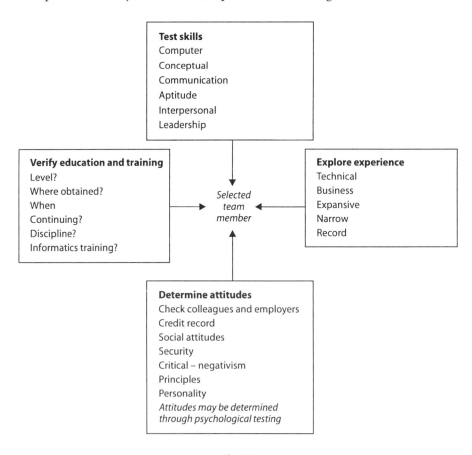

Fig. 2.3

probably not relevant to whether the individual can or cannot do the job. Thus a project manager must identify and select people who will fit into the team environment and be able to succeed in a project task. They must have the appropriate attitudes, skills and characteristics.

When discussing with an individual the possibility of joining the team it is essential that questions be asked that may not have just one correct answer. Also, don't give the answer in the question; think of open-ended questions. For a given project, the questions asked may be different from those for another project. For example, if the project is in a different country that follows different principles, it is no use putting a team member on the project whose principles are different. Therefore questions that can lead to a conclusion on an individual's principles could be important. Readers can make up their own questionnaire, but Fig. 2.3 outlines some areas that could be explored or verified. As individuals, some people may be highly experienced and have the level of skill required, but may not be effective when working in a team environment. Thus attitudes are a very important aspect of the selection process. A weighting process may also be used, with the characteristics in each unit compared with other candidates in order to maximize the likelihood of selecting the right person for the team.

2.5 Personal Commitments

Teamwork and cooperation are the essence of an effective project team. Peters and Waterman stated in *In Search of Excellence*: 'Treat people as adults; treat them as partners; treat them with dignity; treat them with respect... you must treat your workers as your most important asset'. Nothing can compensate for these principles if they are missing. A characteristic of a team player is to feel a sense of individual commitment to the aims and purposes of the team. Players must devote personal energy to building the team and supporting other members. When not with the team, they should still feel they belong to it and are therefore its representatives.

By accepting responsibility for something, individuals establish a business obligation to the manager to do their best to ensure that it is accomplished. As long as they are personally confident that they can meet their committed objectives they will carry the responsibility. As soon as they loses confidence in their ability to meet the objectives, for whatever reason, they will abdicate their obligation. Managers must be aware that this can happen. If the obligation is abdicated, the individuals will cover their tracks to protect themselves from 'unjust' persecution and then revert to doing their best. Individuals, then, are controlled by their personal confidence, which is subjective in nature. The cause may be that workers feel that they do not have the capability or that their judgement is impaired for whatever reason, i.e. they question their own adequacy for the task. This means that personal commitments are more difficult to recognize and control than business commitments. These personal promises, as explained above, only guarantee that individuals will do what they consider their best based upon their judgement and capabilities. What the manager really wants to know is: 'Is the best going to be good enough?'. When a manager asks a team member this question, he or she is trying to determine where the personal commitment lies.

It is natural for team members to say that they are totally committed, because generally they will believe it to be so. Thus the project manager has the difficult task of being able to determine whether the statement is true. Therefore, the traits of the project manager, such as knowledge and experience, are important in making this determination. However, what is also important is to ensure that all team members are being honest with themselves and with each other.

Responsibility cannot be successfully delegated to an individual unless it is accepted with the confidence to deliver an associated product. Acceptance of a responsibility is tentative in nature and is meaningless if the individual's confidence or commitment to the responsibility is lost, for whatever reason. When an individual is no longer confident of fulfilling an earlier promise, the responsibility consequently must be 'shared' vertically with the person who originally assigned the responsibility. This 'sharing' allows management to take whatever steps are necessary to restore an individual's dedication or, faced with no other choice, to accept the consequences of the lost obligation, i.e. best effort. Rarely is a best effort sufficient. If it is suspected that a team member has reneged on his pledge, then the project manager should rectify the situation. Counselling may be appropriate if it is determined that the commitment can be restored. If not, a decision must be made as to whether the member is to be replaced.

No effort should be made to retain individuals who are incompetent, who have indicated that they have lost interest in the project, or have shown personal antagonism toward the manager or other team members. This, if ignored, would almost certainly result in failure to meet any obligation. Even if the obligation was restored, it would probably only be for a short while, because usually the reason that the commitment was dropped in the first place is probably still there, even if it is not expressed. A transfer, or even a demotion, if appropriate (for example for documented incompetence), should be worked out with the team member who has lost the commitment. This should be done without the connotations of a sentence from a judge. However, assuming that the project manager considers the lack of dedication to be purely attitudinal, then through counselling the commitment may be recovered. The emphasis on any action must be on the future rather than the past. A constructive approach must be taken. For example, letting the member establish goals with the project manager would help the subordinate to reach decisions on the specific steps to enable the project to get back on track. Overtime is one approach; another is sharing the task with a more experienced member or simply improving the individual's time management.

There is always the possibility that the problem lies with the project manager. If team members feel that they must hide unpalatable facts, then perhaps some of the project manager's skills need to be improved. This is, however, less likely with an experienced manager, but would be more likely true of a recently promoted individual.

Although the word 'commitment' may be considered strong, there are other words that may be just as good, so they have been used interchangeably; namely obligation, pledge, dedication, promise, responsibility and guarantee. Commitment at first glance may appear to be simply saying 'yes' to whatever is asked of oneself. However, it goes beyond this. Saying 'yes', paying lip service, because it is the easy way can, if detected, be a signal to the project manager that the individual is not truly committed. Sometimes a team member knows that the motivation to produce the deliverable has been lost. In this instance the individual should share this knowledge with the project manager and give the manager the opportunity to offer assistance in reviving the commitment. One way to determine a person's dedication to the project is to measure participation and performance. Setting goals can do this. In the case of a project, the goal of the project manager is to complete the project on time and within budget. As a project is made up of discrete tasks, each member of the project team has a number of tasks. As performance is a function of commitment, using the completion or non-completion of the tasks can be a measure of dedication. To measure this, a project manager needs to have a method of knowing where time is being invested and what is being accomplished. An obligation can be further measured by noting whether the individual participates in discussing the status of the tasks, problem resolution and innovation. A dedicated individual will have a need to progress, since completing a task gives a sense of accomplishment. Project team members would like limits. Tasks left open would leave the person with a sense of not getting anywhere, and any initial commitment would soon be dissipated. However, realize that recognition and appreciation are essential and that those involved know the importance of their contribution.

The project management approach, then, consists of soliciting confident personal commitments for deliverables and then periodically monitoring the pledges to determine the confidence level of the team players. This is mainly an intuitive process. That is, a project manager must be tuned in to the team and obtain this knowledge or cognition sometimes without any empirical basis, and must be able to judge whether a project member's responsibility is still being sustained.

If team members feel confident about achieving the project task and continue to carry their pledges, this will undoubtedly help ensure success in meeting the project's objectives. Of course, the project manager must always ensure that the members' confidence is realistic and not founded on dreaming. It is common practice to be overly confident of completing a task. This is where proper planning and estimating will help in assuring management that the project timeline is achievable.

One of the secrets of good project management is to establish guarantees from individuals for their deliverables and then continually monitor them on a regular, cyclical (i.e. calendar-based) basis. The cycle must be appropriate to the task. In some cases it is daily and at other times it is weekly; but generally a monthly cycle is appropriate. Daily monitoring can be a very useful process if the project is off the rails and needs to be brought back online. For the author, one project on which this worked well was one in which a team was made up of a mix of internal and external staff who did not communicate very well. They simply followed the specifications given to them. The specifications needed interpretation from a specialist, but team members, with single-mindedness of purpose, barrelled along without seeking the appropriate input. At testing time, very few of the deliverables were accepted by the client and it became a 'blame others' scenario. By arranging to meet all members on a specific task at 8:00 a.m. each day to ensure that agreements noted the day previously had been actioned, it became impossible for blame to be given unjustly. What happened was that the members became organized voluntarily rather than being treated as naughty children, i.e. as non-professionals. Here workgroup automation may help the communication process.

2.5.1 Responsibility Characteristics

On the foregoing basis, a set of attributes or characteristics of responsibility are suggested as a necessary part of the project management process. They are:

- For an individual, responsibility is a personal thing and cannot be delegated. Therefore when an obligation is accepted, it becomes part of the team's collective accountability and helps form its culture and *esprit de corps*.

- Things can change so quickly that it is not always possible to wait for any one person to make a decision. It is therefore preferable that team members work in an empowered environment whereby the team can make the decision without having always to refer it upwards. Personal screening and psychological testing of individuals can assist in determining whether the team members have this ability. This is part of putting the right person in the right job.

- Responsibility cannot be accepted (or maintained) without access to adequate authority and resources to meet the obligation. If the person carrying the personal commitment perceives that the resources are not available, the obligation will be dropped and only the minimum will be done. There is only one size for an obligation, namely: 100%. Whenever two or more individuals share an obligation, they each have 100%.

- Sharing responsibility in no way absolves others (team members, management, clients) of accountability. This means not blaming another individual when things go wrong, but collectively sharing the successes and failures in achieving the goal.

- Responsibility will not be maintained unless the individual feels it is being shared. This means that the avenues for this sharing must be perceived to be open and that guidance and support are readily available. Thus when things go wrong, a mutual acceptance of responsibility of all concerned is necessary. In such an instance, blame is not attached to anyone, but a collective resolution is encouraged.

- The delegation and acceptance of an obligation are not one-time events, but, rather, an ongoing relationship. This means that each individual's responsibility must be reviewed on a regular basis and the project manager must regularly reaffirm that it is being maintained.

- Responsibility should always be associated with a deliverable – not an activity. For example, a team member can be committed to programming for a team on an *ad hoc* basis or on an as-available basis, but it is much better to establish that responsibility is for, say, delivering Module A. With this promise to deliver, the member will ensure that all the necessary tasks are accomplished, even those that were not originally planned for because of lack of foresight, lack of knowledge or whatever. The visibility of a responsibility encourages the individuals concerned to carry out their understanding of the task. However, as much as possible, the deliverable should be fully defined by users, including its quality attributes.

It is worth highlighting at this point that the work ethic is not dead. Workers will take pride in their work if they are on a winning team and will be loyal if appreciated.

2.6 Motivation

To enjoy the results from a motivated and loyal project team, members must have the right to participate in decision-making. Although the human relations movement is considered to have waned around 1960, its spirit of inquiry did not die. Rather, it was transformed into a movement called organizational humanism, expounded by writers such as Chris Argyris, Warren Bennis and Rensis Likert. The late Rensis Likert, the 'father' of participative management, categorizes organizations into four types:

1 Exploitative authoritative – in this organization, subordinates are motivated by fear, threats and occasional rewards. This tends to lead to inaccurate information being passed up the line. The answer expected by management is given. Therefore this is rejected as a way to motivate project teams, as workers in the end will not accept such treatment.

2 **Benevolent authoritative** – this is a master–servant relationship with some paternalistic involvement of project team members who would not derive much satisfaction from their efforts. Although preferable to Type 1, it is not conducive to achieving results on time and leads to a *laisser faire* attitude. Therefore, it is not recommended.

3 **Consultative** – with this type of management style, team members are consulted before solutions to problems and decisions are presented to management. Communication upward is an improvement over Types 1 and 2, but the approach is a cautious one. Therefore, generally project members consider their contributions as not always being taken seriously and that they are not appreciated. The manager must therefore guard against listening but not hearing.

Although Type 3 may be considered an improvement over Types 1 and 2, it is considered by some that there is still a better approach:

4 **Participative group** – in this group, which complements the project management methodology, team members are trusted, they are regarded as willingly working toward the achievement of the project's objectives. The manager learns to make requests and not give orders. An assignment is coupled with worker empowerment, i.e. the spreading of decision making within the domain of meaningful information and within policies and procedures. It does not mean allowing an employee or team member to act independently or thinking that freedom of speech implies freedom of action. Empowering individuals, however, will allow them to express confidence and improve their morale and motivation.

The most productive organization in Likert's view is the participative group. Decisions are better because the project team members (informatics specialists, users and consultants) who know most about the issues are collectively joining in problem resolution. This is supportive of ego building. A team member interacts with others and maintains a sense of personal worth. Each seeks and receives the other project member's knowledge, experience and expertise. If the manager accepts equal participation and recognizes good work, the outcome will be that team members will produce better results. If satisfactory results are ignored, the biggest complaint that team members have is reinforced: lack of recognition or not feeling appreciated. Therefore the effectiveness of this approach will depend on the amount of participation encouraged. At meetings you should ask, as an item, who gave out praise recently to their team members? This reinforces the fact that we must keep doing it; when giving it out don't say it as a thank you, but as an effective message, e.g. 'Hey! You did a great job on the project'.

Of course Type 4, the participative style, may not hold up in all situations. Therefore the reader must determine through reading and experimentation what will work best in the current environment. For example, if a manager has an ethnically diverse team, then some of the methods, such as fear, absence of compromise, perseverance and intuition may not work. This would be particularly true if the team consisted of individuals who considered overt intimidation an undesirable management attribute. What this attempts to say is that there is no one correct way to manage under all conditions. Therefore, the situationalist approach is worth cultivating, i.e. use the best approach depending on the situation and the players involved.

Lyman W. Porter and Edward E. Lawler derived another model based on expectancy theory. This model is applied primarily to managers. Thus, although the situationalist approach may be valid under certain conditions, the expectancy theory is based on the idea that the amount of effort (the strength of motivation and energy that a manager expends) is dependent on the value of the expected reward. In addition, David C. McClelland added to the comprehension of motivation by identifying three needs, namely: power, affiliation and achievement. These are relevant to project managers because all must be present to make a project team work well. In that a team needs to achieve its goals, achievement is of primary importance. Power is needed by those who enjoy practising influence and control. In order to satisfy the need for affiliation, a manager could find satisfaction in being accepted by the team players.

Another example in which a different form of management style is appropriate is in that of programming, a highly specialized function. Some managers consider that programmers are interesting examples of individualistic behaviour. It is a misconception that they are undisciplined ne'er-do-wells. They are in many cases referred to rudely as computer nerds or as hackers. The majority, however, fit conventional norms of behaviour and look and act like professionals. They may, though, be considered to have dual personalities. In many instances, normality only lasts until they are faced with an interesting problem. At this time they may adopt a single-mindedness of purpose, sleep the minimum, nibble on food and infuriate those around them when they interrupt a social activity and leave to test a solution. G. Weinberg (1972) suggested an approach known as 'egoless programming.' Until the present time, programming has generally been thought of as an individual creative task. However, the social environment around programmers and the attitude and value system held by programmers has changed. With the tendency to allow programmers to 'hack', we may see a return to programmers becoming attached to their own programs, and this should be guarded against. Programmers who practice 'egoless programming' (and these should be encouraged) expect there to be errors in their code. They enlist the aid of other project team members to help find errors and in turn participate in verifying other team members' code. A major benefit of this approach is that each programmer's knowledge of the whole system will be improved and therefore they will each become a better resource to the company.

This is not to say that 'hacking' (master programming) does not have its place. Sir Stafford Beer claims that programmers' skills cover a 25 to 1 range with the hacker at the 25 end. Although it may carry a negative connotation, there is a use for hacking when there is a need for a complex problem to be resolved by elegant, tight, code. How is it possible to manage these individuals? In his book *A Whack on the Side of the Head*, Roger Von Oech advocates total flexibility. Programmers need to be free to develop and try out new ideas. This freedom may all be very well. However, how does a project manager control the need of the project to be delivered on time and within budget? Obviously there must be an agreed upon discipline, except perhaps in a research environment where researchers are given free rein; we do not consider this approach. Fostering creativity in a disciplined framework, however, requires establishing an overall structure of reasonable discipline, covering such factors as schedules, architectures and specifications. Communication among the team members is paramount. Email may be one solution where people work different hours. Of course, status reporting against reasonable deadlines and regular meetings are also essential, i.e. a process coupled with flexibility will go a long way to ensure success and harmony for all the project team players.

Although not advocating any one model, it is probably true that a mix of all models is probably the best, i.e. any one need could be satisfied in any given situation.

One of the critical challenges facing organizations is how to continuously motivate people to perform. There is a massive lack of motivation within organizations today

A project objective reflects the needs and desires of management, project members and the clients of the end product. Through this, project members' needs, namely to achieve their personal goals and to grow in the job, are important and satisfied. Some managers have trouble giving out bouquets and motivating staff. They pay a compliment as though they expect a receipt. Some overreact. They pour syrup all over people. Some managers, however, refrain from giving praise for good ideas or a job well done simply because of jealousy. If a manager consistently has problematic staff, he or she should ask: 'Why is it that people do not want to work for me?'. Team players are not indiscriminately loyal. They must be convinced that the manager has their interest at heart. Therefore, managers who want loyal team players must work at their development. Managers must deserve loyalty and return it to the players by being sincere, appreciating the members' views, hopes and ambitions. Managers must deal openly and honestly with their staff. Giving them responsibility and sharing the credit, will, with the other factors, go a long way towards obtaining loyalty.

A major problem in implementing any new approach to managing teams is the attitude of some project managers. Many tend to believe that they can know individual components as well as the team. Also unfortunately, they act as if they were experts about abstruse technical problems. This is a quick way to lose respect. However, to maintain respect and credibility it is essential to be able to understand and discuss concepts with staff. Therefore, through reading, seminars, observation and listening it is possible to keep up to date with what is happening in one's particular industry and with globalization throughout the world.

In the past there was much emphasis on the merit system. This is now changing in favour of a more egalitarian approach based upon teamwork. Peer pressure rather than the carrot-and-the-stick approach is becoming one method to drive motivation. John O. Whitney, a management professor at Columbia University, in his book *The Economics of Trust*, writes: 'If we continue with our traditional measurements and rewards, our relative productivity will continue its decline, our quality will suffer, and our ability to compete will wither away'. This tends to support Likert's participative view in that peers working together as a harmonious team can be trusted to get the job done. However, it must be appreciated that the conditions affecting morale are varied and complex. Therefore the need for an individual to receive the traditional motivators based on a STAR system is likely to diminish and be replaced by some form of collective reward based upon the product being delivered on time and within budget. Therefore, the objective is to create a climate for self-motivation.

Numerous organizations are not reaping the hoped-for benefits from their systems development programs. One major reason is that management cannot get employees motivated to support the initiatives or they put the wrong people on a project. Plans to improve quality or boost productivity are often produced against a backdrop of staff cuts, wage freezes or rollbacks. Corporate planning tends to be plastic and individuals do not necessarily relate to it or are not loyal to the decisions that come from the planning exercise. Management must guard against their ideas being seen as a way to squeeze more out of the employees while management reaps the rewards. Money alone cannot motivate employees, albeit that many human resource managers conclude that it is money that motivates people to perform. Because of this approach, many employees are being paid more and more and productivity is lagging further behind as wages increase. It is important to realize that in a tight labour market and a good economy it is more challenging to be able to continuously motivate people. This is especially valid when it may appear that staff appear to be more motivated by money than by a rewarding career. Managers lament the high staff turnover rate. They complain that staff are no longer loyal. They are disappointed that after spending much time, effort and money in building their skills and knowledge they simply leave the organization for a more lucrative job elsewhere.

Performance can be increased significantly if everyone participates in an incentive program. To make it work there must be quality and service objectives. That is, targets must not only be given based on measurable factors, but also on qualitative standards, such as helpfulness and interpersonal relationships. Performance needs to be measured regularly against these objectives. Although it is not easy, there are a few practical ways to put some value on these qualitative factors; for example, observation, polling clients, reviewing project correspondence and one-on-one interviews, where negative attitudes may be discerned. It must always be remembered that employees are a critical link in the corporate chain, and especially so for staff working on a project where lack of motivation can seriously disrupt a project schedule. Therefore, to keep employees happy show that they are appreciated through a participative style of management. Give them a competitive compensation package, give them an opportunity to grow (perhaps through job rotation and training) and upgrade their skills, thus making them feel that they are part of the team.

One way to motivate staff is through incentives according to their performance and recognizing their contribution to the project. For example: in a project one goal could be to meet the target on time for a bonus of, say, x% of profit, but by completing it earlier a bonus of y% could be given for each week it is completed early. It is important to keep the objective broad. In this way, what is lost on the roundabouts can be made up on the swings. That is to say, completing a task late may not affect the overall project because it was not a critical factor in the schedule. However, although a broad objective may appear simple, it may not work on a lengthy project, such as for example the stealth bomber or the Channel Tunnel. In these cases, multiple objectives could be determined. For example, an overall goal, such as 'finish the project on time and within budget', and sub-projects, such as (for the bomber) get the wings done by a certain date or (for the tunnel) get the lines laid by a certain date, could be set. It can easily be seen that adopting this type of motivation encourages all employees. Managers can then link employee expectations with organizational performance.

The motivation problem not only translates to staff turnover; employees who choose to stay on also have motivation problems. They often do not show initiative to take responsibility or take charge of situations. They are reactive in their approach. They undertake many fire-fighting activities instead of preventing fire breakout. They do a lot of maintenance repair and very little preventative maintenance work.

Too often managers are quick to conclude that people lack motivation because of the compensation system. They point out that people do not take more responsibility or become more proactive because they do not know how but because they are not motivated. They point out that people view work as an exchange; they will put in just enough work or undertake enough responsibility to match what they are paid. However, money can be a powerful demotivator if employees feel they are not being adequately rewarded for their efforts. In a survey of 50 Canadian companies, it was found that incentive pay programs that included management as well as non-management staff contributed to higher performance.

The problem with monetary motivation is that it is superficial and does not sustain the motivation level of people once they get used to the increased salaries. The truth of the matter is that there will never be enough money to motivate people. They will get used to the additional money they receive. It will eventually be taken for granted to the extent that it is no longer a motivator. People will always demand more and more if we use money as the main motivator in getting people to improve performance or to try to buy loyalty. In fact, the blatant use of money to motivate people, either to join an organization or to stay on, has created more motivation problems than it has solved. It often creates a system of unfairness or inequity. For example, newly recruited professionals may be paid very much more than existing incumbent staff with similar experience and qualifications. This is a desperate move to attract them to the organization and can backfire; many professional athletes have performed poorly when seduced with high signing fees. Also, staff who resign for better pay and who are being counter-offered may cause a sense of inequity for remaining staff with similar experience who remained loyal to the organization. This cannot be allowed to happen in a project environment. In fact, using money as the only motivator may encourage even the normally loyal staff to resign or look for other jobs to seek 'fairness'. Those who stay on, despite the perception of inequity, may suffer a loss of morale, and consequently commitment and motivation may suffer. The root cause of all these problems can be attributed to the way people look at money and work. If we motivate project team members by getting them to view their activities as being an exchange for money, then we cannot get them to work beyond money.

The motivational approaches highlighted earlier are not completely effective. To motivate people to achieve their best work and produce quality deliverables needs more than money. They need interest, a powerful sense of pride in their work and commitment, with a determination to succeed. A unique event occurred in the Malaysian government when project teams were formed to each prepare deliverables ('Blueprint' and a 'Concept Request For Proposal') in conformance with the Prime Minister's vision of three flagship applications, namely: electronic government, telemedicine and smart schools. What was amazing was that these ethnically diverse teams, from various countries, were asked to rise above their companies' interests and, with no incentive, work together harmoniously. The team players felt good and important to have been chosen, thus enabling them to further develop their knowledge and skills. The project was accomplished successfully because of leadership, personal pride and commitment.

Money never entered the picture. The 'What's in it for me?' syndrome was invisible. Addressing the 'What's in it for me?' question went beyond money, and the team members achieved a sustained motivation level for the four months of the project's duration.

The effective way for the teams to achieve a sustainable high level of motivation was to address their fundamental needs, and the project work served as the key to providing this requirement. That is, team members found that they increased their value through performance and increased knowledge and experience by working among an internationally diverse mix of professionals.

These Malaysian government flagship application project teams supported the fact that people who know that they are building new knowledge, skills and experience, and who are allowed the opportunity to perform, will be more motivated. They know that their value will increase with their record of accomplishment of performance. With increased value, they know that they will be rewarded either internally within their organization or outside. This fundamental need is illustrated in Fig. 2.4, which illustrates a motivation model (MM).

We can now elaborate on the five steps (mind-set; building knowledge, skills and experience; track record; value obtained; reward) in the process of this motivation approach.

2.6.1 Initial Mind-Set

The process of motivation begins with ensuring that the mind-set of individuals is conducive to change, or that they are motivated by the need to improve themselves.

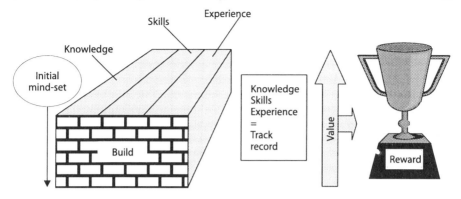

Fig. 2.4 Motivation model.

Many individuals don't know or care how to improve their motivation level or what it is. The Malaysian team members had a positive mind-set to begin with, but saw the opportunity to build upon their experience. They had a mind-set that was conducive for all individuals to apply what they knew to improve their work and impart their knowledge to other project team members.

If you are managing a team, the symptoms of low motivation are usually very apparent. The team members will not do their best. They will not be efficient. Their productivity will be low. They are not creative and proactive in the way they approach work. They do not take charge or possess the self-responsibility to improve work performance. Furthermore, they simply do not get the work done.

As explained, you can discern a lack of motivation in team members from many symptoms. However, to address the root cause, you must go within the individuals. For project team members with a negative mind-set to become productive you must change their mind-set. It is necessary to address their negative assumptions. They may have strong beliefs about the old way of doing things. Their values may not support the work ethic. They may perceive that they are providing value for money and that their effort and performance are not linked to reward and therefore they have little motivation to improve. Others may have a blind spot regarding their weaknesses, such as the lack of knowledge or skills. Some may become complacent with their level of performance; they may not see the value of improving or putting more effort into their work. Until these mind-sets are changed you may not be able to get team players to produce quality deliverables or execute their work efficiently. Thus the first step towards motivating people is to eliminate the undesirable frame of mind that prevents them from acquiring more knowledge, skills and experience to improve.

An approach to getting individuals to change can be as in the Malaysian experience. Project team members should see the project as an opportunity to build knowledge, skills and experience. With this in mind, each team member's value should increase, which should attract higher rewards. This higher value of oneself could be motivating enough, irrespective of whether or not the individual's home organization rewards the person. The truth of the matter is that if an individual's own

organization does not reward that person with an improving record of accomplishment and hence increased value, some other organization will.

2.6.2 Developing Knowledge, Skills and Experience

Once people's mind-sets are changed, they will view the development of knowledge,
skills and experience in a more relevant and positive way.

The role of leaders, be they project managers, line managers etc., is to provide
opportunities for people to increase their knowledge, skills and experience. They can
do this by providing the necessary environment and resources, such as training,
books, videos, computer-based training, on-the-job-training and relevant job
assignments. If time permits, project teams should be encouraged to learn and
experiment with new ways of doing things. This learning must be fun, meaningful
and rewarding, and should be provided in an interesting fashion. For example,
training or team meetings can be conducted outside the building: on the lawn and
under the sun, or by the lake with the birds singing. Project managers should not only
teach, but should also entertain to make teaching lively, memorable and fun. Those
who learn under pleasurable conditions are more open to accepting new skills and
knowledge. What is learnt with pleasure is certainly learnt full measure.

Learning can be encouraged on an individual or team basis. Many organizations
who practice the concept of organizational learning are encouraging team learning,
whereby staff come together to share their knowledge, skills and experience. They
teach and learn from one another. In the Malaysian experience mentioned earlier the
teams had a weekly forum where ideas were expressed, issues raised and concepts
were explored. This allowed cross-fertilization and provided a harmonious
competitive environment where the learning process was fun and positive. This
approach made team members feel good and internally rewarded through knowing
that they were recognized for their knowledge, skills and experience and being asked
to share them with others. This experience was meaningful, relevant and interesting
and thus rewarding and motivating by itself.

2.6.3 Building a Track Record

Encouraging people to learn new knowledge and skills is not meaningful and
rewarding if the staff are not shown how to apply the knowledge and skills in the
workplace. Too often employees do not commit themselves totally to learning, as
they see little relevance in what they have learnt to what they are being asked to do in
the workplace.

To ensure that people find learning meaningful, the knowledge and skills that they
learn should help them improve their performance. Allowing team members to
practice their newly learnt skills on the project is one good way of ensuring the
relevance of training and learning. This can be done by designing work or providing
work assignments that will allow the utilization of the new skills and knowledge
fully. For example, an individual who has recently completed a supervisor's course
could be given a first assignment of supervising two junior team members. Another
team member might enjoy writing, so use that person to write documentation or

minutes. The ways to motivate are endless if you take the trouble to find out what it is that motivates an individual. Thus one of the roles of project managers is to help develop their team and allow them to use the knowledge and skills learnt to improve their performance. Getting team members to learn, grow and improve is an important role, and gratifying inasmuch as those who use their new knowledge and skills to build a record of accomplishment of good performance will feel good about themselves. This good feeling will motivate them further to learn more and perform better.

2.6.4 Increasing Value

Once team players have realized how knowledge and skills can help them build up a good record of accomplishment, their motivation will increase. Their increased performance with the application of new knowledge and skills will help them to view themselves as more capable. They will be motivated to learn more because they perceive that their value has increased as a result of the improved record of accomplishment. By viewing themselves as more capable and more valuable, their confidence and their self-image will improve and their motivation will further increase. Thus, the critical role of project managers is to transform team members' negative mind-sets to positive ones, thus enabling them to take positive action to achieve positive results.

Positive action can be seen when team players see the relevance of their new knowledge and skills to their work. Positive action may or may not create positive results. It is here that everyone needs to encourage the continuation of positive attitudes. When a positive attitude is maintained, team players will appreciate the value of their skills and knowledge, and this will further reinforce their motivation level and their positive mind-set.

2.6.5 Providing Attractive Rewards

One of the great challenges of motivation is to get people motivated first to perform well before they are rewarded. Some ideas about a reward system have been highlighted above. When a project team has performed well, the issue of rewards should not be a problem. The only challenge that remains now is to ensure that the team is rewarded fairly and attractively.

A critical factor is to ensure that the team players who have built up their knowledge, skills and experience, along with their record of performance, do not leave the organization. This is critical, as they have increased their marketable skills and thus their market value. Thus rewards should be fair and attractive. Coupling this with a motivating environment, whereby the staff are given the opportunity to learn, grow and improve their value and confidence, should provide every reason for the staff to remain in the organization and stay motivated.

2.7 The Project Organization

We have spoken of the right people and their attitudes and traits. These must be channelled, so we establish an organization for projects. To accomplish projects an organization attuned to the needs of the users should be established. The organization illustrated in Fig. 2.5 reflects the needs of the different individuals to participate fully in the information systems development activities. To adapt to this need, *the project manager should be complemented by staff functions from line units.*

A *project manager* or *project director* would oversee managers supervising the following:

- Team leaders or project managers would manage *development teams.* The teams consist of analysts, programmers, technical writers etc., who would be assigned to work as a matrix team on the different events, stages or tasks of a project. These events, from a generic SDLC, are initiation, feasibility, analysis, design and development.
- *Implementation* could have its own manager and cover training, acceptance testing, conversion and installation.
- *Information technology*: this would be a technical component, administering and supporting the data communications network and computer operations.
- *Technical administration*: this would function as the administrative arm for the project manager. For small projects, this would probably be done by the project manager. It could also act as a support centre for problem resolution, change control etc. If it were not established, the responsibility would be shared among the team members and the managers.

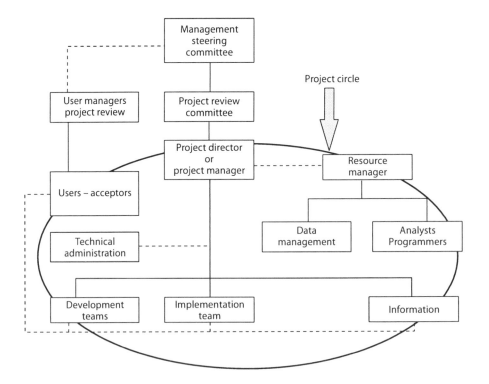

Fig. 2.5 Project organization.

A project management methodology assists the project manager in managing the sum of the component parts. That is, *the project management methodology and the SDLC are complementary, and for project deliverables to be completed both are needed.*

Resource managers would supply qualified staff, such as programmers and database management specialists (who ensure that data is managed as a corporate resource and that data redundancy is minimized), to work on the project matrix teams. These individuals report to their resource manager for day-to-day administration, but to the project manager for project assignments. Thus, at the end of the assignment they return to their resource managers.

Staff functions: to ensure the participation of staff levels, the following are suggested:

- A *management systems steering committee* should be established as a subset of an executive committee to give overall direction to systems activities. The management committee may be considered synonymous with the board of directors.

- For each major systems application, a *project review committee* should be established. The committee would be chaired by the project champion or client (i.e. the executive responsible) for whom the systems project is being conducted. The committee would comprise of individuals (other managers) who have a personal stake in the successful completion of the project. The chairman would report regularly to the management systems steering committee.

  The project manager would report at least monthly to this project review committee, or whenever an issue needs to be resolved.

- *Subject matter staff* should be designated a role on systems project teams to specify requirements, review deliverables and conduct acceptance testing to ensure that the deliverables meet their unit's specifications. These are individuals who are experts in their functional areas and know their subject intimately, e.g. accounting – accounts receivable.

- Each major functional group with an interest in the project's results should appoint a general coordinator who would be the area representative to participate in planning and liaison to resolve issues.

One issue that causes much disagreement is in deciding who is responsible for what. A simple solution is to establish that subject matter specialists decide *what* is required and development professionals decide *how* the requirements are to be met.

The process flow that the functions support in a matrix type environment is illustrated in Fig. 2.6. This shows that overall the project manager sits at the top of a project and is accountable for delivery to the client. To achieve this, project stages should be broken down into phases. As each phase is developed it is tested and accepted. The project review committee acts as the balancer of resources and the arbitrator for problem resolution.

2.8 The Project Circle and Personal Deliverables

Every project and every deliverable within a project must have the following three entities clearly identified:

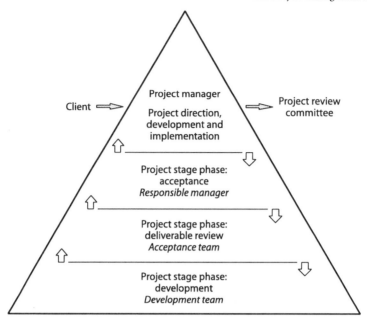

Fig. 2.6

- The *deliverer*, typically the project manager, is the individual responsible for delivering a product. This is the macro view, since all team members can be viewed as deliverers.
- The *end product* – a clearly defined, visible, recognizable deliverable, representing an implemented project or deliverable(s) during development.
- The *acceptor*, i.e. an individual who is responsible for accepting deliverables on behalf of him- or herself or the line manager. Line managers, with many functions reporting to them, would normally delegate the responsibility. It is obvious that if there are numerous projects going on that impinge on a functional area it would be impossible for one manager to be responsible for accepting them all.

The three entities are illustrated in the nodes of Fig. 2.7. Each entity must be clearly defined for a healthy project. A missing or 'vague' node will seriously weaken the effectiveness of the project circle. If there is no deliverer (project manager, team member etc.), the project will wander aimlessly like a ship without a rudder and a coxswain to steer it. Without these nodes, no one will accept the responsibility of being the driving force behind the deliverable.

Regarding visibility, mentioned previously, a question often asked is 'how can something that is invisible be seen?'. Obviously normal mortals cannot see the invisible. However, consider what Jonathan Swift said: 'Vision is the art of seeing the invisible'. A good example of project visibility is the Channel Tunnel visionaries. All across the world, many people are cognizant of the engineering accomplishments, the political problems and the cost overruns. On the other hand, not many people were aware of the stealth bomber's problems, or even its existence, until it was rolled

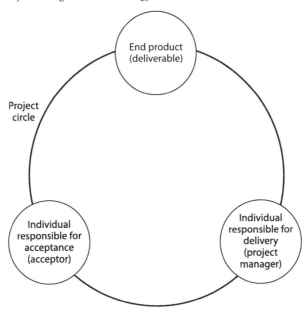

Fig. 2.7 The three entities of the project circle.

out on the tarmac. This invisible project, had it depended on acceptance by the American people, might never have seen the light of day. Although these projects relate to external visibility, the same concept holds true for internal projects, albeit to a lesser degree. For example, some projects are kept 'invisible' because funding may be cut off. On the other hand, some projects have high visibility because they have a high profile for management. Thus, the idea has relevance if you want your project to have the attention you consider it deserves. To reiterate, ensure that it has high visibility.

If products are not kept visible in front of all interested and decision-making parties, they will not be seen until some activity or some event makes it so. This may be too late if corrective action or a major decision is required

If there is no acceptor or designated 'system owner,' the project may never come to a formal end, and may drift into a state of limbo. The acceptor should indicate through a sign-off procedure that the project or deliverable meets or exceeds specifications. One may question how a specification could be exceeded. This can be relatively simple in real life. For example, a specification may state: 'time to obtain the result of a generalized retrieval search is to be no less than x seconds'. However, if, with an improved design, the actual average time were less than x, the client would undoubtedly be happy.

If the 'end product' (project deliverable) has not been clearly defined at the outset, what is delivered is usually a surprise to everyone but the developer. Even starting with the same product in mind, changes during the development process often lead to incredible distortions. This is particularly true if there is no acceptor working with the developer to discuss and agree to changes as they occur. One reason that 'pilots' and 'prototypes' are useful is because they demonstrate working solutions (proof of concept) as the project progresses, although they are not panaceas for poor project management.

Clearly, to avoid these potential problems it is essential to resolve the project circle before development starts. For many projects this is not a trivial task:

- Selection of the project manager can be both difficult and easy. It is easy if an experienced one (from inside or external to the organization) who meets all the criteria explained in this book is available. If no experienced manager is available, then it is probably better to delay the project. If management is willing to take the risk on a relatively inexperienced individual, then it is very important that the principles outlined in this book be followed, because they will considerably reduce the risk of disaster.

- Definition of the end product can be rather elusive when trying to define it in a measurable manner. This is because in many instances the client only has a vague idea of what is wanted. This is why it is important that an experienced should analyst help define functional requirements.

- Selection of the acceptor may also appear impossible for projects that affect more than one area of the client's organization. However, appointing a prime acceptor for the overall project and seconding others for individual components (i.e. forming an acceptance team) will help.

As the responsible manager is accountable for the project (i.e. its champion and a representative from the group responsible for the project), he or she should first ensure the selection of a project manager. Without one, the project is unlikely to get off the ground. The project manager can also help in solving other issues, such as identifying an acceptor. The champion of the project also enlists the project manager's help in determining who is most affected or interested in the end product and, in addition, what skills the person is likely to need to understand the implications in building the product. Based on this input, the champion should then select someone who can be given the time to carry out the responsibilities of the acceptor.

Generally, for large projects, an acceptance team would be established (from representatives of the users) to ensure that all areas are properly covered. This group is not to be confused with the project review committee, although some individuals may serve in both roles. This team should not be formed until the project manager and the acceptor have both defined the end product. It is not uncommon for the nature and scope of the project to change quite dramatically during this initial phase of the project. Therefore, initially the number of people involved should be kept to a minimum until the three main players, namely the champion, the project manager and acceptor, are certain of the project's end product and the required resources are identified.

Understanding the project circle will enable all participants in the project to formulate a clear answer to the classic question that arises during project work: 'When does the project end?'. This also helps answer the classic questions 'Why is it being done?' and moreover 'What is the point of this?'. Obviously, the project ends when the acceptor accepts responsibility for the end product. Before this event, the deliverer (project manager) is fully responsible to the client for completion of the end product. This visibility highlights the fact that the completion event depends on the subjective personal commitment of an individual. The event is controlled by the deliverer's desire for acceptance at the earliest moment. This is to relieve the project manager of project responsibility. On the other hand, a requirement of the acceptor is to delay acceptance until his or her personal confidence level is high enough to accept full responsibility for the end product. *This is an extremely important and valuable point, because the deliverer wants to get the project accepted within time and budget and may try to give the acceptor a less than 100% product. The acceptor, on the other hand, wants to ensure that the product meets specifications 100% and may review or test* ad nauseam *and delay acceptance.* If both developers and acceptors understand this point, then it will undoubtedly have a beneficial effect on the development process. That is, the acceptor would normally have a continuous, active and useful role to enable taking over from the project manager as soon as appropriate.

Approval of a deliverable is an important event and is made visible by the personal acceptance document – a sign-off sheet with a difference. The signal that this document sends is that 'I (the acceptor), accept responsibility for such and such a deliverable'. It is important to understand that the signing of this document is not merely the 'approval of an event', but is the event itself – (i.e. the completion of the project is the signing of the personal acceptance document). The objective elements of completion (e.g. the programs, system documentation) are then subordinate to the subjective element of the acceptor accepting personal responsibility. Success will be measured by achieving completion of the deliverable agreed upon at the start of the project.

When this concept is applied to some of the typical project problems, some interesting and simple answers are given. For instance, why is there difficulty in accepting a deliverable when there is no single 'user' or systems owner? It is argued, somewhat weakly, that this is bad because a single interface is needed with the user department. When there is no acceptor or no single individual to accept responsibility for the end product, it leaves the completion event as a round table discussion, with multiple interpretations of the value of the objective deliverables. Often this means that the project manager cannot get a sign-off. The application of the project circle will make clear to all concerned the wisdom – indeed, the necessity – of a single acceptor.

How about the question 'Who is responsible for system specifications: the user or the analyst?'. This has always been a difficult question because one may have knowledge of the subject and the problem, but no specification skills, and the other may have the skills but no knowledge of the subject or problem. Applying the model to this question introduces the element of time. Have the specifications been accepted? No! Then the analyst (deliverer) is responsible – yes – and then the acceptor is responsible.

The project circle can be applied to any project of any size. For instance, when someone, your boss or your spouse for example, says, 'Will *you* (X) do *this* (Y) for *me* (Z)?', he or she is setting up a project. Similarly when an individual says, 'Will *you* (X) do *this* (Y) for *him* (Z)?', he or she is also setting up a project and a commitment is still required.

2.9 The Project Management Process

The project management process (Fig. 2.8) is driven by the project manager. All the tools or documents are designed to be managed in order to solicit and monitor personal commitments, ensuring that the project moves along according to an approved plan. Because these documents (described in detail in this book) are to illustrate the sharing of responsibility, they enable the project manager to monitor the status of an individual's dedication to the project on a regular basis. This approach assures optimum involvement of the essential project principles, as well as displaying accurate, credible status.

The process begins with the project initiation and the assignment of resources. At this time, it is necessary to be assured that there is acceptance of a personal commitment from the project manager to deliver the end product. Approval of the project plan is the vehicle for accepting this obligation.

The project manager starts the project circle by soliciting from the client the appointment of an acceptor and an agreement on the role's responsibilities. Resource managers are also approached and the assignment of resources negotiated. Note that

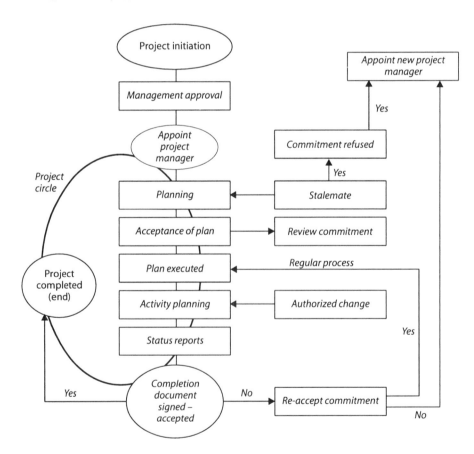

Fig. 2.8 The project management process.

the option of refusing to accept a personal commitment *must be available*. The avenue for sharing that responsibility will be perceived to be closed and promises will be dropped if it is not possible to refuse a commitment.

After the project plan is submitted and accepted (i.e. bought into by all parties) and resources are committed, the project manager then manages the project by executing two periodic management cycles. The first, a weekly cycle, is used to solicit and monitor continuing progress. The vehicle for facilitating this is the weekly activity planning schedule. The second cycle is the regular weekly, monthly or quarterly cycle for sharing responsibility upwards. The requirement must be arranged by the project manager. It can, however, change depending on circumstances. In a crisis, for example, the cycle might be daily until the crisis is over or under control. At this time, the regular cycle would be reinstated. This sharing of responsibility is facilitated by project review committee meetings, the submitting of status reports from the project manager to the responsible manager (client) and the signing of acceptance reports by the acceptor. Through these meetings and reports the project manager illustrates that the views of all individuals have been solicited and the obligation to project completion is reaffirmed. That is, a personal commitment for the project on a regular basis is demonstrated. Therefore the avenues for sharing responsibility are kept open: upwards to the responsible manager, downwards to the individual project team members and sideways to the acceptor. The project manager drives these two cycles, managing the project until the acceptor accepts responsibility for the end product and thus completes the project.

For small projects the cycles for status reports and activity planning could be less than monthly, whereas for larger projects monthly would suffice. The longer the time span between reports or meetings the less chance there is of picking up something going wrong. Thus the control cycle must be appropriate for the size and complexity of the project or event. That is to say, a mix is generally appropriate: daily, weekly or monthly, depending on the situation. A daily meeting could be appropriate when something is obviously going awry and causing a stoppage or delay: for example, development staff blaming the acceptor(s) for not signing off on a test, thus preventing progress. In such a situation, they (developers and acceptors) pass the blame back and forth, which may distract the project manager from the real issue. Remember that people cause problems and that they fix them. The solution is to get all the individuals that can be part of any solution together on a regular (hourly, daily etc.) basis until the project is back on track. These meetings will minimize the buck-passing and cooperation will become the norm. Another technique that can work when a decision is required is to hold a meeting late on a Friday afternoon. Bear in mind, however, that only in soap operas are crises resolved by Friday; do not expect the impossible or unreasonable.

When a real or perceived problem arises, the completion of a situation analysis can help in its resolution. Of course, a project manager cannot sit back and await, for example, a monthly report. It is important that continual project monitoring take place and the automating of many project activities using groupware could be beneficial. If an incident occurs, it is imperative that it is communicated for general dissemination, explaining any impact and corrective action that has been, or which needs to be, taken. For example:

- A key project member may leave.
- A deliverable signed off needs to be reinstated.
- The specifications might change.

In many cases, the impact will be a change in the project schedule. The corrective action taken will depend on the circumstances. If an essential employee has resigned, the action may be as drastic as dropping or freezing the project, or parking it for a while. Usually it is not so bad. However, if allowed to go unnoticed there could be a domino effect. Thus, one incident that by itself might be inconsequential could initiate a succession of events that could put the project in jeopardy.

2.10 Project Delays

Projects are susceptible to delays, and there are many reasons, causes and excuses for them. Generally they are not technical in nature, but relate directly to the style of the organization and its people; for example, unqualified staff, autocratic management, *laisser faire* attitudes and effective but inefficient organization. There should be good, clear reasons and not excuses for any delay. Management should not accept finger-pointing or the well-worn excuse 'technical problems' without a clear explanation. A project manager should ensure that the team members are asked, 'How will my and/or your actions contribute to project delay?'. They should know the answers. Monitoring progress and recognizing the following traps may help to prevent a disaster:

- Imposing a deadline not based on work to be accomplished but on a deadline to obtain a contract. The user can also translate this into unrealistic or ill-defined requirements.
- Inadequate planning, such as leaving out testing by users, no time being planned for reviews, sickness or training, and no time being allowed for holidays. Therefore it is important to have a contingency plan that answers the question 'What if?'. One project that the author was responsible for did not consider sickness, as the team was all in good health. However, an important individual became hospitalized, causing a delay of three months to the project. This was compounded by the fact that the external staff's productivity was affected, and costs increased as they were on a time and labour contract and the staff could not be redeployed.
- Procrastination also can be a major delaying tactic. As mentioned by many: 'Do what you can do today and leave nothing for tomorrow or you will regret yesterday'.
- A project that crosses organizational boundaries where there is infighting (e.g. Sales fighting Accounting) is bound to cause strife. Perhaps one of the functional units will not even supply competent subject matter staff.
- Lack of upwards, sideways and downwards communication will ensure that nobody can understand what is happening, so how can they design a system?

- If a project is perceived as lacking in any urgency, i.e. priority, then other jobs will take precedence.
- Lack of staff will surely cause a delay. This does not mean a simple lack of numbers. If the project requires an analyst and only a programmer is available, then the project is going to be late. Perhaps a problem is that the organization cannot attract competent staff because of its work environment.

This list could go on and on, and some project managers have had to become creative at explaining why a project is late. Project managers should ask themselves three questions each morning:

- What's delaying the project now?
- What will delay the project if I don't do something soon?
- How can I shorten the project?

These questions, coupled with following a structured methodology, will allow one to anticipate many problems and take appropriate corrective action.

2.11 Project Visibility

Although visibility has been mentioned several times already, it is still worthy of discussion as a topic by itself so that the management principles behind the project management cycle may be understood.

Visibility is the project manager's greatest ally. Usually, the only things 'visible', i.e. known to all persons, about a project are the project manager and the deadline date. This type of 'visibility' makes for lonely project managers – lonely because they can expect to bear the burden for all problems, even when the environment is changing beyond their control. We all know from experience that the only thing that doesn't change throughout the project is the deadline. Using the tools in this methodology will promote visibility of the project and ensure through change control and status reports that any deadline that is changed is based upon decisions made by the appropriate authorities.

Visibility of responsibility promotes responsible behaviour. Everyone should know the responsibility line for a project, i.e. the project organization. Thus, project communication among groups with a vested or peripheral interest is essential. *If you can stop anyone from these groups, who should have knowledge of the project, and ask them the following questions and get the same names and answers from all people questioned, then you can assume that you have good project visibility:*

- 'Who is the project manager for the project?'
- 'Who is the acceptor?'
- 'Who will management blame if the project fails?'

The people named will probably understand their project responsibilities because they will know what others in the organization are expecting of them.

Questions could also be asked of other management and staff on the objectives of the project. Poor communication of these would lead to misunderstandings and facilitate failure.

The personal acceptance documents explained in later chapters visibly make the responsibility for acceptance by using personal pronouns in describing the acceptance event.

When the scheduled goal is visible, i.e. known by all groups concerned, the team members will work towards this end. If you ask people on the project team 'When will this project end?', and you get the same response, then your project has a high probability of at least meeting the schedule. This is because everyone, assuming a commitment, is striving to meet the goal. Therefore make sure that the goal is visible. To help visibility, post the personal acceptance documents and/or the deliverable acceptance matrix on a wall where they can be seen, thus reinforcing the goal. Further, ensure that progress is visible, as this promotes confidence – in the team members and in the acceptors. However, be careful of negative visibility. This is where inquisitors are attracted to the project and team members may need to be shielded from them. Otherwise they could be disruptive to progress; for example, do not encourage inquisitors to ask for demonstrations of interesting components of the system.

All the tools associated with this methodology have visibility in mind. The project manager should take every opportunity to use visibility to promote the project's interest.

2.12 Summary

We have explained some common traits of a good project manager, such as the need for diverse management experience (business and technical); participative management; motivation; and how technical, interpersonal and conceptual skills are appropriate at different levels. This chapter's theme covered the importance of the project circle, motivation, personal deliverables and commitment. The importance has been explained of making a project visible and illustrating how it contributes to success. It was suggested that there is a need to replace the 'star' reward system with a collective reward system. A project organization has been illustrated that outlines who is responsible for what. Furthermore, the make-up of project teams now consists of people from different cultures, religions and values. Therefore it is important to understand their values and work within them. Being oneself and being open minded do this. Team members are volunteers. Treat them well and make an effort to understand them and you will have them working for you instead of against you. They will also volunteer for future projects that you manage.

We now move to the next chapter, covering quality management and testing. It is important (for ISO 9001) to realize that the role these play in the success of producing quality deliverables is a function of how much effort and resources are given to the function. A project manager should always ensure that all deliverables pass through some level of examination, which can be simply a review and/or a walkthrough. We mention this here to alert the reader to the fact that it is an ongoing function through all stages of producing an acceptable end product.

3. Quality Management and Testing

3.1 Introduction

It is no use having a project management methodology and a systems development life cycle in place without giving some thought to the quality of their deliverables. Quality management can be defined as a program of planned and systematic activities. These determine, achieve and maintain required deliverable quality. As in ISO 8402, 'Quality is defined as the Quality characteristics of an entity that bear on its **ability to satisfy** an implied need'. What is needed therefore is 'conformance to requirements'. In innumerable instances quality may be given a low priority or even overlooked within the development process. A quality program is needed in the processes of development, maintenance and planning and will transcend organizational boundaries. For example, before proceeding with any implementation it should be required that all participants sign-off on the project plan to demonstrate their commitment and the duly signed document filed in the project workbook.

One reason for quality management being overlooked, or given a low priority, is cost; another is the demand of many managers to get things done and clean up later. This latter approach is fraught with danger, as the cost of retrofitting something invariably exceeds the cost of doing it right in the first place. Therefore the question is not whether to implement quality management, but what, when and how?

During the systems development life cycle, total quality management (TQM) should be considered of prime importance. It can be defined as company-wide quality management. It is clear that the target is 'quality'. This would include partnerships among the units with a personal stake in the quality deliverable, e.g. users, acceptors, analysts, developers and trainers.

However, beware of blindly following the concepts of 'total quality management'. Many papers have been written about it, and under certain circumstances it has proven itself. However, the costs associated with it can be more than the effort is worth. Therefore, to reiterate, the question is not whether to implement quality management, but what, when and how? It is important to determine through rigorous examination what the real costs associated with specific functions are. Then determine whether the money available to be spent will contribute enough quality to make it worthwhile. For example, in determining the usability of a system much effort can be spent on obtaining the opinions of many individuals, where perhaps only a few important employees need be given the task. Thus, when planning, specific

Table 3.1 The quality requirements in accordance with the ISO 9001 standards

Quality requirements	Measurement criteria
● Ensuring that the required level of quality for the solution has been defined and that it can be measured	Acceptance plan
● Ensuring that actions have been defined, planned and will be executed which will measure the quality being delivered, throughout the whole life cycle	Project plan Development plan Implementation plan Conversion plan Change control procedure
● Assessing the deliverables and the process used to produce them	Project monitoring record
● Solution standards	Functional specs Design specs Conversion specs System manual User manual

quality activities must be built into the plan (Table 3.1), such as review of design, testing of programs and editing of written reports (e.g. requirements analysis).

3.1.1 Benefits

With the implementation of a proper quality function in the development process, and attention to real costs, management should expect most of the following benefits:

● systems that are easy to learn, maintain and operate
● systems that are easier to maintain and whose components can be reused
● systems that are testable to ensure that they perform as intended
● systems that meet users' requirements with accuracy, completeness and timeliness
● optimal use of hardware
● systems that have good security methods
● systems that meet Open Systems Integration requirements

In trying to explain quality, it can be said to have much in common with sex, as explained by Philip Crosby:

Most nearly everyone is for it (in certain situations);
Everyone feels they understand it, but would not want to explain it;
Everyone thinks execution is merely a matter of following one's inclinations; and
Most people feel that all problems with it are caused by other people.

If the project is large enough, an acceptance team should be appointed. The purpose of such a team would be to assure quality by reviewing and evaluating deliverables and conducting acceptance testing. The level of involvement would depend upon the deliverable to be reviewed, the required expertise (subject matter or technical) and the level of detail. The point is that 'error detection' should be carried out at every step of the project, and is most cost-effective in the early stages. For example, it has been calculated that the costs of error correction during the requirements phase of the systems development life cycle increase by a factor of 1000 by the acceptance phase and by a factor of 3000 at the completion of implementing a system in production. In following a systems development life cycle, two major types of costs are incurred, namely:

- those to produce the deliverables
- those incurred to ensure that quality is obtained, i.e. an overhead

One way to minimize quality issues is to ensure that development teams follow policy, standards and specifications. The policy should address not the *what* to do but the *how*. The *how* should focus on standards and planning. For example, the policy could be that a standard project management methodology should be followed to manage the stages of the systems development life cycle. Specifications should clearly explain *what* is required. These would help significantly in ensuring the quality of deliverables.

Managers are under pressure to do more with less, to produce higher quality and to get it all done on time. Some questions frequently posed by management are:

- Why does it take so long to get the system finished? In answering this question, ensure that you are not panicked into speeding up the project at the expense of quality.
- Why are costs so high? One answer is that competent, qualified professional staff come at a premium. Also, the cost of quality can be a significant item, but must be calculated so that the costs resulting from errors found during development and production are recorded. This will help justify programs for improving quality and reducing quality costs.
- Why can't we find all the errors before the system is put into production? How many readers remember the multimillion-dollar expenditures and aborted Mariner 1 space mission? The computer program had a hyphen missing that caused the rocket to go off course, so that it had to be blown up.
- How can we measure progress? Time should be recorded and project team members must be focused on spending their time on the main sequence of tasks. If time is recorded, lost time in producing deliverables, caused by interruptions and rework, can be highlighted.
- What tools are needed to do a better job? A project management methodology, following the SDLC and implementing quality management are three important tools.

By implementing some form of systematically developing systems and standardizing on some form of TQM, e.g. a project management methodology, the above questions would be answered or even not be raised. *Thus the solution is primarily a management issue.* Managers must realize that workers must become more effective by 'working smarter', i.e. managing time and the development process better. Therefore, in a systems development project, the team as a whole must take the lead in producing high-quality deliverables. Keeping data on past performance could be useful in verifying that deliverables were done on time and accepted by the client. By comparative analysis between projects, some issues may be highlighted and corrective action taken. An old saying goes that what gets measured gets done. This was just as important yesterday as it is today and will be tomorrow. Reports from the data could also be used to determine whether past problems had been corrected.

3.2 QM Organization

To establish a quality management programme it is essential that the functions be agreed upon between the different factions within an organization. The placing of the function should be clearly thought out and a decision made whether it should be in the Informatics Division (MIS etc.), in audit or in some other unit. When established, the mandate of such a unit could be to develop partnerships between other units (finance, security, informatics, audit etc.) and users to ensure conformance to requirements. Such a mandate would ensure that the requirements supported business objectives in achieving zero defects. However, the major role of the programme is to be useful in ensuring that quality is satisfactory and that without it the cost of deliverables would increase.

Some of the functions of a unit charged with quality management or quality assurance are:

- Defining what to do, i.e. prepare plans, including resourcing and requirements. Quality requirements need to be specified at the early stage of project management. A quality plan provides the tool to do this, i.e. to do it right the first time. An example of a typical table of contents of the plan is provided in Appendix B, at the end of this chapter.
- Defining how to do it by developing standards, procedures and conventions and monitoring their effectiveness. The quality plan can be the plan for determining how it is done, because it captures all the essential elements for successful project execution, i.e. it can be a flow chart or a set of procedures.
- Reviewing or ensuring that deliverables are passed through a quality control cycle.
- Reviewing systems configuration management – change control.
- Maintaining records of plans, specifications, logs, results, sign-off etc.
- Promoting awareness of the function.
- Identifying practices that can be improved.
- Conducting post-implementation reviews.

For the testing of business functions it is preferable to organize the testing into groups of users around the function they perform. Therefore, if an accounts receivable function is being tested, users from this unit should be assigned the task. It is in the functional area's management's interest to ensure that this occurs. The manager is a stakeholder in the results, and functional staff are the best able to determine whether the deliverable is satisfactory and is what they want, i.e. usable.

Acceptance should therefore come from an agent of the responsible functional manager, i.e. the person most interested in ensuring that the deliverable meets specifications. During the development of any deliverable, it belongs to the project manager; after acceptance it belongs to the acceptor. This is why it is important to establish criteria and decide what is to be tested and when.

3.3 Quality Management Approach for Systems Development

There is a need for management attention in ensuring the quality of the systems produced. One way is to implement quality management, and an approach to developing a quality management programme could be to:

1 Develop a quality plan
We consider that the process of quality assurance development starts when the project commences, and it focuses on quality requirements. Once these requirements are defined, a set of standards is established that will ensure that all the project deliverables meet the requirements.
The following draft quality plan fits into the quality requirement efforts:

- Development of the project plan
- Change control procedure
- Development plan
- Implementation plan
- Conversion plan
- Acceptance plan

Adhering to the plans illustrates that the project manager is committed to maintaining a high degree of quality assurance in the project.
2 Develop an organizational model
3 Develop the quality goals
4 Determine the quality management framework
5 Decide quality criteria, e.g. for:
(a) Network management:
– System response time, data integrity and usability, e.g. level of transmission quality.
– Availability of systems and facilities, e.g. network availability, level of accessibility and level of sufficiency.
– Optimization of the use of resources, e.g. compliance with standards and optimal use of resources.
(b) Production and computer operations:
– System response time, e.g. processing turn-around, on-schedule completion and on-line response time.
– Data integrity and usability, e.g. legibility of output and output available for authorized users.

- Availability of systems and facilities, e.g. capacity of CPU and storage, compliance with planned facilities, level of downtime (MTBF and recovery times).
- Optimization of the use of resources, e.g. establishment of standards and methods, compliance with procedural standards, and the ability to optimize resource utilization.

6 Establish quality measures. Examples are:
   (a) System response time:
       Average time-sharing response time; total number of jobs submitted versus the maximum allowed; total log-ins versus the maximum allowed; swapping area transfer rate; disk transfer rate.
   (b) Availability of system:
       Total hours of downtime (average and peak times); effective production time; system overhead; network utilization; total tape and disk mounts.
7 Prepare a detailed plan of quality assurance.
8 Implement and subsequently evaluate the quality management programme.

The strengths and problems of quality management vary from one organization to another. In some cases, the strengths cited by some organizations are problems within others. However, its strengths appear to be directly linked to the support or lack of support by management. One aspect that should never be compromised is quality assurance of deliverables. However, what is quality? A good definition is one that can be objectively measured. In defining it, be careful of traps, such as using the words *conformance* and *meeting*. These are subjective terms and can therefore be arbitrary. Some might say that the deliverable 'meets user requirements' and therefore that this is the prime quality standard. Consider the development of a poor product that could be considered 'high quality' because it met requirements. Ask yourself the question: is it of such quality if the requirements were not defined adequately in the first place by the user? Surely this is where the QA team must review the requirements from a wide perspective and ensure that if there are perceived gaps they can be filled in before the project starts.

3.3.1 Quality Assurance (QA)

QA is part of a total quality management programme. It can be defined as the finding of errors or as a destructive process used in manufacturing. Its function is to interpret test results to determine product reliability and process improvements. Analysis techniques are used to identify or map test cases to some aspect of the deliverable in order to determine coverage in that area. Basic automated tools are used to determine the percentage of lines of code and path logic covered by sets of tests. Some automated tools report on the input needed to achieve additional coverage. The process of quality assurance ensures that deliverables, which may be, for example, documentation, are in all respects of sufficient quality for their purpose. A standard is published as IEEE Std. 829XXXX, where 'XXXX' is the year of the latest publication. In all cases the purpose is to find errors before they get into a process, be it manufacturing, a computer process or a procedure. A project manager who develops good testing plans and strategies will go a long way towards ensuring that the deliverable meets specifications. However, it is important to realize that this is not random hacking away by a user or programmer, but a systematic way of approaching the process. It is also not the correction of errors after the fact, or debugging a program from diagnostics, or processing data in a standard way.

The process is demanding, and must start as early in the project cycle as possible. The process of testing is one that demands discipline and controls that must be strictly adhered to in order to test systematically and efficiently. This is because errors differ in severity, and if all the rules that can be thought of are covered and classified then the evaluation of test results will indicate where the system is falling short of specifications. Thus the focus must be on the 'rule' that handles a class of data. Not only must individual conditions be tested, but also combinations.

One reason why testing is a neglected component of project management is because it can have an impact on deadlines. Project managers must resist any attempt at cutting it out or reducing it to meet a deadline. It should be realized that one objective of testing is to uncover systematically groups of errors with as little effort as possible. Some groups of errors to be considered are syntax, data and logic. The result of testing is to confirm that the deliverable is acceptable and that it works and meets acceptable quality control measurements. For example, it is no good having something that works but takes so long for the function to be performed that it is next to useless. For instance, if the system response time criterion was x seconds, but it actually took y minute(s), then the deliverable would not pass the quality management criteria established. Documentation could be measured by its style and usability. The standard might be to use Playscript style for the documentation, yet the writer might have produced it in free-form style. This, of course, would not pass a review.

To ensure project success it is necessary to check the quality of all deliverables. Thus, approval to continue with the project should be obtained before moving through subsequent phases. What this appears to be saying is something that in real life does not generally occur. That is, work stops if the deliverable is not signed off. If a dogmatic approach is followed, developers will see it as an impediment to progress, and those who impede as traffic cops and nuisances. Thus one would be faced with a start–stop situation, and this, if accepted, would not be conducive to team morale or keeping the team together. Realistically, acceptance is presumed and sign-off is concurrent with continuation of the next task or stage.

3.4 Sources of Error

As can be seen from Fig. 3.1, testing can be linked to each phase of the systems development life cycle. Validation is agreeing on 'What are we doing?' and verification focuses on doing the job the correct way.

As highlighted earlier, errors become more costly to remove as each phase of the SDLC is completed. Therefore it is important to catch them early. Many consider initiation to be the most important phase, because if the correct requirements and problem have not been identified, then the project is in trouble from the start. The

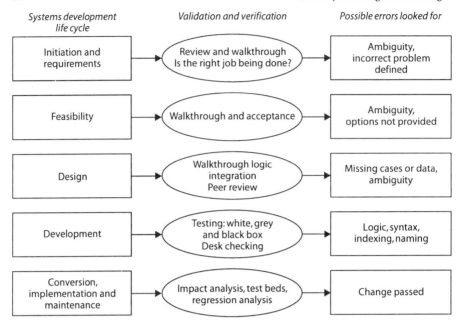

Fig. 3.1 Testing and the SDLC.

whole project could be done based upon the wrong input. This can be contrasted with a program bug, when work can move on to the next phase after the bug has been fixed; in this case the business scope is not affected.

Most error sources can exist in many of the SDLC phases and affect the system like a plague. Thus, as with antibiotics and bacterial infections, it is necessary to catch the error (disease) early. Although there are some very rigid methods, common sense must prevail. But be cautious. For example, the author was managing a large development project that used a database management system (DBMS) that had stood the test of time. Therefore a calculated risk was taken, upon approval of management, to forego the testing of the DBMS. It was felt that it would prove nothing and time would be better spent on testing the functionality of the unique requirements of the client. This was found not to be the correct approach, and some form of modified test would have minimized some frustration at the user testing level.

There are many reasons why systems fail. They can fail from business or technical perspectives. The author was involved in an after-the-fact development of a system that had taken twice as long because the developer kept convincing the client of the advantages of adding bells and whistles. There was no user sign-off at each stage of development and no walkthroughs of the stages. Had a group or committee review taken place, the project might have been kept in bounds and time and cost would not have escalated. When the client moved on and was replaced by a new client, the project deliverable couldn't be implemented because it was too complex for the user to understand. The new client just did not have time to comprehend all its functions, so the project was restarted with less ambitious goals. This was a problem of not implementing quality management and a methodology that, with its checks and balances, such as reviews and acceptance sign-off of each deliverable, might have prevented the project from getting out of hand. I say 'might', because sometimes management can be persuaded to continue a project because they do not have time to fully appreciate the impact of their decisions. What happened in the case cited was that everything was frozen, the design revisited, and a system implemented that was functional, although it might have been considered a less than perfect technical solution. Subsequently, configuration management for changes was implemented and the system evolved. Bear in mind that 90% of the functional requirements were met and the cost of the remaining 10% could not be justified by a business case.

One major reason why systems fail is because of lack of testing or poor testing strategies. However, testing cannot be done without good quality test data, tools, good environment, skills and methodologies. Thus in a systems development environment, project management must be of good quality and the manager must have the right skills, as discussed in this book. Having found a suitable manager, other components, such as the definition of requirements, planning and control, design, development and implementation, with quality control and testing at each stage, are essential. Another overall aspect not to be ignored is the training of individuals on a project team and users.

3.5 Fault Types

There are numerous fault types. However, a fault as defined by the IEEE, is the manifestation of an error that can lead to failure. In addition, the American National Standards Institute produces many publications related to errors. The type of fault can be classified broadly, with some being more destructive than others. A few are illustrated in Table 3.2, and the reader can add or obtain further literature on the subject.

Table 3.2 Classification of types of error

Types	Description
Ambiguity	Some things can be read in more than one way. Thus precise wording can help, or a change of wording may be required.
Cross-referencing	A data dictionary can help in ensure that the correct data elements are used and referenced.
Input/output	Communication with external devices.
Logic	One of the most common types of error. Some tools can help to avoid or minimize this type of error by checking the logic automatically.
Syntax	Common, but like logical errors these are usually easier to detect.
Documentation	There are many reasons for this type of error. A project manager should always ensure that documentation is written, reviewed and tested as the project unfolds.

3.6 Testing in Perspective

Testing is the exercising of system components to find previously undiscovered errors. Therefore, a good test case is one that has a high probability of finding new errors. Referring to a previously mentioned time when testing was not undertaken, it is undoubtedly true to say that the probability of finding a new error was low. However, a successful test would have provided a test-bed for reviewing usability, detecting errors in a deliverable and verifying that deliverables were acceptable for production.

Testing is usually considered the testing of programs. Although this is a very important component, all aspects of a project deliverable need to be tested, e.g. the procedures listed under the design heading. Testing can usually catch poor analysis and design before they lead to project failure. Evaluation of products is a form of testing, but to distinguish it we shall call it simply 'evaluation'; the reason for this will be explained below.

3.7 The Testing Flow

Executing a test not only tests the specifications but also the test case design itself. When a test case does not work, it is sometimes the fault of the test case rather than the program executing it.(Indeed, both the test case and the item being tested could be faulty.) Thus you can see that a successful test may in fact be in error, due to the test construction being faulty. We will discuss test design in detail in the sections on black and white box testing. A typical schematic of a test flow is outlined in Fig. 3.2.

3.8 Test Design

This aspect includes those techniques involved in generating the large number of tests required to achieve desired quality levels. Good test design involves defining the test cases required for determining branch and path coverage, data flow coverage and reliability. There is a major labour component involved in building proper test suites. Thus this is a key area for automation.

A test design document should detail a strategy, plan, methods to be used and test types. These are explained in the following sections. One important aspect is determining who should be chosen to test. Testing is a function of the project and acceptance teams, and also the users. The skill of the tester depends on the type of test being conducted. When a tester signs off, there is an implicit guarantee that the expected result has been achieved and the product is verified as working satisfactorily. However, the primary skill of all testers is to be methodical. They must have an attitude that allows them to want to prove that the deliverable does not work. Thus, a penchant for detail, if not perfection, coupled with the stamina to persevere and be hard-nosed is mandatory. Without these, the results will be slipshod. Having

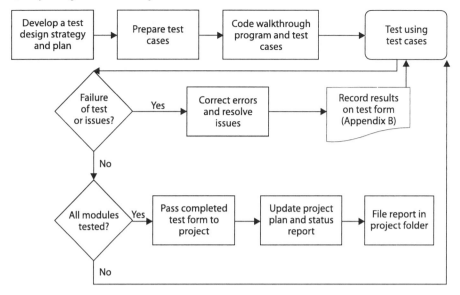

Fig. 3.2 Schematic of a test flow.

illustrated some traits that may be considered negative, it is important to realize that the outward appearance of the tester is one of diplomacy.

3.8.1 Strategy

The objective of a test strategy is to reduce the need for continuous testing for the same case. A test plan must be implicit in detailing a strategy and the test design and document how the strategy will be structured. The more detailed objectives are to verify, validate, maximize resources and improve quality.

There are two basic approaches, namely top-down and bottom-up. You can apply them both to systems and program architectures. Generally, top-down is used for systems architecture and bottom-up for programs. However, sometimes a combination is used, known as the 'sandwich strategy'. It is assumed that an architectural design has been approved and is documented.

3.8.2 Test Management and Planning

Management consists of the tracking of test data, including test cases, procedures and defects. The purpose of a test plan is to describe the scope, approach, resources and schedule of testing activities. The plan identifies the items to be tested, the features to be tested, the tasks to be performed, the roles and responsibilities of those involved and any risks associated with the plan.

The plan itself is a dynamic document and should be usable by users, the project manager and the acceptor. The document is a working document that is used from the conception of the project. Thus, on completion of the project it reflects a history and provides an audit trail.

In planning, it is important to determine what results are required. This is what the acceptance team or tester will use as a criterion. Mapped onto the plan would be schedules, times and resourcing. These can be derived from the project plan and schedule. That is to say, the planning concepts in this book are as valid for testing as they are for any other project, i.e. testing is a sub-project. However, in some industries plans for testing are elaborate – imagine the testing that must have gone into the Space Shuttle. In fact, anybody doing work for a specialized industry must know the bible for that industry. It is an objective of planning to get the highest quality for the least expenditure of resources. Approval, therefore, is acceptance of a certain quality level. Thus, the test plan is a major part of any project plan.

Walking through a plan with all parties concerned is an excellent approach to ensuring that the who, what, why and when are clearly delineated. A useful document on this aspect is the U.S. Military Specification 1521B. Walkthroughs are also an important approach for giving the audience an immediate response. If a program, for example, is walked through, then it encourages programmers to check their work rather than let a computer do it, which promotes a *laisser-faire* attitude. One purpose of a walkthrough is to detect errors that are perhaps not detectable by the computer.

Some components which can be used as a check list to be considered when writing a test plan and which are additional to standard planning principles are:

- A description or purpose of the functions to be tested should be produced in order for testers and the client to be clear as to what approach is going to be taken in the testing process.

- Test reference items should be identified and references to appropriate documentation made.

- Environmental needs, such as communications, software, hardware, security, testing tools and other items, such as publications, should be spelled out and approved before testing starts.

- Resourcing must be determined and approved by the appropriate resourcing manager. The skill level of the individuals, together with any specialized training, should be spelled out and approved.

- Functions/features to be tested/deferred or demonstrated, and if deferred, why and until when? If not all functions/features are to be tested, it is important that agreement is reached with the acceptor. *Modern Structured Analysis* by Edward Yourdon (Prentice Hall, 1989) can help in this aspect.

- The approach should be described, i.e. static or dynamic testing. Static testing can be a boilerplate for most organizations. It consists of walkthroughs, deskchecking and an evaluation of test results by the client. On the other hand dynamic testing, such as unit, string, acceptance, stress and response times should be conducted by computer operations for both operability and testing of the facilities.

- Selection of input. Appropriate input that will be used live should be derived.

- The pass/fail criteria to determine whether a test item has passed or failed need to be approved. For example, must the test run from start to end? Under what circumstances may it be resumed in the middle? Are there to be checkpoints in long tests?

- If any risks are involved, they should be spelled out so that a proper evaluation on supporting the project can be made.
- Suspension/resumption criteria (rules that the tester will use to do the test).
- Metrics – results of measurements. Any measurements that can be taken, such as in stress testing, should be recorded and used as input to the analysis.
- Analysis of results, i.e. a test report. This would consist of test logs as appendices and a written report that indicates the state of the deliverable.

3.8.3 Test Execution

Here we apply test cases to the code under test and provide data about the software's performance. The results that are monitored during test execution may include the software output or some internal measures, such as code statement coverage. Capture/playback is considered necessary for any test execution: this is the most common of all automation tools.

3.8.4 Walkthrough (Peer Group Reviews)

A walkthrough is a quality control function and at least one should be *considered* for each phase of the systems development life cycle. An example of where it may not be considered appropriate for all phases is in a small project. There are different types of walkthrough, and the most appropriate should be selected for the audience. That is to say, for example, technical specifications should be walked through with technical staff and not general management. The walkthrough itself is a detailed formal review of a deliverable conducted by a group of knowledgeable peers and prospective users of the deliverable.

It should be used continuously throughout the systems development process to ensure optimum communication and to produce the best product by spotting errors as quickly and economically as possible. The primary purpose is to provide a guideline that helps to expedite the process to ensure quality and completeness without sacrificing flexibility and utility. This can be likened to 'egoless programming', whereby the deliverable is put up for scrutiny and errors or improvements can be expected. Undoubtedly the lack of walkthroughs would result eventually in poor-quality deliverables. Additional information can be obtained from references such as *Structured Walkthroughs* (Yourdon Press) and *Technical Inspections* (Freedman and Weinberg, 1982). A typical process is spelled out below, although it may vary from organization to organization.

1 Well in advance of the walkthrough, schedule it and distribute relevant material.
2 Ask reviewers to be prepared to discuss at least one positive and one negative comment about the material content.
3 Ensure that the presenter gives a quick overview of the subject before opening the subject to the audience.

4 Obtain comments from the reviewers at the walkthrough by getting the chair-person to go around the table and ask each individual present to point out an error.

5 Ensure that the walkthrough does not become a brainstorming session. Let the person whom the comment is aimed at consider corrective action outside of the forum. This is especially important if the individual disagrees with the person making the comment. That is, record the comment for action later.

6 An hour should be aimed for as the maximum time for the walkthrough.

7 Record the results of the walkthrough. They may be decisions or suggestions, depending on the level of authority of those attending.

3.8.5 Documentation

Documentation is one of the most neglected areas in project management. Testing is no exception. Users don't want to do it – they are quite happy to sit down at a PC and check functionality by using a user or training manual as a guide. The result is super-ficial. Therefore it is important to realize that four documents are key to successful testing, namely:

1 *Test Design Specification* – this would include specific plans to test functions, e.g. test identifier; what is to be tested; pass/fail criteria; platforms if appropriate; approach; individual test IDs; statistics and analysis; and any special requirements.

2 *Test Case Specification* – this explains how a test will be run and can be very technical. It is essential for mission-critical systems and high up-time require-ments. Governments tend to require a detailed document that can require a lot of overhead to prepare. The document might be maintained on a table grid, as illus-trated in Appendix C.

3 *Test Procedure Script* – These are the procedures for the acceptance team or user who will be carrying out the test. They can be complex or simple depending on the complexity of the deliverable being tested. They are especially useful to opera-tional staff, who must interact with the system. Some aspects that must be considered are: purpose of the test, any special requirements or training that may be required, procedural steps, and identifying errors and how they will be handled. In such a script, one approach is to use the user manual and the screens that are illustrated to check what will be displayed when the procedure is followed. In this way, the user manual can also be verified.

4 *Test Log* – Records what happened during the testing, and is used for subsequent reporting. This is a tool used to correct errors, and the log becomes a change document. Subsequently, when compared to the next test, it can be determined whether or not the changes were done. Since most errors tend to cluster together, a review of the log will indicate possible common problems. In such a case, the cluster could be more vigorously stress tested to ensure it is stable.

3.8.6 Management reporting

A good test plan is necessary as a base for reporting. Reports to persons with a personal stake should state what occurred versus what should have occurred. To minimize reporting, only the exceptions should be noted. The plan should be kept up-to-date and used for future estimating.

3.8.7 Methods

Traditionally, five common methods are used to determine the acceptance of a completed deliverable. They are:

1 The most likely conditions have been tested and pass scrutiny.
2 The project manager, the boss or the client says enough is enough.
3 All conditions have been thought of and an 'else rule' used for all other conditions.
4 Best and worst case scenarios have been tested.
5 A developer has run out of user patience, money, ideas, time and his or her own patience.

It is apparent that some are risky, e.g. number 5, which, if followed, could be disastrous, although it might be a solution to a non-mission-critical application. Numbers 1 and 3 should be used regularly, although one cannot escape the fact that number 5 happens many times, especially when it is apparent that returns are becoming marginal. If asked, 'what would I advocate', it would be Number 3, because at least invoking the 'else rule' one would catch all conditions.

3.9 Test Types

Testing does not guarantee that a system has no errors. It will, however, reduce the probability of errors occurring during system use. It is also effective to do comprehensive testing at an early point in time to minimize the future costs of error correction. There are numerous overall tests that need to be conducted on the system environment to be assured that performance is satisfactory. In *Datamation*, 15 February 1988, p. 67, an article entitled 'Passing the Systems Test' outlined the importance, nature and procedures involved in systems testing. For example, an operations unit must be assured that applications fit its technical platform (hardware and software), that the application operates reliably and that there is a restart/recovery procedure.

It is appropriate to define some test terms. For example, 'unit testing' or 'white box' apply to the testing of program modules, i.e. each program module is tested individually to ensure that it works. The purpose is to test a program's logic to ensure that it meets specifications.

There are criteria to determine the coverage of a program's logic, namely: statement, path, decision/condition, multiple conditions, program integrated testing, and walkthroughs and code inspection. However, a module may not work when grouped with other modules. Therefore, a module is grouped with other modules to perform string tests or job streams. White box testing (verification) is an approach to testing the structure of the internals of individual modules and is primarily conducted by programmers to prove the correctness of program implementation. The structure of the program is examined and test data are derived from the program's logic. The primary approach to this testing is to sift through lines of code or structure charts.

Following white box testing is black box testing, or integration or system testing, i.e.; the testing involves all job streams, including backup and recoveries. It should be done in as close to a production environment as possible. This testing validates inputs, functionality, consistency, help features, access and security, performance, ease of use, documentation and output. It is done primarily by analysts and users. It is concerned therefore with what functions are performed.

When this is accomplished satisfactorily, acceptance or usability testing (grey box testing) is conducted to give the user a chance to experience the human–machine interface. This should be done as early as possible so that suggestions can be incorporated into the interface design and implementation. Prototypes can be used to accomplish this, but beware of the issues of using this approach. With acceptance testing, if the software passes the tests, systems ownership passes to the user. This should be predefined and lead to the formal sign-off. Users need to be assured that the deliverable meets their business needs and is usable. Usability covers the human–machine interface, i.e. it must be user-friendly.

Another reason for developers to use grey box testing is to demonstrate the ability of the software to do black box testing. Such software quality testing detects errors to allow black box testing to be conducted without finding significant program code errors. We commonly consider a graphical user interface as being friendly. Documentation is also tested to ensure that it is readable and conforms to a standard. A reference on this subject is *The Art of Human–Computer Interface Design*, edited by Brenda Laurel, 1990. The foregoing processes of white, grey and black box testing are illustrated in Fig. 3.3.

Stress tests are performed focusing on volumes of transactions and numbers of concurrent users. For example, an email stress test could be conducted at scheduled times by following a pre-tested script with the purpose of determining at what threshold the system becomes degraded and unusable. This aspect can very easily be overlooked or considered not worth the effort. Consider for a moment implementing email for, say, 1000 or more users on local area networks connected through a wide area network. Perhaps the vendor's demonstrations and customer references all indicated satisfactory performance. However, a stress test may confirm that the quality management criteria could not be met with the current network topology. Therefore the network would need to be upgraded before the email could be successfully implemented. Eventually black and grey box testing could be conducted by the users and hopefully the email favourably received. The point of the story is that stress testing is an important aspect of overall quality. It should not be cut out due to deadlines or resource constraints. And even if the tests all have favourable results, do not forget the human component, i.e. can the change be assimilated?

Static testing is conducted throughout the SDLC. This can be defined as the testing of some components before executable code is produced, e.g. desktop checking. However, as a project moves through the SDLC, data becomes increasingly dynamic, i.e. it requires program execution to test. This dynamic data generally provides the data for static testing in reviews.

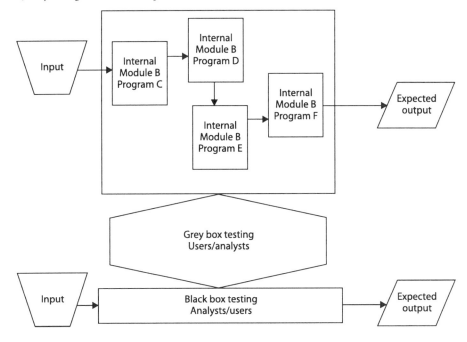

Fig. 3.3 White, grey and black box testing.

3.10 Summary

For the benefit of project managers and readers who may be unfamiliar with the importance of quality management, this chapter and its appendices provide an overview so that its importance is highlighted. An experienced project manager may use it as a checklist or to suggest that junior staff follow the principles outlined.

It has been explained why quality management and testing are essential in the production of deliverables with minimal defects. There are many quality assurance methods, both manual and automated, and a reader with an interest is advised to do further reading. Management treats many aspects of quality management, such as walkthroughs, superficially because of their overhead. However, the use of QM and its component parts can produce significant reductions in the number of errors that would normally go undetected. Testing is hard work, and it should be structured and complete. The objective of testing is to produce deliverables with as few defects as possible within the constraints of time, money and resources. This is achieved by performing systematic evaluation throughout the project life cycle. For systems, it can be defined as any activity that can be checked by means of actual execution to determine whether a system or component behaves in the desired manner. Other components of the systems development life cycle can be verified through reviews and walkthroughs. It is clear that automation is necessary in order to meet minimum quality standards. Software development is virtually impossible without test automation. While individual tools can be successfully introduced, new bottlenecks of manual procedures will surface in the testing life cycle.

Documentation is one of the most neglected areas in project management. Testing is no exception. Users don't want to do it – they are quite happy to sit down at a PC and check functionality by using a user or training manual as a guide. The result is superficial.

A practical product evaluation approach has been illustrated that contributes to testing the functionality of vendor products and compares them in order to determine the best fit for an organization.

The next chapter outlines the systems development life cycle and this needs to be quality managed and integrated with the project management methodology.

Appendix A: Testing Examples

These examples are provided to aid the project manager in understanding the different tests so that they may be considered and if appropriate, included in any project plan.

A.1 White Box Testing

This tests a program's logic to ensure that it runs without error and verifies that it meets programming specifications.

Assume we are testing a System A and that the program modules are related to each other in parent/child relationships. At the highest level, we have structure charts – a system architecture that depicts functional breakdowns. For example, in Fig. 3.4, System A consists of Function A and Function B. As can be seen, all functions and

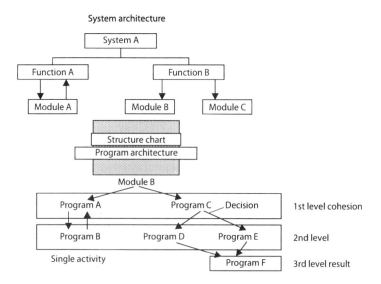

Fig. 3.4 A structure chart.

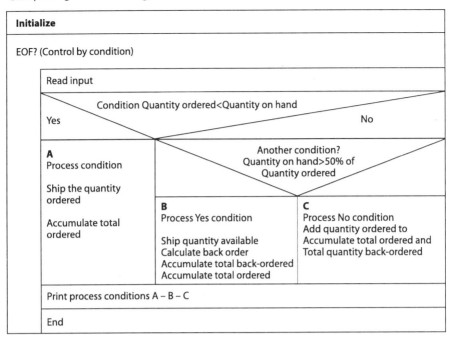

Fig. 3.5 A Nassi–Schneiderman (Chapin) chart.

their modules break up the entire system into subsets and these can be broken down into other subsystems and so on.

At the cohesion level, we can see illustrated how strongly the elements within a module are related. The strongest cohesion occurs where each element in a module is a necessary and essential aspect of one function; e.g. Programs A and C are related.

Test sources for white box testing can be obtained from numerous sources. Some of the most common ones are:

- CASE tool outputs, such as key inputs and outputs
- Decision tables and Nassi–Schneiderman charts (Chapin charts), as in Fig. 3.5
- Business forms
- A data dictionary
- Live data
- The original functional specifications

As many sources as possible should be used, bearing in mind that testing is an overhead that is not always supported by management. Thus, select that which will give you the best chance of successfully testing the system within the constraints that may be imposed.

If the chart of Fig. 3.5 were written in English, it would appear as follows:

- Read order
- Continue to read the orders until end of file

- Read Quantity ordered. If = or < Quantity on hand, ship Quantity ordered, Accumulate total quantity ordered; end of If statement
- If Quantity on hand is > 50% Quantity ordered, Ship quantity available, Calculate back order, Accumulate quantity back-ordered; end of If statement
- Add Quantity ordered to Accumulate total quantity back-ordered; end of If statement
- NEXT
- At end, print totals for Ordered–Shipped–Back-ordered

A decision table (Fig. 3.6) is also an excellent tool for determining whether all logical combinations have been covered. The basic construct is illustrated in the matrix of the figure. It can easily be seen that it has two components, Conditions and Actions, e.g. If only Condition 3 is positive and all other conditions negative and Question 2 is positive do Action 1. Many developers do not use decision tables because they can become large and unwieldy. This is why they are excellent: they contain every possible condition. However, to simplify the many conditions, it is possible to combine them where they activate the same actions. A compromise is the Nassi–Shneiderman or Chapin chart (Fig. 3.5). These are considered a replacement for the traditional flowchart. They have one point of entry and one point of exit and consist of a construction of sequence, selection and repetition. Their deficiency lies in the fact they cannot be used for designing data structures. They are also not easy to produce and do not link to data models or dictionaries.

Many individuals will not believe that program testing begins before coding. This is called desk checking or dry checking, and the objective is to keep bugs out of programs and save on the error removal costs. One way to do this is by verifying the program structure chart. These charts can be used to identify and eliminate logic and specification errors before coding. Programs can be represented by noting the sequence, selection and iteration constructs.

Flowcharts, a common documentation technique for program logic, are not considered a good technique for describing structured programs because they do not represent hierarchical structure, although they do help in writing programs. However, a useful graphic representation of program flow is the flowgraph (Fig. 3.7). It can be likened to the state diagrams that engineers use. The process is to represent a program flow. It is then possible to determine the number of independent paths in

	1	2	3	4	5	6	7	8
1. End	n	N	n	n	Y	y	Y	y
2. Question 1	y	Y	n	n	–	–	–	–
3. Question 2	y	N	y	n	–	–	–	–
Actions								
1. Do this	x		x					
2. Calculate		X		x				
3. Do this		X		x				
4. Do this	x	X						
5. End					X			

Fig. 3.6 A decision table.

the program being tested. This is known as the cyclomatic complexity. The purpose of this number is to determine the error-proneness by predicting where errors are most likely to occur. Design errors are likely to occur where the number is >10 and coding errors <10. More information on flowgraphs can be obtained from Dr Roger Pressman's book *Software Engineering: A Practitioner's Approach*. The cyclomatic complexity value gives the maximum number of conditions; the conditional program statements tell you the specific conditions to test. This information, plus end-point conditions, gives a set of scripts for the program to be tested. Boundary testing is elaborated under black box testing, but can be used here for the testing of internal programs. The purpose of complexity analysis is to test the most complex parts of the program code. The number derived represents the number of compares. For example, Fig. 3.7 and Table 3.3 illustrate a simple chart with nine steps and a cyclomatic complexity number of 4.

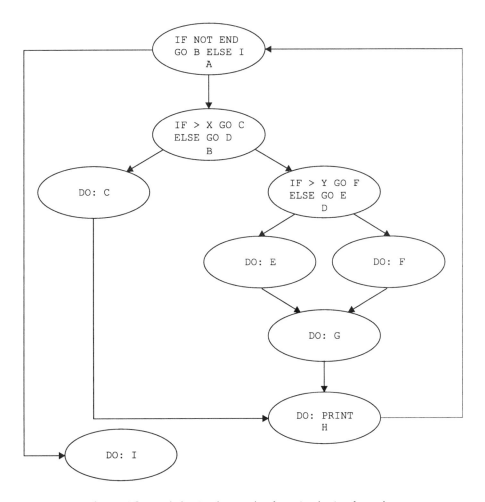

Fig. 3.7 A flowgraph showing the procedure for testing the size of a number.

Table 3.3 Deriving test cases from a flowgraph. In this case, the cyclomatic complexity (i.e. the number of paths) = 4.

Case	Path	Procedure
1	A–I	If End go to I Process I
2	A–B–C–H	If >X go to C else go to D Process C Print
3	A–B–D–E–G–H–I	If >Y go to F, Else do E, G and H
4	A–B–D–F–G–H–I	If Not >Y do E, G and H

A.2 Evaluating White Box Test Results

To do this type of testing is as tedious as the program is complex. Some source code errors can be caught by the compiler or program analyzer. Others may be caught during program execution. However, the errors that keep programmers mumbling are those avoidable by prior design review using structure charts. We will therefore outline some guidelines for locating logical and other internal processing problems in the debugging unit. Using test beds, test scripts and test cases the following errors should be caught: reference, computational, comparative, control flow, interfaces, and input and output.

A test script is a group of test cases designed to find errors in a function. There may be a very large number of these test cases. Therefore they are usually maintained in a catalogue or library of data called a test bed. They have many uses but are mainly used in regression testing, that is, verifying the integrity of systems after changes have been made. The test cases should consist of input and expected results from processing. At the white box level each module or path is verified. In a black box process, the programs are tested from a transaction point of view. In this case the focus is on the input and output legs of the structure chart.

A.3 Black Box Testing (Functional Testing)

As mentioned earlier, this is the testing of input and interfaces, done primarily by analysts and users. This is an overall test to ensure conformity to the system requirements. An organization usually has this done independently of the programmers who are given the results to debug the programs. To determine whether black box testing should be done at any stage, it is usual to show that the unit test (grey) has not produced an unreasonable number of errors. The measurement of unreasonableness can be statistical, i.e. if x per cent of errors are found, continue with debugging until the number is reasonable.

If we look at a system architecture structure chart, we will observe that it is a good source of black box test data. Such a structure outlines the test data and corresponding procedures: on-line versus batch, equipment etc. In fact, it is necessary that the architecture be established before testing, because if this is wrong it is difficult to correct. A walkthrough is a good approach to ensuring that the architecture is correct. For example, consider the effect if, in a client–server application, a function was designed to be processed on the server yet it was obvious that it should be done on the client machine.

A.4 Black Box Specifications

These are specified in much the same way as for white box testing. However, white box testing concentrates on a module or program test, i.e. internals. Black box testing is concerned with functionality, so the test script concentrates on the business side and is usually performed by subject matter staff. This again is something that must be negotiated between the project manager and the client. A plan and schedule are essential to inform the client when the people will be required. This is another reason why regular reporting to the project review committee and all other interested parties is necessary to keep them informed so that they know when the project is lagging behind or ahead of schedule and that their resources will be required at a time other than originally agreed upon. The specifications analysis is used to establish test cases using different methods.

A.5 Testing Methods

Exhaustive testing requires that every condition be evaluated. This, of course, is not always practical or necessary, and domain testing in various modes is done. One method, 'Equivalency testing', for example, can be done to test a representative sample of data *within* a domain boundary containing valid values. It is a judgement call as to what constitutes such a sample. Boundary testing uses values on the boundary, such as maximum and minimum values. Then there is *outside* boundary testing, which tests invalid values such as depicted in Fig. 3.8.

A.5.1 Outside Boundary Testing

It can be seen that A–R and 1–10 are within the domain; that 11, 12, 13, 14 and S are on the boundary; and that 15, J, K, U, W and Y are outside, i.e. invalid. The approach is invaluable whether you are using black or white box testing. This is a two step process, namely:

1 *Identifying the equivalence classes*
   The first step is to identify the equivalence classes. These are identified by taking each input condition (usually an attribute) and partitioning it into two or more groups. Two types of equivalence class are identified: valid, i.e. those that repres- ent valid inputs into the system; and those that represent all other possible states of the condition, e.g. erroneous input values. Given a set of attributes, identifying the equivalence classes is largely a heuristic exercise. Guidelines are:
   (a) If an attribute specifies a range of values, e.g. value can be 1–99, identify one equivalence class (value is >10 and value is <100) and two invalid classes (value is <10 and value is >99).
   (b) If an attribute specifies the number of values, e.g. 1–10 owners can be listed for the house, identify one valid equivalence class and two invalid equiva- lence classes (no owners and more than 10 owners)

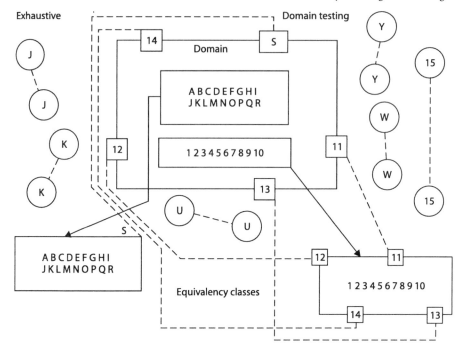

Fig. 3.8 Outside boundary testing.

(c) If an attribute specifies a set of input values and there is reason to believe that each is handled differently by the program (e.g. type of house must be bungalow, semi-detached, detached x bedrooms, four storey), identify a valid equivalence class for each and one invalid class, e.g. apartment or flat.

(d) If an attribute specifies a 'Must be' situation, e.g. X must equal Y, identify one valid equivalence class (it is equal) and one invalid equivalence class (it is not equal).

(e) If there is a reason to believe that elements in an equivalence class are not handled in an identical manner by the program, split the equivalence class into smaller equivalence classes.

2 *Defining the test cases*
   The second step is the use of equivalence classes to identify the test cases.

(a) Assign a unique identifier to each equivalence class.

(b) Write a new test case covering as many of the uncovered valid equivalence classes as possible until all valid equivalence classes have been incorporated into the test cases.

(c) Until all invalid equivalence classes have been covered by the test cases, write a test case that covers one, and only one, of the uncovered invalid equivalence classes.

   The reason that invalid cases are covered by individual test cases is that certain erroneous input checks mask or supersede other erroneous input checks. For example, if a specification states: 'enter book type as (Hardcover, Softcover or Loose) and an amount (1-9999)', the case expressing two error conditions: XYZ 0 (Invalid book type and amount) will probably not exercise the check for the, amount because the program may say 'XYZ is unknown book type' and not bother to examine the remainder of the input. Therefore the test should be broken up into separate test cases, namely:

- A book entered as XYZ is in error but the value 88 is correct and may not be tested, i.e. the test should be set up to prove that the input is wrong and has been detected.
- A book entered as Loose is correct but the value 0 is in error, i.e. the expected result is that the value is proven to be wrong.

Thus, as can be seen, both error conditions have now been tested through correctly designing the test case.

A.5.2 Boundary Value Analysis

Boundary value analysis is a method to develop test cases to test the areas where valid and invalid values meet, e.g. a field that can only contain valid input between −1 and +1 could have the following test cases: −1, −1.01, 1 and 1.01.

The other important part of designing test cases is to cover the operational, performance, input and design limits of the code. The idea behind this is to subject the software to conditions or inputs that are in some sense extreme. For example, if a database is designed to handle 20 transactions a second, the program should be subjected to rates of 19, 20 and 21 transactions. In general, boundary tests cover the first and last, lowest and highest, longest and shortest, and slowest and fastest conditions that the code logic was designed to handle. Other boundaries are available at run-time, reload and initialization, and critical event timing.

A.5.3 Cause–Effect Graphing

While the above techniques do not attempt to deal with the problem of testing combinations of inputs, cause–effect graphing does. It is a method of creating a set of high-yield test cases. Through its use of decision tables, it helps point out incomplete and ambiguous specifications. A cause–effect graph is a natural language specification translated into a formal language. See Myers' book *The Art of Software Testing* (1979) for detailed information about this technique. The following process is used to derive test cases:

1 Break specifications down into attributes.
2 Identify cause and effect. Cause = a distinct input condition or an equivalence class of input conditions.
3 Assign each cause and effect a unique number.
4 Create a basic graph by linking the cause and effects using Boolean graph symbols.
5 Add constraint symbols to complete the graph. These describe causes and/or effects that are impossible.
6 Convert the graph into a limited entry decision table where each column represents a test case.

7 Convert the columns in the decision table to test cases.

A.5.4 Stress Testing

This technique is applicable to volume testing. A heavy stress is a peak volume of data encountered over a short span of time. In many instances it is not undertaken because everything from other testing appears normal. *However, it is essential to ensure that the system operation conforms to a given threshold, which should be specified in the requirements analysis.* Stress testing is applicable to programs that operate under varying loads or interactive, real-time and process control programs. For example, if an email system supports up to a number x of users, subject the system to extreme pressure by determining the number of users that could be sending messages and measuring the load on the network and server by transmitting a predetermined script for half an hour at a scheduled time, say twice a day for five days. It should be understood that the script should be tested beforehand.

A.5.5 Evaluation

The approach is to review reports, screen displays and other output and is valid for black, white and grey box testing. Test check-out is laborious and an intellectually challenging process. If possible, automate this function as much as possible. However, it is important to verify results with the stakeholders in those results. Also, retain any automated data in test beds for future use, since testing is not a one-time event. To maintain these test beds is a function of quality assurance. If a support or help desk environment exists, use the staff to assist in testing, as they will be the front line support individuals when the system goes into production.

An important function of quality assurance is to determine reusability of components. With object-oriented programming, this reusability will become a major benefit. With a library of reusable code, testing will be reduced because the reusable items will have been pre-tested.

A.6 Test Inputs (Test Data)

Inputs into any testing should be examples of data that will be used in a production environment, together with the original requirements document. In addition, software analysis tools may be available and, if appropriate, used.

Each type of system has its own different test design. For example, in a batch process steps are standard and it is relatively simple to establish an input that can be verified against an output. Therefore a test log can be used indicating the input, the function to be tested and the expected output. If the output is not what was expected, an error can be assumed.

For interactive systems, an approach is to lead the tester through the functionality by following a script, with the screens expected being displayed along with the result. This is a time-consuming operation because it entails the tester sitting at a PC and following the script to its conclusion. In order not to frustrate the user it is desirable that the scripts be broken down into, say, half-hour stages. The tester should then complete a script report before doing another script. If this is not done, users will find many reasons why the script is wrong, or why they are not available etc.

Consideration could be given to having a reward system, where a prize is given for each problem found. This could be collective or individual.

When testing *per se* is completed, volume testing should be considered. This means taking live data and passing it through a stable tested system. However, it will not contain all conditions. Therefore it can only be seen as a quality measurement criterion for timings etc.

A.6.1 Test Summary Report

This is an important document and as a minimum should cover an assessment, the results of testing an evaluation and recommendations. It can be used as a predictor of project quality inasmuch as, for example, if there are frequent errors of the same type then there may be cause for alarm. Management should then keep a close watch on the project deliverables and perhaps implement more frequent reviews.

A.7 Program Debugging

How many of us have made simple errors like the missed hyphen mentioned earlier or leaving out a full stop at the end of a statement? When I first started programming an IBM 1401 in Autocoder (1966), I insisted to the IBM consultant at least a dozen times that I had put word-marks in all the correct places. Needless to say, I had not, and it took an experienced IBM consultant to verify the program and find the problem. The moral of the story is that it is common to find that another programmer can be more successful in finding errors in a programmer's code than the individual who wrote it in the first place. To reiterate: programs that are tested using program charts or other tools require less debugging after coding. This is because it is easier to change structure charts than code. Therefore, do not use the computer to do the full testing. A walkthrough with peers, i.e. egoless programming, will improve the quality of the deliverable. Let the computer, when used, catch such aspects as syntax errors. A simple strategy should cover how the error can be replicated and then corrected based upon an analysis of the error. Thus the objective is to identify the conditions through testing, isolate them, follow a change routine and then verify that the change has worked. For those individuals involved in the debugging exercise some guidelines are necessary. It is preferable, for example, to isolate one error at a time and use tools such as traces.

Some CASE tools can scan a program and derive its structure. They determine what the program does. This is reverse engineering, i.e. determining 'what' from 'how', and making corrections is the underlying principle of debugging. These CASE tools are continually evolving and improving in functionality. If an organization has a maintenance problem these tools can be very useful, since the code is the only constant and can be trusted. This is because, over time, documentation is lost or no longer reflects the program; the original and subsequent programmers have long departed; and the designer has probably retired or become a consultant.

When mixing languages, debugging can be difficult. However, Simon Peel, who manages Micro Focus's OEM and directs Unix support teams in Palo Alto, California, suggests an approach for COBOL and C. He suggests that, when debugging COBOL, one should use Animator (a debug tool) and a C debugger. Simply debug the C executable; then, when you hit a call to COBOL, Animator will be invoked, and when you exit or call another C program you will drop back to the main program. This seamless interface between Animator and C debuggers means that both languages can be used to their full potential.

A.8 Program Changes – Regression Testing

The purpose of regression testing is to verify that a program works after changes have been made. All systems are changed, and this is usually done through configuration or change management. After a change has been completed, regression testing can verify that the systems still function correctly after each iterative change has been made and that it has not regressed. When a change has been approved, do some form of regression testing before and after the program has been modified.

Regression testing therefore verifies that the functions that should not have been affected by any change were in fact not changed. Therefore, the purpose is to prove that the new code works and that, furthermore, the previous version of the code works as it did before the changes were introduced and new bugs have not been introduced. Corel, the developers of Corel Draw, found that, through automated regression testing, errors are found at a much earlier stage in the development cycle.

A.9 Automated Tools

Testing approaches can be labour-intensive unless some form of automation is used. The use of tools that record, for example, keyboard, mouse and screen operations, into a script and subsequently plays them back on a later software release verifies consistent operation, i.e. regression testing (checking that the software has not regressed to an earlier state).

By the year 2000, it is expected that the use of automated tools will be a common occurrence. This is because the problems associated with software quality and costs are becoming virtually impossible to control. The demand for distributed systems, graphical user interfaces and highly interactive applications demonstrates the significant growth in the complexity of software. Many companies are relying on procedures that have been in use since the beginning of the computing era, and most testing is being performed by engineers operating manual tests. Therefore you should approach the implementation of automated tools in a holistic way by continually monitoring the process and listening to feedback. Further, ensure that the skill set exists, manage resistance, and determine participation and the impact of change, e.g. will the 'creative artisan' type of developer leave?

There are, in many programs, so many combinations that it is virtually impossible to test them all. If you, the project manager, don't know how to determine the paths of a program, it is impossible to know whether they have all been tested. The traditional 'seat-of-the-pants' method is not and never has been a satisfactory method. It is becoming even less so when the number of users that are able to write programs is increasing substantially. Some tests would not be done without automated tools.

Many development organizations now claim to need a larger staff and larger budget to test software than to develop it. Often such uneven staffing requirements result in using expensive contract help to try to break through the testing bottleneck. As this becomes acute within a company, it will adopt its first automation tool. The resultant labour reduction realized by developers utilizing testing tools more than justifies the capital equipment and training costs associated with the approach (Fig. 3.9).

While cost benefits are one yardstick for justifying the initial expenditure on automation, the expense of not improving testing procedures is quite another. Unfortunately, there are many examples of disasters caused by buggy software that has been released into production. AT&T's long distance communications networks have crashed causing thousands of customers to be without service. In one instance, there were nine hours of national long-distance telephone chaos in the USA in 1990. American Airlines' reservation system has had service interruptions that cost the company millions of dollars in lost revenue. Ashton-Tate fell from being a market leader based on a single bad software release. Microsoft's Windows NT, shipped to customers in August 1993, was electronically tortured, beaten and brutalized until it broke – thousands of times. Competing teams alternately sought to build and to punish the huge system (millions of lines of code). The purpose of extensive and exhaustive testing, fixing and almost daily building was to try to ensure that the system worked in its first released version.

For those companies with external markets for their software and services, the economic risk of making similar mistakes is nothing short of a potential financial crisis. However, no less a crisis can occur for buggy and delayed software developed by internal development teams. Literally hundreds of 'clients' whose effectiveness might be compromised due to faulty or unavailable software could adversely affect the organization's profit and loss account.

Although complexity, payback and release risks are reasons enough in themselves to justify test automation, an even more fundamental reason remains:

> The most important reason to adopt test automation is that contemporary software development is almost impossible without it. If anything, manual testing error rates increase as the tedium of doing yet another boring test run increases. If the process itself has bugs, this creates an uncertainty about the bugs that are found. Real bugs are missed. False bugs are discovered and the software 'fixed', thereby introducing bugs. (Boris Beizer, author of *Software Testing Techniques*)

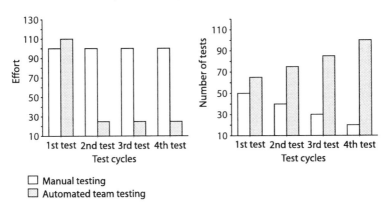

☐ Manual testing
☐ Automated team testing

Fig. 3.9 Comparison of automated and manual testing. Left: testing effort; right: number of tests.

While the benefits of adopting test automation may be clear, most organizations have yet to understand how to approach the overall process of testing in general, or how to adopt automated tools in particular. A common scenario is for a company to buy a single tool to automate a manual bottleneck, such as test execution, and then discover that its expectations for major productivity and quality improvements were not met. Even with the successful implementation of an automated tool, the testing bottleneck merely shifts to the next step in the process.

After making the decision to adopt test automation, the next logical step is not to start reviewing and buying specific tools. Rather, it is best to first understand the overall testing process and the procedures that will need to be supported, then start to incorporate the tools that best meet the requirements you have set forth.

A.9.1 Approaching Automation

A simple way to introduce automation is to review questions commonly asked of those responsible for software testing and quality assurance. For example:

- How many bugs have been found?
- How long has it taken to find them?
- How complete is the testing?
- If it is not complete, when will it be?
- How reliable is the software?

While the first two questions might be answered by those still using manual methods, the last three questions are far more meaningful to an organization, and they can only be answered by those using automated tools. Test automation has to be approached by defining what data will be collected and what analysis will be used to determine when the testing is complete. One such approach is to collect failure data based primarily on functional tests. This data is then fitted into a software reliability growth model to determine the software's readiness for operation.

A second approach is to establish measures of testing completeness based on some criterion and collect the associated data to measure progress. Common among these are such measures as statement and branch control flow coverage and data flow coverage. Either or both approaches can be used.

No matter which approach is selected, the volume of data required to support automated testing, and resulting from automated testing, is enormous. Thus a test repository (database) (Fig. 3.10), must be established as a place to save test items and measurement data in a structured, retrievable way. It is not uncommon in a modest testing program to require tens of thousands of test cases and to generate thousands of test incidents. A program of this scale will also require a team, whose members need accurate and timely access to this data. A test repository will provide this access.

A.9.2 The Automated Testing Model

Most software authorities agree upon the basic steps within a proper testing process as well as the general order for integrating automated testing methods into an organization. However, since it is impossible to test all possible combinations of input and expected results from a system with any meaningful level of complexity, it

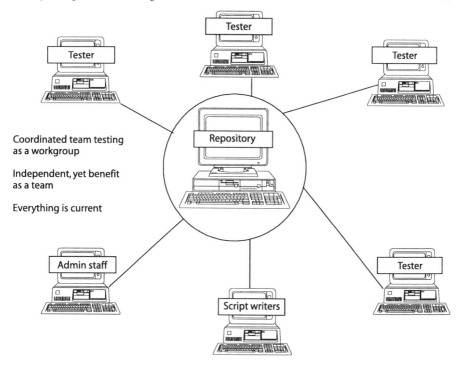

Fig. 3.10 Test repository.

is necessary to analyze and understand the areas of high risk in order to maximize return on testing investment. Effective testing is defined as testing that achieves its objectives of covering or minimizing risks at an acceptable cost. A system view of software testing illustrates several interdependent activities. Various automation tools are associated with each area.

Taken together, the overall components of the system testing model would be integrated as shown in Fig. 3.11.

- *Test design* includes those techniques involved in generating the large number of tests required to achieve the desired software quality levels. Good test design involves defining the test cases required for determining branch and path coverage, data flow coverage and reliability. There is a major labour component involved in building proper test suites. Thus this is an essential area for automation.

- *Test execution.* These highly labour-intensive steps apply test cases to the code under test and provide data about the software's performance. The results, which are monitored during test execution, may include software output or some internal measures, such as code statement coverage. Capture/playback execution tools are a basic requirement for any test effort and are the most common of all automation tools.

- *Test management* consists in the tracking of test data, including test cases, procedures and defects. Test planning, including scheduling, is included in this activity.

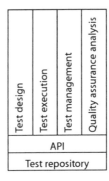

Fig. 3.11 System testing model.

- *Quality assurance* applies broadly to all of the activities. Its function is to interpret test results to determine product reliability and process improvements. Analysis techniques are used to identify or map test cases to some aspect of the product in order to determine the coverage in that area. Basic automated analysis tools are used to determine the percentage of lines of code and path logic covered by sets of tests. Some tools also report on the input needed to achieve additional coverage.

A.9.3 Implementation of Automated Testing

While full implementation of test automation must address all of the major test activities mentioned above, several issues must be considered as preparatory steps. The first is to define the testing goals with measurable and objective criteria, such as requirements coverage, path coverage and reliability.

The next step is to establish the measurement and management system to be followed. This will allow the test results to be interpreted in terms of the defined criteria. For example, if software reliability is a test criterion, then the measurement system must support the data collection needs, such as failure times in terms of execution times. It must also have the capability to produce metric data from reliability models.

Initial testing methods will probably be functional, testing software against specified requirements. Automated test drivers, such as capture/playback tools and automated management and analysis tools, will most likely be the first tools considered for implementation. As test automation advances, structural testing techniques will be introduced, probably starting with branch testing and progressing to dataflow and domain testing. Such advanced testing procedures are only possible when automation has been implemented throughout much of the overall testing process.

In order to assess the merits of commercial test tools, it is first necessary to examine the system and architectural issues involved in applying automation to the industry's accepted model.

A.9.4 Test Repository

At the core of the test system architecture is the test repository. This central facility is used to store, organize and validate all the information necessary to support a robust departmental and ultimately corporate-wide testing and quality assurance program. Examples of information maintained in the repository include:

- *Test documentation*: such as test plans and the specifications for test design, test procedures and test cases.
- *Test procedures*: a set of test activities used to exercise the application.
- *Test cases*: a measurement of software performance at a point in time.
- *Test logs*: records of all procedures, cases etc., indicating such test data as results, dates and times.
- *Failure data*: incidents and problems.
- *Reference information*: IEEE, Department of Defense, ISO standards and corporate standards.

The repository also provides access to existing source code libraries to enable, for example, automated static analysis, code metrics or structural test case generation. In addition, the repository must support group testing efforts with security and record-level locking features.

A general schematic of the repository and associated data facilities would be as illustrated in Fig. 3.12.

The BBS/email provides for the sharing of information before its submittal to the repository. The library is the storage facility for the test assets themselves, test procedures and test cases, and such variable length test data as core dumps and test images. The database is used to cross-reference all test data to maintain configuration control in an evolving product release cycle. The archive is a facility for securing periodic copies of the repository and for storing historical information, which facilitates the journalizing of changes.

All of the test automation tools use the repository as their information 'back plane'. The data model for the repository must be fully disclosed and access to it facilitated by published access methods.

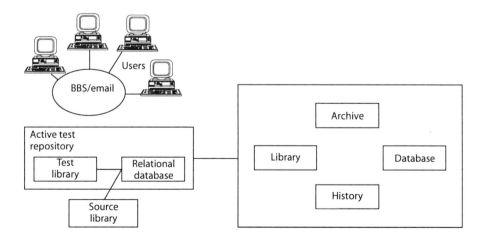

Fig. 3.12 The repository and associated data facilities.

An organizational testing entity could be established as a workgroup. In such an environment a tester could run any test in the library and immediately verify the results. The administrative staff component would keep everything in synchronization and resolve problems.

A.9.5 Test Execution

There are five basic test execution requirements for process automation:

- automatic playback
- automatic logging of test results
- automatic queuing of scripts based on test results
- extensive error handling, including crash recovery
- automatic collection of coverage data

Execution tools automate the application of test cases to the software under test and provide data about the software's performance, functional or otherwise. 'Capture/playback' execution tools are the most common, with a wide variety available which cover a wide range of prices and functions.

Transactional test tools involve the simple capture of all system transactions and the subsequent playback of those transactions on a designated host computer. Character-based tools record what the user sees and play it back for review. As the name implies, these tools can only address character operations, not icons, mouse movements etc. Client–server execution tools address local area networks and visual interfaces. Client–server configurations and graphical user interfaces for OS/2, Unix and Windows applications have placed a major emphasis on testing that occurs at multiple locations.

Advanced execution tools can record all of a client's keyboard, mouse and screen operations, capture them into a script and subsequently play them back on a later software release to verify consistent operation; this is regression testing (checking to see that the software has not regressed to an earlier state). The better versions of these tools make the script editing much easier by recording it in a high-level scripting language and integrating it with a standard programming environment, such as Visual Basic or C. These high-level scripts communicate directly with the operating environment, e.g. Windows, and translate the captured information into high-level operations:

```
Window Focus ('NotePad')
Menu Pick (Open File)
```

Conversely, tools that yield only low-level scripts typically require advanced programming skills and communicate with hardware rather than the operating environment. The scripting language itself is more difficult to interpret:

```
Mouse Down (320,245)
Mouse Move (320,248)
```

Imagine you have a full suite of regression test cases and your developers change 'Notepad' to 'Scratchpad'. With high-level scripts that change can be quickly made. With low-level scripts, the time required to find all the mouse movements that relate

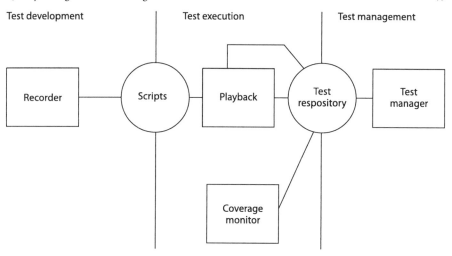

Fig. 3.13 Automated execution process diagram.

to 'Notepad' could be significant. When the goal is to generate test scripts that are easy to interpret and easy to maintain, only high-level scripts are feasible.

Test execution tools provide many ways to monitor the software's performance. Built-in test cases allow screen images to be compared, output data to be examined, file or window existence verified, interprocess communication to be monitored and correct file contents to be checked. User-defined test cases can also be integrated into the scripts. A process diagram of automated execution would be as illustrated in Fig. 3.13.

Other software or system performance can be monitored with test execution tools. System resources, i.e. memory, stack usage and disk space, can be monitored. Performance of the software under varying system configurations can be measured. Coupled with test design tools that analyze the structure of the software, test execution tools can also capture information about test coverage, i.e. statement, branch, path and data flow.

A.9.6 Test Design

Of all automation tools, test design tools are destined to become the most important elements of the software testing tool suite for two fundamental reasons. First, they will remove the large labour component in building test suites. Second, design tools are the only instruments for generating the large numbers of tests that will be required to achieve 'adequate' testing.

Test design requirements for process automation include the following capabilities:

- Generate tests from existing sources, such as source code, recorded scripts, load maps and functional/requirements specifications.
- Generate runnable scripts.
- Generate coverage data such as path definitions, control flow and data flow.

Test design can be addressed for functional (acceptance) or structural (unit) tests. However, design automation tools for functional tests are hampered by a lack of formal software requirements or functional specification languages. Consequently, the test coverage has to be defined by interpreting natural language descriptions. Automation tools can be applied to this activity to catalogue and organize the test coverage points and associated test cases. That data can then be used to easily generate reports of coverage completion.

Structural testing better lends itself to automated test design because the software code exists as a formal description of how the software operates. From this formal description structural test design can be highly automated, as Fig. 3.14 demonstrates.

The code analyzer is specific to the source language and parses it into a canonical form. From this form, control flow or data flow graphs can be developed. From the flow graphs, the particular coverage elements can be generated. Coverage elements are paths, branches, all-uses data paths, domains etc., depending on the coverage criterion. These elements are then used by the code instrumentor so that coverage can be monitored during program execution. The predicate interpreter retraces the code predicates (conditional statements) to the software inputs. These inputs become test cases that are applied to the software with a test driver. As the driver executes the software, the instrumented code logs information becomes the measure of coverage completion.

Variants of this test design system, based on different testing strategies, can be developed. The important point is that many of the most effective testing strategies are too difficult to undertake without an associated set of design tools.

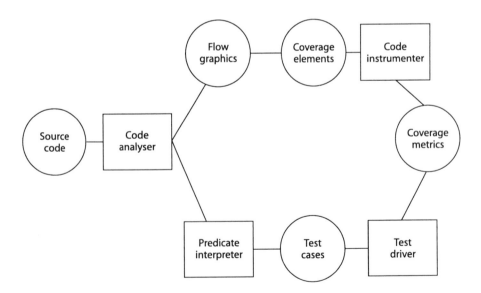

Fig. 3.14

A.9.7 Test Management and Planning

The management of a software test and QA program requires a system to monitor progress and measure results. This system requires a sophisticated tool that must be integrated with design and execution tools so that all are accessing a common set of data. Test management tools maintain the test repository, and analyze and report on the data stored in it. These tools empower engineering management personnel to see a unified view of the status of a testing program.

Planning involves a careful review of the software specification, followed by a definition of testing goals with measurable and objective criteria. It will typically include designated methods for both functional and design testing. The test plan is the key to the design of specific automated software tests.

A.9.8 Benefits

If we compare a manual approach to an automated approach, we would find that the automated one is far superior. The test suites built for the first test cycle are an investment. Payback will be realized in subsequent cycles, as it will be seen that they can be run in a fraction of the time that it would take to run them manually. As more tests can be conducted in the same time frame, if there is a deadline there is less likelihood of major errors through using automation because the majority of errors are found in the early stages of testing. This is also beneficial in that the effort required for automated testing will decrease over time, as many tests can run unattended.

A.9.9 Inputs, Outputs and System Integration

When implementing test automation tools, it is helpful to consider the information flow required between the various stages of the testing process. In essence, the outputs from one test activity need to be reviewed in relation to the required inputs of the following activity. Table 3.4 gives a list of such inputs and outputs.

There are tools available to aid the process of testing and debugging. For debugging, learn them before they are needed. Some of these tools are highlighted below, but as software is a changing platform it is important to learn the state of the art at the time testing is being planned. Some tools and techniques available are illustrated below, but this should not be taken as an endorsement. For research on automated tools available, review *Data Pro* and *Data Sources*.

Computerworld, 19 October 1989, In Depth, describes some tools. It features automated regression testing (ART) as a useful tool. Some other automated tools are:

- *VERITAS ViSTA™*. This product has simulation techniques and libraries to exercise and increase coverage of hard to reach code or physically difficult to replicate test scenarios. Other facilities include error-seeding, code complexity and presentation graphics. The company in Santa Clara, California, distributes a free evaluation kit.

- *The Evaluator*. This is a software test system that automates the testing and retesting of software. Software can now be tested unattended, 24 hours a day,

Table 3.4 Inputs and outputs

Inputs	Test activity	Outputs
Software specifications Functional design Standards documents	Planning	QA plan Test plan
Software specifications Software Test plan	Design	Test design specifications Flow graphs
Test design specifications Software Flow graphs	Development	Procedures Test cases Coverage instruments Test drivers
Procedures Test cases Coverage instruments Test drivers	Execution	Incident Problem Test log Test results Coverage
Incidents	Analysis	Problem reports Coverage analysis Reliability

seven days a week. The product automatically generates a report for each test conducted. Because Evaluator can test graphics and text-mode applications there are few applications that it cannot work with. The product features three main test facilities: Learn, TCL Programming Language and C Test Library. These provide a comprehensive environment for regression and stress testing. The company may set up a two-week evaluation.

- *Q/Auditor* by Eden Systems Corp. is a software tool that calculates the cyclomatic complexity number to determine the effort required in developing and/or maintaining programs. This tool enables programmers to build quality into COBOL programs during new development. Furthermore, it avoids introducing error-prone conditions in maintenance, virtually eliminating time-consuming code reviews. On a PC, a Common User Access method uses standard pull-down menus and one-key operations. New programs are migrated to production only if they receive a top quality code rating. Existing programs must equal or better their previous grade to re-enter production status. It has over 450 metrics, such as function point estimating, complexity scoring, IFs without corresponding ELSEs and data elements that are not referenced, to name only a few.

- Bender & Associates have a case tool product that does requirements-based testing. Mr Bender was manager of Software Testing Technology for IBM and as a programmer was one of the few to have received IBM's Outstanding Invention Award. Requirements are validated by identifying all functional variations and inconsistencies. This is an aid in project management to the extent that quantitative measurements are provided of the testing process.

- *Ferret* is an automated software testing system by Tiburon Systems Inc. It is designed to increase software quality while decreasing development costs and shortening the delivery schedule. It performs regression testing to verify that repairs to code or software enhancements have not caused additional software bugs. The graphic capabilities offer a solution to handling the complex requirements of OS/2, Windows and the Macintosh. Once connected, the system allows a test or quality engineer to develop and execute automated test procedures. Its major features are:
  - Non-intrusive hardware and software
  - Platform-independent
  - Operating system-independent
  - Variable playback speed
  - Area-of-interest, window-of-interest or full screen image comparison
  - Selectable areas of inclusion or exclusion
  - Synchronizer for real-time playback
  - Test control language
  - ASCII-based scripts
  - Video window
  - Interface to CASE
  - LAN interface
  - Expandable

Another approach is to create one's own automated tools by building programs that can create files for analysis by, for example, comparing known values with generated values. This may take a little time to think through, but it can be well worth the effort. However, the best tools are those that are integrated, i.e. a complete suite that addresses the total environment. In using a suite of tools, a good approach is to learn them on a working program or system. If your company does not have procedures for testing you could write them by experimenting and then have the procedure adopted by your client or company. *Computerworld*, 9 October 1989, In Depth, describes how to 'Pack your Testing Toolbox'.

A.9.10 GUI Testing

There are special challenges with testing graphical user interface programs. Although such applications give users more control over their workflow and workspace than traditional applications, this gives a corresponding increase in the number of situations that need to be tested. Thus, speed in creating and modifying test procedures is critical. The most productive paradigm for this is the record/playback technology built specifically for GUIs. Traditionally it has been possible to test on positions and time. However, with a GUI we have unpredictable behaviour. Objects appear in new locations, with different sizes or at different rates than in previous tests. Thus test scripts that automatically compensate for this unpredictable behaviour are essential. The benefits are more reliable and more maintainable test procedures. In moving from character-style applications that have approximately 2000 points to inspect on a screen to a full-size GUI window with from 300 000 to 800 000 individual pixels to inspect one can easily see the need for automated testing in a GUI application. Such testing requires state-of-the-art image comparison technology.

A.10 Quality Audit

An audit is an integral part of any TQM. It is a management tool to evaluate, confirm or verify activities relative to quality. If it were practised throughout the life cycle of systems development then there would be fewer overruns and failed projects. It is not performed to apportion blame, but to continually improve the project manager's skills. Generally the audit process consists of three components:

1 Planning the audit
2 Conducting the audit
3 Implementing recommendations

The audit requirement is important in the context of ISO 9000.

Appendix B: Quality Plan

The following outline of a Table of Contents is a tabulation of a typical quality plan. Refer to ISO 9004-5: Quality System Elements – Guidelines for a quality plan.

1 *Purpose*
The purpose of the quality plan shall encompass the product quality objectives, scope of work, and time periods of validity.

2 *Management responsibilities*
It is essential that the organization responsible for undertaking the project be identified. The acceptance team should also be identified.

3 *Quality system*
Any quality system that is in use within the organization should be highlighted.

4 *Contract review*
If a contract is part of the project, a procedure for its review should be in place. In addition, the responsibility for the coordination effort should be specified.

5 *Design control*
The plan should indicate where in the design process its validation and verification shall take place. This would ensure that it conformed to requirements. The interface of client and users should be detailed. Any applicable study, codes, standards or documents relative to deliverable objectives should be specified.

6 *Document control*
Any documents and their management should be detailed. Here an automated document management system may be worth considering.

7 *Purchasing*
   If deliverables are obtained outside the organization, the requirements, selection and methods of acceptance should be specified.

8 *Quality control*
   A process for acceptance should be specified and a test plan should be prepared.

9 *Records*
   A database of errors found and corrective action taken should be implemented so that they can be rectified easier in future or prevented from occurring. Document control may help.

Appendix C: Test Cases and Results Form

What is to be tested	Project manager	Schedule
Special requirements		

Client	System	Version
Module:	Run:	Revision:
Specified by:	Date:	Reviewed by:
Tested by:	Date tested:	Tester's signature:

Test item #	Input/action	Expected result	Pass (P or ✓)	Fail (F or X)	Result description/comments	Action

Appendix D: Example of Processes for Evaluating a Product/Deliverable

In addition to the standard testing conducted during systems development, there is a need to evaluate vendors' products/software to verify functionality and that it will work in the organization's technical infrastructure. To evaluate a deliverable it is important to determine its technical features, quality of documentation, whether it works with the organization's equipment and operating systems and the effect it will have on user attitudes. There are numerous ways of doing this and the following is one.

From an evaluation point of view, the foregoing can be categorized into three components, namely:

1 Technical quality of input/output and error handling

2 Modelling, i.e. the adequacy of the model used in simulating a real-life application

3 Documentation, i.e. the supporting materials and instructions available in print and on the screen

An acceptance team consisting of users and technical staff should consider, for ranking purposes, a four-point criterion-based scale as follows:

- Technical quality
  - Level 4: Exemplary. The technical quality of the software is extremely high with respect to user inputs, software outputs and lack of system errors.
  - Level 3: Desirable. The level of software is not as technically adequate as Level 4 because of minor flaws in design. The flaws may be regarded as slight inconveniences, not serious enough to detract from the overall functionality of the software.
  - Level 2: Minimally acceptable. Software at this level has distinct weaknesses that are, at the very least, constant annoyances to the user and, at worst, a distraction from efficient learning of the system.
  - Level 1: Deficient. This software has flaws that hinder efficient usage of the system, regardless of the technical content.
- Modelling
  - Level 4: Exemplary. At this level, a highly realistic portrayal of a real-life situation is provided, yet its complexity is within the grasp of the intended user.
  - Level 3: At this level, the software has a less adequate, though usable, model.
  - Level 2: Minimally acceptable. The model has significant weaknesses, although the model is still usable in carefully controlled situations.
  - Level 1: Deficient. This is generally considered unusable, regardless of its strengths in other areas.
- Documentation
  - Level 4: Exemplary. Software at this level has clearly written, concise documentation that fully explains how the software may be used in the user's subject area and provides technical information from a data processor's point of view.

- Level 3: Desirable. Like Level 4, documentation at this level explains how the software may be used in the user's subject area and technically; however, it contains minor deficiencies or is not considered well written.
- Level 2: Minimally acceptable. This level of documentation contains a minimum amount of usable documentation and the technical aspects have minor errors and omissions.
- Level 1: Deficient. Documentation at this level is clearly inadequate to support the use of the software, either technically or by the user or both.

D.1 Use of the Criteria

An acceptance team using the criteria will enable the team to arrive at a complete evaluation of software that is both meaningful to the user and will be reliable. The evaluation itself contains two components:

● Ratings on the three criteria
● Written summary comments by the evaluation team

D.2 Steps

Step 1: Study Evaluation Criteria

Study the definitions of each of the important characteristics of the software together with the descriptors for each level of the scales given.

The sample evaluation illustrated later should be looked at carefully to give an idea of how the criteria are interpreted.

Step 2: Familiarization

Become familiar with the software being evaluated. First, read the software documentation and work through the software to get a general idea of how it flows. Second, emulate a practical problem to test the functionality of the software, its error handling ability and its ability in interactively giving advice. If, during this step, the software contains programming errors serious enough to prevent it from operating as described in the documentation, discontinue the evaluation and skip to Step 4.

Step 3: Assign Ratings

The evaluation team should reach a consensus on the level that best describes the software in each category: Technical Adequacy, Modelling and Documentation. There are no half-points on the scales: the software must be given a rating of 1, 2, 3 or 4 for each category.

Undoubtedly it will sometimes be found that none of the levels perfectly describes the software being evaluated. Nevertheless, select the level that has the most features in common with, or is most similar in nature to, the software currently being used. A rule of thumb is that, if one is uncertain which of any two adjacent levels on any scale to assign, choose the lower of the two. This will prevent 'inflation' of the ratings. Also, try to rate each characteristic independently, without allowing the rating of one characteristic to influence the rating of another.

Step 4: Write Evaluation Notes

After the software has been rated on all relevant scales, brief evaluation notes should be written on the team's overall opinion of the software. These notes should be as constructive as possible. For example, wherever appropriate, point out ways in which the software can be improved, how it could be integrated into the functional unit and what the implications might be if it were used outside design. Guidelines for preparing these notes are given in the next section.

After the evaluation is finished, it should be entered on an evaluation report form similar to Figs. 3.15 and 3.16.

Software or deliverable name:
Developer or vendor:
Date: **Version:**
Cost:_____ (if evaluating proprietary software)
Configuration:
Description:
Evaluation team:
Date of evaluation:
Equipment used:
Evaluation team ratings: **Technical:**   _____ **Modelling:**   _____ **Documentation:**   _____
Comments:

Fig. 3.15 Evaluation report form.

Software or deliverable name: Accounts receivable module	
Developer or vendor: Information Architects	
Date: 3 March 1992 **Version:** 4.0	
Cost: Dependent on whether in-house or proprietary software (being evaluated)	
Configuration: *Workstation:* Compaq Pentium, 32 Mbyte RAM, colour graphics card, colour monitor, 200 Mbyte hard disk *Network:* WAN operating system: Banyan Vines *Server:* IBM 4086 Unix O/S and Ethernet NIC	
Description: This program is designed to assist accounting staff in the recording of accounts receivables based upon standard accounting principles.	
Evaluation team results	
Date of evaluation: 27 November 1997	
Equipment used: Workstation: AST Bravo connected to a Token Ring LAN and Ethernet backbone	
Evaluation team ratings: *Technical:* 2 *Modelling:* 3 *Documentation:* 4	
Comments: The evaluators were in strong agreement about the quality of the documentation. However, there was some disagreement on the technical quality of this program. The project manager asserts that the system is functional according to the specifications. One evaluator agreed with this assessment. All other evaluators doubted that the system would be easy to learn and are uncomfortable with the way the module programs are fragmented. As technical adequacy is important, this module should be rejected and changes made.	

Fig. 3.16 Sample evaluation.

D.3 Guidelines for Writing Evaluation Notes

Step 4 in the evaluation process requires that brief notes be written on the evaluation team's overall opinion of the software. They are intended to supplement the scale ratings, not to restate the characteristics of the software conveyed by the ratings. In practice, evaluators find note-writing to be the most tedious part of the process. This is probably because the notes must be reasonably brief to give the reader a quick overview of the software, while providing sufficient detail to be of use. As an integral part of the evaluation process, notes should be written carefully. To help write the notes, the following guidelines are offered:

1 Aim for notes to be about 150–250 words in length.
2 Write in complete sentences, preferably in the third person singular.
3 Avoid the use of technical terms or jargon.
4 Make sure the written comments are consistent with the scale ratings. For example, if Technical Adequacy is rated 4 (exemplary), don't refer to it as of little value.
5 Avoid restating the criteria set forth in the scale ratings.

If the deliverable or software is not acceptable, then corrective action must be taken. The function of corrective action is to make corrections to the deliverable or if necessary change the specifications.

A formal presentation from the acceptor, or project manager on his or her behalf, may be appropriate to an acceptance team and/or the project review committee. This is done to satisfy other users who may be affected by the deliverables of the project, before the acceptor is in a confident position to sign.

The foregoing can be used to evaluate proprietary software or in-house developed applications.

D.4 In-House Deliverable

For an in-house program deliverable, a simplified version of the above could be simply to document on a sheet of paper the functionality to be tested (grey box testing), with a subject matter specialist simply stating that the component has passed or failed. Of course, it is necessary to indicate what result is expected from the test. The sheet would then be passed to the project manager who would follow a change procedure to get the deliverable upgraded to an acceptable level. Other components, such as documentation, could be based on a review by interested parties. An evaluation might also be as simple as listing total functions in the products being considered and simply ticking whether the product has the functionality or not and determining which one has the least 'no's. However, this approach can be dangerous if the product is complex.

Appendix E: Procedure for Implementing Quality Management

In Fig. 3.17 we show the steps to establish and maintain a quality management process.

Details of each of the steps in the process are given below.

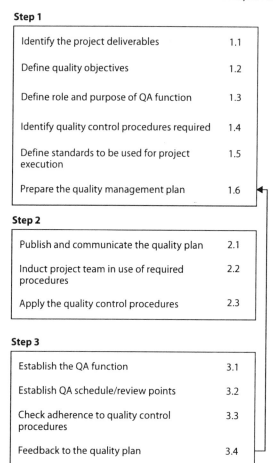

Fig. 3.17 Process for implementing quality assurance.

Step 1: Establishing the quality management process

1.1 *Identify the project deliverables*: Identify from the overall project management plans and scope the project deliverables (intermediate and final) which shall be subject to quality control.

1.2 *Define the quality objectives*: For each deliverable define the required quality objectives in order that, taken together, the service level delivered will meet the project requirements.

1.3 *Define the role and purpose of the quality assurance function*: Define the role and purpose and gain agreement to this with all parties. This can be drawn from the collective experience and capabilities of project team members.

1.4 *Identify the quality control procedures required*: Prepare these based on general practice and using the procedures currently in use in the organization.

1.5 *Define the standards to be used for project execution*: For each type of deliverable list the standards to be used for measurement. Examples of standards include (the list will not be limited to this):

- records standard
- management review standard
- internal quality audit standard
- documentation standard
- document control standard
- staff training standard
- purchasing standard
- development project review standard
- testing standard
- maintenance standard
- change management standard

1.6 *Prepare the quality management plan*: The results of the above are summarized into this important project document. The quality plan covers the following areas:

- quality objectives within the scope of the project
- quality management organization, roles and responsibilities
- documentation requirements and records to be maintained
- quality control procedures
- applicable standards
- tools, techniques and methodologies to employed
- review responsibilities (item by item)
- revision and update of the quality plan

Step 2: Implement Quality Control

2.1 *Publish and communicate the quality plan*: Issue the quality plan throughout the project, to nominated individuals who are responsible for updating their copy.

2.2 *Induct project team in use of procedures*: Hold presentations and discussions with all projects groups to explain how the procedures will be used and how this will benefit the project.

2.3 *Apply the quality control procedures*: The detailed application of the procedures is the responsibility of those carrying out the work on the project. However, if there is a quality assurance manager in the organization he or she would ensure that the project has the capacity to apply the procedures correctly.

Step 3: Implement Quality Assurance

3.1 *Establish the QA function*: Set up the organization roles and people to fulfil this function.

3.2 *Establish QA schedule/review points*: Identify key points within the project schedule related to stages in the development of the deliverables.

3.3 *Check adherence to the quality control procedures*: Monitor the formal output from the quality control procedures and ensure that this is complete and accurate. Hold QA audits to check compliance in more detail and submit the reports to the project director for action and endorsement.

3.4 *Feedback to quality plan*: Ensure that the quality plan is modified to incorporate lessons learnt during application of the procedures and that changes are issued to holders of the quality plan

Resourcing for Quality and Commitment to ISO 9000

If a quality assurance individual is not available within the organization, engage an outside consultancy team to manage independent quality assurance for the project and to ensure that ISO 9001 standard procedures are being set up and implemented correctly. The organization should have preferably received ISO 9001 certification for its QM work in information technology projects.

Independent Assurance

The consistent application of quality management to achieve delivered quality is the responsibility of the project director. To assist, however, quality assurance services would be provided by an independent quality team who review all project quality plans and monitor their subsequent application through a systematic audit programme, as described in detail above.

Summary

The approach to quality management will provide the following benefits:

● Assurance that the project will deliver a service that meets the requirements
● A common language for discussing and addressing quality issues so that they are dealt with in the shortest possible time
● Wide usage and acceptance of the system and the value it will bring to the project
● Greater confidence that the project targets are being met
● Confidence that the systems being used are consistent with ISO world class standards.

4. *Systems Project Development Activities*

4.1 Introduction

We have seen the importance of individual commitment and making a project visible through communication. In addition, it has been illustrated that significant changes are occurring that will need strong project management to ensure that the diverse components are glued together, i.e. communications, technology and people. The importance of the SDLC, quality management (QM) and testing have been explained as being a necessary component in the process of delivering a quality deliverable. All three, QM, SDLC and PMM, are separate, but all are complementary to each other in contributing to the success of a project. It is now appropriate in this chapter to link the systems development life cycle (SDLC) to the project management methodology (PMM).

Project managers should use the PMM process to help ensure that they proceed in a structured way by following certain principles and procedures on how to manage a project. The SDLC, on the other hand, is a methodical process that outlines *what* deliverables are required at each step during the building of the project objective. The SDLC consists of stages, with each one consisting of a number of phases. Figures 4.1–4.3 outline three of the numerous systems development life cycle models. In the pie model, each slice represents a stage and each item within the stage represents a phase. A stage is a discrete event. Within the event there are sub-events made up of tasks that, when completed, generate deliverables. Deliverables can be documents that report, for example, recommendations, specifications, analyses and planning for subsequent stages. Other deliverables would be programs, test results etc. Each deliverable would also be subject to some aspect of quality management.

Implementing a project management methodology is in itself a significant benefit in guiding the management of projects so that deliverables meet specifications. For the development of a deliverable, a complementary component to a project management methodology is used, i.e. the systems development life cycle. Other professions also have their own development life cycles, but all are based on similar events; for example initiation. The linear model and the waterfall SDLC models serve their users well. The iterative model and prototyping, although also offering some benefits, are considered not proven for large projects. Such projects are difficult to plan and control because they lend themselves to continuing with iteration after iteration.

Not planning the development of a product in a methodical way will result in exaggerated development time or, even worse, a product that does not meet

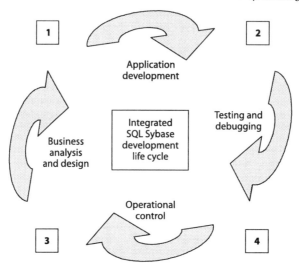

Fig. 4.1 The automated SDLC.

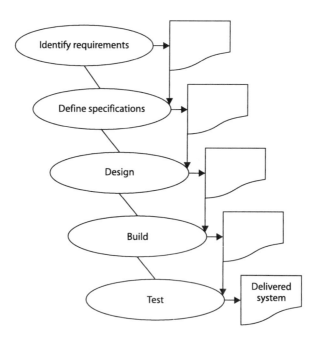

Fig. 4.2 The waterfall model.

specifications. This is where the SDLC is an essential component in the development of systems. There are several models of the cycle such as: linear, waterfall, spiral and iterative. Illustrations of some are presented below. A quick glance will show that they all consist of more or less the same events, albeit with different names, e.g. development and build. It is within the subsets that there are differences. It is not the intent

Fig. 4.3 The pie model.

of this book to go into a detailed explanation of the pros and cons. Many reference materials explain each one individually. (DeGrace and Stahl's book, *Wicked Problems, Righteous Solutions*, describes and evaluates approaches to software design.) The main consideration is that an organization has a systems development life cycle (Figs. 4.1–4.3) that is followed by internal and external developers, i.e. standardization. Thus the process becomes accepted and is agreed upon by all parties working in the environment.

4.2 Business Analysis and Design

If a systems development life cycle (SDLC) is used (Figs. 4.1–4.3), the systems project management methodology activities, forms and documents that apply to the project are carried out or created as appropriate throughout the evolution of each of the

Table 4.1 Deliverables expected at each stage of the SDLC

Event stage	Deliverables
1. Initiation	Preliminary analysis report and functional requirements
2. Feasibility study	Feasibility study report
3. Analysis	User detailed requirements
4. Business system design	Design document
5. Computer system design	Design document
6. Business system development	User manual
7. Computer system development	Computer system documentation
8. Acceptance testing	Report
9. Conversion and installation	Completion report with sign-offs

SDLC stages. These can be designed to be used in an automated workgroup environment.

Some events occur only once, e.g. initiation and business system design, while others, e.g. stage completion, completion of deliverable acceptance documents and control activities, occur repeatedly throughout the project. Others are repeating activities that occur at fixed intervals, such as the project status and cost reports (monthly), and others occur on an as-required basis, such as specifications change request, staff meetings and project review committee meetings.

An example of what deliverables should be expected from each stage is illustrated in Table 4.1.

4.3 System Project Management Activities

Systems project management methodology activities have been separated into four distinct events. They are those dealing with:

- Project initiation
- Project planning
- Project control
- Project or stage deliverable completion

Each of the foregoing events is composed of a series of forms, standard documents and tasks. Detailed descriptions, purposes and methods of use for each of these are described. These four events are described in subsequent chapters. It is important to realize that at each stage some form of quality management is necessary to ensure a quality deliverable.

The first stage of the SDLC consists of project initiation. The tasks to complete this can be conducted by users independently of, or in conjunction with, an informatics specialist. When a project manager is appointed, the other three events (project planning, project control, and project or stage deliverable completion) are managed by this individual. The project management functions are carried out for all three groups, i.e. project planning, project control, and project completion. This is where the use of a systems development life cycle is integrated with the development of a deliverable for each stage of the life cycle (stages 2–8 in the systems development life cycle outlined in Fig. 4.3).

The automated model (Fig. 4.1), from Sybase, depicts a completely automated development environment that integrates the entire process of designing, building, debugging and deploying SQL applications. Such an environment offers a project team quick and easy tools needed to build applications. It consists of four stages that are summarized as follows:

- *Stage 1*
  For the business analysis and design stage, relational database management system (RDBMS) integration, with forward and reverse engineering of form definitions and schemata between major RDBMSs is available.
- *Stage 2*
  In the application development stage, a form-based application development environment is available. With interactive decision support the guesswork usually associated with database design, maintenance and tuning is removed.
- *Stage 3*
  During the testing and debugging stage technology can help developers to identify and correct SQL code logic and performance problems early in the process.
- *Stage 4*
  Operational control automates the functions of SQL systems administration in multi-server environments.

This is not an endorsement of the Sybase methodology but an illustration to show how the development of applications, even with automated tools, still uses an SDLC. However, the automation of the SDLC does not remove the need to put the organization's logic into the application.

4.4 SDLC Stages

Here we describe the application of the project management methodology as it relates to each separate SDLC development stage. These descriptions can be used as a checklist of required project management methodology tasks during each stage of the SDLC.

Originally, the SDLC was a linear model followed blindly by many a project manager. with complete disregard for the client until the product was finished. The problem with this was that on completion of the project the client stated it was not what was wanted, or had left and the new incumbent said it did not meet her requirements. This led to prototyping and the iterative approach. However, irrespective of the approach adopted, the fundamental events (stages) are the same. The objectives of having a systems development life cycle are to define the events that must be carried out in a system project; introduce consistency among the many systems projects in an organization; and provide checkpoints for go/no-go decisions.

The procedures and guidelines pertaining to the SDLC will be of assistance to a project manager. The cycle organizes the events and their activities. This makes it more likely that the project manager will address the right ones at the right time. It is no use worrying about the development stage if the design stage has not been completed.

This overview is intended to provide only general direction and a process for controlling what happens during system development. Exactly how the activities within the stages should be performed, or sometimes not performed, is the responsibility of the project manager and the individuals on the project team/task force. Therefore experience with an SDLC is desirable and most informatics shops should have a standard.

Each stage is made up of activities that produce deliverables characterized as end products to be produced. They take numerous forms, such as: software – programs; documentation – user manuals etc.; and presentations.

Quality management, consisting of presentations or reviews, should take place regularly throughout a project and can take more than one form. These are:

- *Walkthroughs*: These are conducted by team members who work together to review a technical product for correctness and quality. They are usually characterized by an informal environment.
- *Formal reviews*: These are usually in the form of a presentation to management. They provide an opportunity to obtain an official stamp of approval for what has been done. The result is usually permission to continue as planned or a decision to halt or change the direction of the project.
- *Milestone reviews*: These are usually milestones that a project team works toward. These, when reviewed, provide a gauge of the validity of the project plan. As a project progresses, they provide a time when plans can be adjusted for any unknowns that may surface.

4.5 Systems Development Life Cycle Details

The following is an example of a summarized generic SDLC.

Stage 1: Initiation

Event 1, Stage 1, Initiation, would commence with a document from a user (client) that is approved by management. It concludes with the writing of a preliminary analysis report. The corresponding project management methodology (PMM) used to initiate a project is as outlined in Chapter 6. At this point all parties have an oversupply of enthusiasm.

Phase 1.1: Project Initiation

This activity identifies the objectives or the *raison d'être* for the system and establishes the foundation for the system development project. The project initiation document, as defined in the project management methodology, is what is used to communicate the scope etc. When completed, the document is reviewed and accepted or rejected by the client, management and the project review committee. From a testing point of view, it constitutes the *what, why* and *when?* Developers should avoid trying to 'justify' project effort when completing this stage.

Phase 1.2: A Preliminary Analysis

During this activity the purpose, objectives and scope for a new or modified system are presented and the functional requirements determined. An analyst would assess the size of the problem or opportunity; determine the scope of the potential area; and provide sufficient information so that development priorities and resources may be set. This will serve as a framework within which to conduct a feasibility study. Determining functional requirements at this stage causes problems for many individuals. It is a simple concept: determine *what* is required, not the *how*. It is a good idea to obtain a copy of a functional requirements document and use it as a boilerplate.

It is important that an approved project initiation document be available as the medium for approving the assignment of resources.

Stage 2: Feasibility Study/Cost–Benefit Analysis

The feasibility study provides an assessment of the operational and business case for various options. It concludes with a recommendation of what option should be developed and the first-cut of a development plan. The general scope for the deliverable is defined, problems are identified, objectives established, constraints determined and a high-level architecture documented.

We consider it an essential critical success factor. As mentioned in an earlier chapter, everyone is in a hurry to start and produce results. This could be because the project start-up has been delayed and lost time must be made up, or because competition is heating up and the project must be completed to provide critical marketing information, or for any of a number of other reasons. Starting a project without fully understanding its impact usually results in a restart.

During this step, the study is conducted to ascertain that there is sufficient justification for development to take place. It should also determine the most appropriate solution in terms of economic justification, organizational capability and technical feasibility, within the scope and objectives of the system and the project. In sizing the system, as many externals as possible should be identified. However, since the development cost will vary with the number of externals, it is important that an assumption be made regarding how many additional externals will be identified during the subsequent analysis stage. This information will be useful in estimating if there is an algorithm that converts the number of externals to lines of code.

The objective of this stage is to create a schematic of how the system will function at a conceptual level. This 'creative process' is a very important aspect of any application's success. It will identify sub-systems, objects and links between each sub-system and major interface points. The first activity is to create a schematic of how the system will function at a conceptual level. This should be done in a 'joint application development' session with the client and the project manager.

Doing a study will answer at least three important things:

1 What the project is all about. If we start by defining the wrong problem, then we will produce the wrong result. Thus a project mission statement should be prepared that explains the project's goals, objectives, its scope (enterprise-wide or Local), the problem, whether there are any constraints, e.g. budgetary, and the client's vision. This can be in effect a macro summary of the project. An example: 'To write script for Mathematics and prepare a marketable multimedia product for Grade 1 Students by 1 January 20XX'.

2 Should the project be undertaken? It is important to ensure that the project is not undertaken purely to satisfy egos or politics. However, if an executive asks for a project to be undertaken it is probably no use spending time on this question. However, time is well spent on providing options, and these could include the recommendation not to continue. You can detect some reasons why a project should *not* be undertaken, such as:
   - No champion can be found who is willing to sponsor it with resources
   - Political issues are unresolved
   - Costs and benefits are not strong enough to recommend proceeding
   - Internal staff lack the knowledge and experience to undertake the project successfully. Outsourcing is too expensive
   - Project risks (substantiated by a risk analysis) are too high, i.e. the risk/reward ratio is unfavourable.
   - The requirements keep changing based upon who they are being discussed with
   - Key users do not want to participate
   - Planning is superficial

3 How the project should be implemented. This involves developing a high-level project plan to provide management with a time-scale

Steps in the Feasibility Study

The steps are simply illustrated in Fig. 4.4.

Stage 3: Business Analysis and Design

Stage 3, analysis, provides specifications based on a detailed analysis of the accepted option presented in Stage 2. Business system design outlines a design for an efficient and effective system that complies with the specifications produced in the analysis stage. This includes specifications for manual interfaces and user procedures.

Phase 3.1: User Requirements

This phase completes the requirements of the required system in the context of the solution approved in the feasibility study. A report is prepared that illustrates what the system must do and at what level of service. If correctly done, all persons involved will understand what is being built and what benefits will be derived.

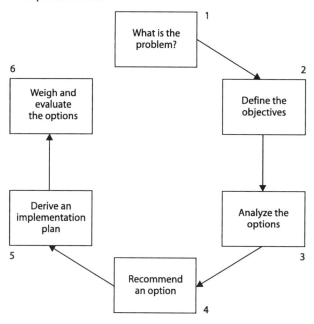

Fig. 4.4 Steps in the feasibility study.

The major activity is to interview the users face-to-face and perhaps with a questionnaire. A clear definition of user views and expectations must come from this activity. However, user requirements may be unrealistic. Therefore, adjust user requirements to what is possible.

Phase 3.2: Analyze Business Functions

During this phase, the purpose is to get a thorough knowledge of the general subject matter. The business processing cycle, procedures and transactions are also analyzed in detail.

In analyzing the process some points of note are:

- Sequence the processes in the order they are performed.
- Focus on major business transactions.
- Review all business functions with users. During this review, also identify current system deficiencies.

Stage 4: Computer System Analysis and Design

Stage 4, computer system design, is a deliverable with a detailed design of the computer system structure and module specifications.

Phase 4.1: Computer Systems Analysis

Covered during this phase are the detailed computer system requirements, conversion plan and implementation plan.

At this point a review is undertaken of the conceptual system model, with business function descriptions, the business system design and the entity/relationship model; technical constraints such as physical facilities are incorporated. From this review, an entity/relationship diagram is produced, together with detailed computer systems requirements and conversion and implementation plans. Users are interviewed to gather detail information. Critical transactions and processes are analyzed together with the activities for each process. System activities are grouped into subsystems. Draft system flow chart and process charts etc. are developed.

Phase 4.2: Computer Systems Design

From the detailed computer system requirements is produced an optimum design that satisfies those requirements that were approved in the user requirement phase. User requirements are turned into program specifications for systems development staff.

To do the design, analysts would familiarize themselves with the technical environment and review the system graphics charts, process charts and detailed flow diagrams. From these would be produced a functional design, hierarchical mapping of functions and options selected for each business function. The input and output processing for each function would also be defined.

Phase 4.3: Database Design

At this phase, the objective is to map from the entity/relationship model (logical data model) into the physical database and produce a schema. Database flexibility to handle changes would be verified, as would the impact of security considerations. During this verification, a review of the database access method and the physical database would be done with data management staff. A quality management criterion to be considered would be response time, which is directly related to database structure and access mode.

Stage 5: Computer Systems Development

Stage 5, computer system development, comprises the writing of actual code, testing of each unit of code and white box testing.

Phase 5.1: On-line Prototype

If it were decided to build a prototype at this phase, the objective would be to build skeleton on-line programs, using the computer system design, with transactions testing capabilities. A review of the I/O should continue until the user is ready to accept. All three units, i.e. subject matter staff, technical manager and development team must work closely together.

Stage 6: Business System Development

Stage 6, business system development, provides plans for installing the developed system, new or changed administrative procedures, detailed instructions for manual or computer system use and a new or revised user manual.

Phase 6.1: User Procedures

By using the user requirements report and business and computer system design report, policies and procedures would be developed for each user on how to operate the system. This phase can run in parallel with the computer systems development phase. Maintaining it as a separate phase, however, gives it significance and visibility. It could be arranged to give the user the responsibility for writing the user manual.

Phase 6.2: Develop System Test Plans

In this phase, detailed plans are established for setting up and carrying out system integration, acceptance and beta tests. Activities include:

● Developing a global testing strategy
● Reviewing the global testing strategy with users
● Reviewing test requirements: software/hardware, data, human resources etc.

Phase 6.3: Execute Integration Test Plan

The purpose of this phase is to ensure that the system operates effectively in all its aspects and to verify that all module components of the system are integrated.

During this phase, data conversion requirements for system performance tests would be carried out. Test case objectives and expected results would be confirmed. Reports, batch and update components would be tested. Performance of on-line/batch components under normal system load and on-line/batch components under stress and CPU overload would be tested. The execution and evaluation steps are reiterated and errors fixed until acceptable results achieved

Phase 6.4: Acceptance Testing

The phase objective is to ascertain that the completed functional computer system, with all its processes, is reviewed by a team rather than the development team itself. To verify that all the system processes are working efficiently, standards are adhered to and the technical environment is best utilized. A prerequisite is a working, fine-tuned system. Acceptance testing covers the pseudo-operation of the whole system by an acceptance test team. The deliverable would be an acceptance test report that would show what functions did not conform to specifications. These would then become part of a change function.

An acceptance team should be established and acceptable criteria defined. It is also appropriate to:

● Review system performance test results
● Review fine-tuned system structures
● Perform walkthrough sessions with development team

- Review standards
- Review response time
- Review all operational aspects: backup and recovery etc.
- Perform corrective actions if applicable

Stage 7: Conversion and Implementation

Conversion and installation cover the migration of data or databases and installing the system in a production mode.

Implementation of systems involves the production of executable code. However, good coding cannot make up for poor analysis and design. Therefore the preceding stages are extremely important, because having reached this far it is virtually impossible to back out.

Phase 7.1: User Training

During this phase, client training would be carried out according to the client training schedule. The purpose is to get users to the point of using the system 'on their own'.

For the training, establish and communicate clear terminal objectives.

Note: One well-trained user is better than ten confused ones.

Phase 7.2: Execute Conversion Plan

The purpose of the conversion plan is to carry out the data conversion process and to ensure that all aspects of the system are ready for a beta test and/or implementation.

Success is measured by the data being converted to a database with integrity. This involves converting all operational files, converting all user data, and verifying conversion results.

Fine-tune implementation strategy and conduct operations training. Finally, evaluate operational efficiency, bottlenecks etc.

Phase 7.3: Execute Beta Test Plan

A fully implemented system would be installed into the model office as though it was a production implementation. The system is thus implemented on a limited scale and volume tested to ensure stability. All parties involved in the test should understand their roles and reporting requirements.

The data required for the beta test must be initialized. It is also an opportune time to reintroduce the clients to the system operation and documentation.

Phase 7.4: Execute Implementation Plan

This is perhaps the most important phase, i.e. turning the system over into a full production environment. Any work done to the system will now be classified as a different project.

Sometimes a system will never be 'all-completed', so the project manager should allay any fears that the clients have by making him- or herself accountable.

Stage 8: Post-Implementation Review

After the system has been running for a reasonable period, evaluate the system against the original objectives and cost–benefit estimates to ensure that it is running smoothly and satisfies user requirements.

4.6 Summary

This chapter has illustrated how the project management methodology and the systems development life cycle are complementary to each other, i.e. one represents *how* to manage the production of a deliverable and the other is *what* is delivered. The next chapter will explain how the management of the *what* is organized to deliver quality products. It should be recognized that there are numerous SDLC models. such as the Software Structured Analysis Design Methodology, the IEEE model and Hoskyn's Prism. The structures of any methodology can be customized to suit each project. The deliverables will be obtained differently depending on which process is followed: whether CASE tools are used or not, using object-oriented programming will be different from writing an application in Oracle. However, the events are generally the same. The combining or modifying of different models may also be considered to achieve the most effective approach by deleting deliverables determined to be unnecessary. Their common theme, however, is a staged process with numerous events within the stage. Thus the entire development is a process that can be controlled, measured and improved. This then gives an understanding of the major processes of project management, systems development and quality management. Readers are advised to review the literature to determine what would be appropriate in their environment.

Now that we have determined the *what*, the next chapter will outline the project roles and responsibilities of individuals in getting the *what* completed.

5. Project Roles and Responsibilities

5.1 Introduction

Organizationally, informatics organizations are still evolving, but they are generally mandated to carry out all information resource management functions, such as administration, planning, policy and procedures, systems design and development, data processing operations, data management, technical support, and data communications. These functions can be located and controlled centrally or decentralized to be closer to the expertise in user areas. The necessity for an informatics organization, however, is to be able to respond to an ever-changing environment. Project management is the author's preferred organizational entity for obtaining quality results when a product has to be delivered, such as the development of a computer system, introduction of a new product or construction of a building. However, the cherished principles of organizational axioms are being overturned.

A fundamental concern with project management is to determine to whom the manager reports. If possible, it should be the client. However, in general there is no right or wrong organization. In determining an appropriate project structure for systems development, it has been the author's experience that a team of domain specialists from different functional areas, crossing organizational boundaries, working together as a cohesive team, under an experienced project manager, produces the best results. An important aspect is the ability of the manager to work with a disparate group of individual people.

Some of the inherent characteristics of the project approach can be summarized as follows:

- Management attention is focused and tends to be strong.
- As the team tends to work together for the common cause, the risk of failure is low when compared with dispersing responsibilities among different functions.
- The team approach lends itself to job enlargement and a broader development of the individual team member because of technology and experience transfer.
- If the team has experience in the area being served, it follows that the level of knowledge of the team will be greater than that of staff added from a pool.
- Generally, group morale will be high as the members are supportive of each other and they tend to bond together and reflect their pride in doing a good job.

The project manager reports to information technology management for administration, standards, planning and direction, but would be responsible to a project review committee for development of an approved deliverable. Team members report through their functional resource managers for administration etc., but to the project manager for day-to-day project responsibilities. With this concept, teams become knowledgeable about the areas they serve and better able to serve their clients. A concern, however, is the ability of members to be comfortable in reporting to both functional and project managers. Under this approach, each team would be headed by a project manager with technical, organizational and business analysis skills, with a core of technical staff and subject matter specialists working as team members in a participative matrix-type organization. With this type of flexibility, businesses can match their business model to the organizational setup. To complement the team, consideration should be given to the use of consultants as a means of quickly obtaining technology transfer.

As explained, the project team is a matrix of subject matter and technical specialists reporting to the project manager, who reports to the chairperson (client) of a project review committee. However, for it to work the idea must be supported by all levels of management in the company. Providing service only to a specific user could imply developing systems without necessarily considering the integration of data or corporate needs.

In aligning or restructuring the systems functions within organizations, it should only be undertaken to improve service, increase productivity and strengthen client liaison. Collectively the executive in charge of informatics, the project manager and the systems project development teams should be the primary vehicle for delivering the service. In selling the idea of project management, it is more than necessary to explain the role of the project manager to the functional areas. For example, the project manager should be responsible for technical aspects and the functional area staff for non-technical matters. General definitions of these terms are:

- *Technical*: hardware and software specifications, evaluations and acquisitions. It also covers the managing of feasibility studies; systems design and development; implementation of systems; support; networking; and operations. It also includes developing policy, procedures and standards, i.e. *how* things will be done.
- *Non-technical*: determining needs; participating in systems planning; and reviews and endorsement of feasibility studies, systems design, and implementation plans. That is, being responsible for *what* is required.

Areas may overlap, but the foregoing does give some broad parameters. In addition, Table 5.1 can aid in separating who does what. Although the model does not illustrate operational control, staffing a project with a mix of individuals creates an environment of ideas and frees individuals from the cognitive constraints that could be imposed by any one individual manager.

User participation is an essential element in successful development of systems. It is the essential component that enables the users to indicate what their requirements are. However, in many cases they have abdicated this responsibility to the technocrat. Therefore the degree of involvement and its form are unique to each organization. This is where a project manager with business and technical skills is a distinct asset.

Table 5.1 Organizational relationships

Data providers	Database coordinator	Information users
• Capture data • Ensure data quality	• Determine who will provide the data • Develop practices to ensure data quality • Understand user's business needs • Communicate data applicability and availability • Justify data access restrictions • Specify business requirements • Establish data definitions • Ensure data quality satisfies users • Coordinate changes with other groups	• Specify information requirements • Use appropriate data

Ongoing professional support

- Ensure data definitions for architecture
- Provide repository tools
- Facilitate integration issues
- Manage change
- Assist in implementation
- Assess impact of data changes
- Coordinate changes
- Manage data environment, e.g. backups, distribution
- Manage the data
- Provide consultation, design, development and implementation services

With the paradigm of technological change, the user environment is also changing. Tomorrow's environment will need to take into account the human factors: job satisfaction, behavioural and cultural diversity. Many systems fail because of not considering these and not realizing how interdependent tasks, people, structure, technology and culture are. Any change in one will result in a change to some of the others. Failures in implementation can be due to negligence in recognizing these variables. Thus harmony, as described in the next section, recognizes this aspect.

5.2 Harmony

For projects to be successful, it is imperative that all functional units in an organization, involved directly or indirectly, pull together harmoniously. The sum of the individual parts must be stronger than the individual components. In many instances, excellent staff leave because of poor management. Therefore, it is essential that one looks at giving up the captain before giving up the ship.

Each layer of an organization has a set of responsibilities that rely on a layer of people and systems beneath it to support its continuing well-being. This is illustrated in Fig. 5.1. It can be viewed as a living entity where the project manager is the head and brain that plans, organizes and controls. If this atrophies, then the rest of the body suffers. The functional areas can be perceived as the body that contains the stomach of the organization, where everything churns around in it until it meets the requirements of the appropriate units. The bottom part is the arms and legs, e.g. a

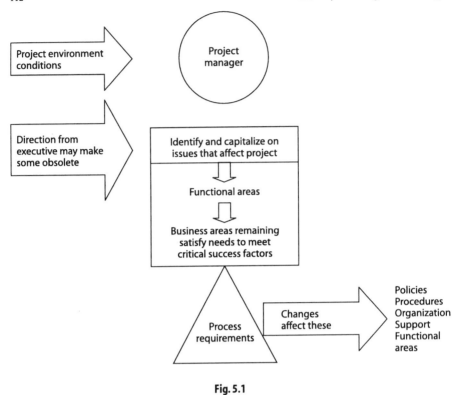

Fig. 5.1

project team, that supports the stomach and performs the work that keeps the rest of the body healthy. As project managers change, all interested parties must constantly be cognizant of their responsibility to direct this change in a proactive fashion. Unless this is done in a harmonious fashion, dysfunction will result. Thus, in paying attention to the users who make up this component, it is important to understand what makes them happy. Happy campers will go a long way in successful implementation.

As shown in Fig. 5.1, the individual parts are not independent. Each has an integral role to play. If one malfunctions, it can have implications for the other parts. It is important that they remain well balanced throughout any initiative during the systems development life cycle stages.

Getting to the future requires consideration of the transformations of each entity, and early identification of changes and their impact is essential. This balancing act continues throughout the systems development process and will ensure that harmony is achieved.

5.3 Systems Development

Policies and procedures should be adopted that define the roles and responsibilities of users. However, whereas, in general, professional informatics staff develop systems, the development of high-level languages, application generators, computer application software engineering packages, computer-aided software engineering and other tools that can be applied directly by users has led some domain subject matter staff to believe they can do the development function effectively. This is undoubtedly true in a limited way, but may be false economy if a highly paid professional is writing code. The demand to do or manage one's own development is evident across most organizations, and can have implications affecting an organization's stability, accountability and even development methodology. Although 'empowerment' may be a word much bandied about, it does not mean everybody is empowered to do their own thing. Empowerment must be explained for each organization. In the context of this book it means that employees may do their own thing within the information supplied and policies and procedures, i.e. prescribed limits. The personal computer (PC) has done more to make individuals believe that they can develop quicker and simpler systems than professionals trained in analysis, development etc. In fact, while PCs were standalone devices the condition could continue with minimal interference or support from a professional group. However, when the computer is linked to a local or wide area network, the rules of the game change rapidly. There are standards (X.400, X.500 X.28 etc.) to be considered. There is planning required for types and capacity of servers. Operating systems cannot just be selected by individuals who subjectively prefer this or that based simply upon what they like. Even with open systems, the more heterogeneous the environment the more support is called for. Therefore, as the infrastructure environment gets larger and more complex, the need will be more than ever for skilled, trained, professional staff, managed by experienced project managers working with standards.

A fundamental question is: why should users be managing information systems development? Rather than saying 'managing' let's turn the question around and ask: why should they be involved? There are many good reasons for users to be involved, for example:

- Participation by users is an essential element for the successful implementation of systems. It is an important avenue whereby they can express their own functional requirements and express their own personal, cultural and behavioural needs. What is needed is to ensure that, in allowing individuals to speak up freely, they do not have freedom of action.
- Users want to be involved is an issue because of their increasing computer literacy.
- Users usually know the subtleties of their business processes better than a professional informatics person does.
- As users become more knowledgeable in managing systems development they will become able to carry out, without informatics, those operational local applications of low priority (but which are useful nonetheless) and which informatics would never have the resources to act on, i.e. the backlog diminishes.

A companion question is: why should staff not be allowed to develop or manage their systems without involving informatics professionals? Some good reasons are:

- Informatics staff have technical expertise. For example, their knowledge of hardware and software compatibility, open systems integration, testing techniques and other technical functions is all-important and is not usually found in other functional unit staff.

- Objective views are needed.
- Someone needs to ensure that methodologies are written and followed and that proper documentation and standards are produced.

In determining to what extent different functional units should be involved in systems development the following organizational issues must be considered:

- Any exclusive mandate for a central group for systems development is inconsistent with the trend to decentralization. Therefore, mandates for the different units should address what role they play in informatics. For example, is the role in determining requirements, providing application support, or providing training?
- If subject matter staff are to play an increasing role in what has been a technical area, technical training and adequate support capabilities beyond first-line support must be provided.
- If standards and controls are not available, they should become a priority for development. If, however, they exist, they should be regularly maintained and promulgated to all interested parties.
- Determine how corporate systems planning and user participation will be integrated into any final informatics function and other functional areas' planning processes.
- Find a process where unique operational systems can be developed without impinging on resourcing assigned to developing strategic systems outlined in the corporate systems plan.

What are the overall risks and drawbacks of involving users more in the development process?

- If not managed properly, day-to-day operations may suffer. Taking users who know their subject matter and putting them on systems projects or letting them spend time on systems development may degrade their operations. Therefore a balance must be met.
- There could be an explosive growth in costs for processing, paper, diskettes, software purchases etc., because users will engage in experimentation.
- Potential loss of key personnel. As users develop systems, they acquire a new and different skill set that is marketable.

Some success factors that will be prominent in a user development environment are:

1 Existence of systems and operational plans that are linked and are followed.
2 Management commitment and involvement.
3 User participation.
4 Staff qualified with appropriate tools and methodologies.
5 Use of effective systems development and project management methodologies and other standards.

6 Manageable scope of projects.

In many cases, the organizational environment does not fit the trend to distributed processing and dispersion of responsibilities in getting closer to the users with all aspects of computing. In determining an appropriate organization structure for managing systems development it has been the author's experience that a team of subject matter specialists working under a project manager produces the best results. One school of thought suggests that the project manager does not have to be experienced in informatics but could be a subject matter specialist. In the author's experience, understanding information technology and the domain of the application leads to credibility within the team. In addition, understanding the domain will help in understanding some decisions. Irrespective of what is right or wrong, it is necessary to ensure that the individual has the skill set, traits and ability to manage a project.

5.4 Project Organization

You cannot manage a project unless each member of the project team knows:

What their individual responsibilities are and what the other members' responsibilities are, i.e. 'Where do I fit into the organization?' and 'Who is concerned when the team member is having difficulties?'. In other words, what are the avenues for sharing responsibility?

The project manager is obligated to the responsible manager for delivering the end product to the acceptor. To help in doing this the project manager has a project team and the acceptor an acceptance team. These and other project responsibilities are described further on. The responsible manager is the champion of the project and usually the executive for whom the project is being undertaken. The acceptor is his or her agent. It is sometimes necessary to explain their roles and responsibilities in a project contract. In some cases, the principal characters will perform more than one role. Two that should *never* be performed by the same person are those of project manager and acceptor. However, the responsible manager may be the acceptor. In the following sections, the principal roles (Fig. 5.2) will be referred to as if they were filled by separate individuals.

5.5 Teleworking

One aspect of project organization is the ability for more and more employees to work from a place other than the official workplace (Fig. 5.3). The concept is not new, and millions participate in North America and Europe. It may be a useful approach to downsizing staff, whereby they are encouraged to work at home part-time while they look for a new position. This may save the cost of a golden handshake, to the extent that the money could be used to keep them employed at home but retaining company benefits. However, in the context of Fig. 5.2, development team members

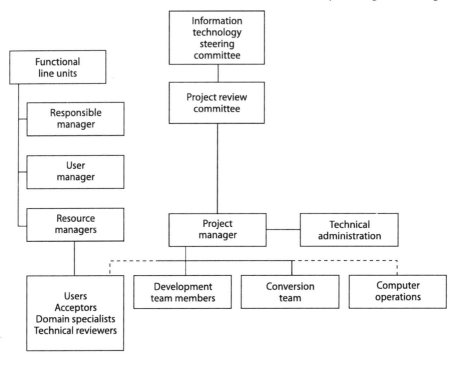

Fig. 5.2

and the project manager could work outside the main office. There are many advantages to this, but it is also important to realize that there are also disadvantages. Managing a team working in different locations needs strong project management and communication skills and a plan that is followed, i.e. everybody knows what must be done and when. If you are working at home and have a child, for example, consider for a moment having a deadline and a child demanding attention. An advantage, of course, is that the family unit becomes closer. As humans are considered social animals, it can be difficult for a gregarious person to discipline him- or herself to knuckle down and work in a consistent manner. This was brought home to the author, who used home workers to do programming. Invariably the individuals came into the office regularly to talk about sports, social functions etc. This became very disruptive and the effort was abandoned. Nevertheless, there is a place in an organization for employees working in a teleworkplace. These places may, for example, be the home or satellite offices where small workgroups are established. Workers would go to them rather than the main official workplace or combinations of places. Consider also the office in the air for time-strapped staff flying long distances. This is becoming viable with high-technology innovations such as laptops in seatbacks, live radio news, and satellite telephones and facsimile machines that let you dial out from anywhere. Bombardier, an industrial organization in Canada, is developing a Global Express with these features, planned to enter service in 1998. The thing to remember is that the only constant is the *official workplace*.

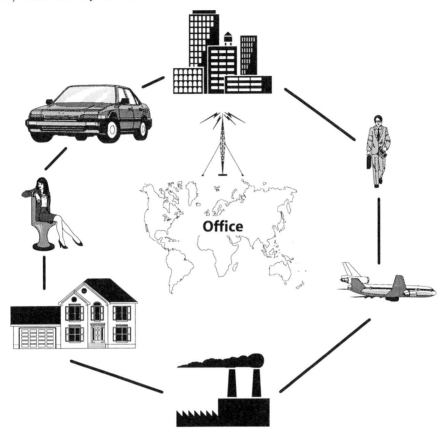

Fig. 5.3

A project manager who accepts teleworkers as part of the team must guard against complacency, i.e. thinking that work is being done. With teleworking (telecommuting), it is important to control a project and ensure that regular contact is made with the team. They should be brought together regularly for project reviews using the plan as a yardstick against progress. Acceptance of teleworking will, however, allow employees to strike a balance between their work and personal lives. In fact, the most striking evidence that the concept works comes from consultants who work much of the time from home, but who, by the very nature of their vocation, have trained themselves to work independently with minimum supervision. However, what is appropriate when it comes to teleworking is difficult to answer. The old organizational rules may no longer apply, and the new rules have not yet been written.

The theory surrounding telework is based upon the belief that mature responsible adults do not need to be closely supervised to perform their work. As teleworking becomes more of an accepted form of work, we can expect many benefits to the population at large.

Digressing for a moment, consider the benefits, social and business, such as:

- Reduced crime because of the increased presence of adults in their homes.
- Reduction in traffic congestion and pollution due to the reduced use of cars.
- More disposable income (in the region of 20%), attributable to not having to use the car (parking, petrol and parking tickets) or bus as often and not eating or drinking out at break and lunchtime.
- The employer can gain, with less office space and a corresponding reduction in heating and insurance.
- A further gain, from the employee's point-of-view, is the reduction of stress. In an office situation it builds up over the working week until 'Thank God it's Friday' is reached. Stress, on the other hand, can be shaken off at home as it occurs.

We shall consider the aspect from an employer–employee relationship rather than a self-employed consultant. We will call working at home telework because it involves the use of computers and generally the ability to communicate by email through a local area network or via a host computer. Considering the important principles of teleworking, we can conclude that it is a logical extension to a project organization. Some questions to consider are:

- Is it operationally practical and has it the support of management?
- Is the department, section, project manager etc. organizationally ready? One aspect to be considered is jealousy of other employees, who may not be selected to participate. This may be a concern when a program is first introduced. If a pilot of, say, six employees is decided upon, how are they selected?
- How is a loss in productivity guarded against? Allowing employees to come into the official workplace at any time could, for example, be disruptive. It may be necessary to establish performance indicators for some workers. This is particularly desirable if the same work is being done in the official workplace by staff who do not volunteer to do the work elsewhere. This may be overcome by a commitment to produce a specific deliverable.
- Is it voluntary and does the employee fully understand any downside? It must be open-ended so that it may be terminated by either party. In addition, it may be appropriate to counsel the volunteer on the practical considerations of teleworking. The organization may also consider having written guidelines to ensure that there is no misunderstanding. For example, can the employee's supervisor or other employees go to the employee's teleworkplace? This may be necessary if a computer being used at home belongs to the organization and something needs to be changed or serviced. Who pays the extra costs that an employee will incur if the home is used, e.g. insurance, electricity and office space?
- Will extra non-voluntary costs be incurred by either the employee or the employer? If so, who absorbs the burden?
- Will unions be amenable to the idea? Unions warn that unless workers' rights are specifically spelled out in collective agreements they may be overlooked or abused. It is suggested that workers could be required to work longer hours, in improper work environments (working at a table rather than at a desk, and sitting on a kitchen chair), without overtime pay (a Carleton University study of 6000 federal public sector workers showed that individuals with home computers work

an average 2 hours longer each day) or the protection of workers' compensation. In Canada, the Public Service Treasury Board has issued a policy that establishes the same rights for teleworkers when working at home as when working at the office. There is considered a risk that organizations will use telework as a substitute for nationally available, publicly subsidized childcare, therefore forcing women to work long into the night in their combined role of worker and parent.

- Does a contract need to be agreed between the employer and employee with clearly stated terms and conditions? How, for example, will value for salary be determined?
- Does the selected teleworkplace conform to any legislation regarding homeworking, safety and health conditions?
- What process has been developed that explains how support, if any, will be given to the individual working at home? For example, what safeguards are necessary regarding harassment or costs involved in travelling to give service?

There will be some work–family conflicts, and someone from the home organization will be expected to eradicate management's entrenched resistance to flexible schedules, work-at-home arrangements, job sharing and leave.

Following a systems development life cycle of initiation, feasibility, design, development and implementation, we will address how each component lends itself to teleworking.

Initiation is done by the project manager in conjunction with the client. Therefore there is little that can be done at home. However, it is a small component of the total project activity.

The feasibility and design stages lend themselves to teleworking, as a large amount of time being allocated to these could be done away from the home office. The effort away from the office would be primarily geared to analysis and writing of the report. Walkthroughs and discussions with peers, clients, vendors etc. would however take up time in the office. However, if a team is needed it may be necessary to get together at a central place.

Development is an endeavour that lends itself very well to teleworking. This is because programming and testing consist of deliverables and are more easily defined and measured.

Implementation is one where a minimal amount of time can be spent at home, because activities such as training generally take place at the offices of the organization and the implementers must attend. However, this may not be true, for example, if data capture is being done as a cottage industry. In this case, it may be necessary to arrange training at a central site. Of course, training materials could be prepared at home, routed by way of email to reviewers, and followed by subsequent attendance at the training facility to give walkthroughs and the actual training.

5.5.1 Information Technology Steering Committee

This committee is comprised of senior managers (decision-makers) from the organizations. These are the executives who approve project priorities and funding.

They are not involved in day-to-day operations and probably only meet twice a year or as appropriate to provide overall guidance.

5.5.2 Technical Administration

This function administers the ongoing communication between clients and the project team and, in addition, any other responsibility deemed to be administrative for the project team. It should be kept as small as possible. It can take many forms, from the use of a secretary to a full project office. However, establishing a formal project office is only appropriate for large projects that cut across organizational boundaries. With teleworking, the function will become more important in order to administer the workers' different demands.

5.5.3 Project Review Committee (Project Working Committee)

For all major projects, a project review committee should be formed, consisting of a chairperson (who should be the project champion) and the line manager (client) for whom the system is being built. Other members should include the executive in charge of information technology and other functional area managers (audit, finance, marketing, information systems division etc.) who have an interest in the system's success and functionality.

The committee should meet as often as required and be responsible for project monitoring and problem resolution. Therefore appointees should be individuals who can make decisions for their functional areas. Specific responsibilities include being accountable for accepting the development of project deliverables, progress reports, plans, changes, pilot test results, and making operational decisions outside the project manager's scope. In addition, the committee is responsible for accepting and recommending (probably to the information technology steering committee), the estimated resources (human and financial) required to complete the project. Having obtained approval for initial expenditures, any subsequent costs exceeding those approved for any particular stage of the systems development life cycle (SDLC) would be reviewed by the committee. On an ongoing basis, members would provide guidance and direction to the project manager. This aspect is very important when differences arise between different organizational units.

5.5.4 Responsible Manager

This manager is chairperson of the project review committee and responsible and accountable to the organization for the project. The project manager is accountable to this individual for the project deliverable. The acceptor is appointed as an agent of the responsible manager. For example the executive responsible for finance could be the responsible manager for financial systems and the acceptor may be the manager of cost accounting if the system is primarily for this functional unit. It all depends upon the size and span of control within an organization. In some cases, the responsible manager and the acceptor could be the same person.

Each organization must decide how to ensure responsibility and accountability for the results expected from the responsible manager, who, in addition to being the chairperson of the PRC, has the following major responsibilities:

- is accountable for project results to the management steering committee, if one exists, or some other designated authority, such as a board of directors
- confirms that the proper project management processes are being followed by the project manager
- makes sure that project control by the project manager is adequate and includes commitment maintenance, reporting and meetings
- ensures that deliverable and project acceptance status reports are reviewed before acceptance
- assigns an acceptor and ensures that the individual is personally committed
- keeps the project manager committed and ensures that the resources required are available. This may mean persuading other managers to assign staff to the project. This can be especially difficult when crossing organizational boundaries. An approved corporate information management resource plan would go a long way to alleviating any conflict
- helps the project manager when required (avenue for sharing responsibility upwards)
- resolves discrepancies, disagreements or issues that cannot be handled effectively at a lower level
- verifies that the project manager satisfies the acceptor
- ensures delivery of a quality product as specified for the resources used, i.e. value

5.5.5 Project Manager

The project manager is the 'driver' of the project cycle. All the cycle tools, indeed the project itself, are dependent on the personal dedication of this individual. Without such dedication, a project has little chance of success. This individual has overall accountability to the responsible manager for the project and must be capable of managing any situation. Therefore it is important for a team to work well for a project manager and that some rules and conditions are accepted, namely:

- Project managers should have the right to approve or reject team members. Line managers must not be able to force project managers to accept members that they feel unable to work with, or whom they feel are incapable of doing the task.
- Project managers must have the right to decide members' tasks and hand out assignments if they are to be held accountable for their team's work. They must also have the authority to control the direction of the project. Line managers should make sure that project managers understand the big picture and stay away from the day-to-day work of the team.
- Line managers must have the right to make final judgements on performance reviews and salary increases for their staff assigned to a project. However, project managers should have the right to evaluate team members' work and suggest merit raises or bonuses.

- Project managers should have the right to initiate removal of employees from their teams. If some team members don't work out, then the project manager must have the authority to begin the process of removing them. This does not necessarily mean firing them, but just getting them placed elsewhere in the organization. Line managers who insist on keep unwanted members on a team against the project manager's wishes eliminate one of the primary conditions of accountability.
- Consider carefully before letting teams choose their own leaders. In the same way that the team as a group can't be held accountable for a piece of work, it can't be held accountable for choosing its leader. This does not mean that managers should avoid asking for advice, but the final decision is management's responsibility.
- The project manager should set deadlines and help in getting the necessary resources from other functional units. It is not satisfactory to ask a project manager to arrange for someone from another unit to attend meetings or do certain tasks if that individual has not been assigned to the team. Of course, we all know individuals who will always help without being officially part of the team. However, to use people without them being recognized as a team player can lead to problems.

The project manager is the essential interface between the development activities, the acceptor and the responsible manager. The responsibilities of the project manager are:

- To be accountable to the responsible manager for completion of tasks and for ensuring acceptance of the project's final deliverable
- Executing the project management processes on behalf of the responsible manager.
- Developing and following project plans.
- Controlling the project by maintaining his or her own commitment and that of the team members; reporting routinely to the responsible manager and acceptor; and meeting as necessary with management, the acceptor and individual team members and continually re-planning for completion.
- Ensuring delivery of quality deliverable(s) relative to the resources used (i.e. value) and ensuring they are accepted.
- Managing the budget and the financial performance of the project.
- Keeping the responsible manager, acceptor and team members informed of all relevant issues.
- Minimizing disruption in completing the end product by establishing a change control process.
- Completing the project on schedule (updated as appropriate).

These responsibilities are given by management when they appoint the project manager. However, to be able to be all things to all men would need a superhuman being. Following the principles in this book and complementing them with the individual's skills and experience will help in getting the job done.

The job of a manager is to understand what his or her people are really looking for. Managers may think it is financial compensation. The truth of the matter is they want appreciation of work completed, to be noticed and to participate in any discussion of what is going on. They want to be in a position where they can continue their education. They want to be challenged by the work they do. They want to see some consistency in the way managers interact with them. They want to feel they belong. If you think you can be a project manager and boss others, the following story is worth repeating. The story goes of a recently appointed underground shift boss who was quizzically asked by an old time mine captain 'if he thought he was good enough to boss others?'. The new shift boss answered affirmatively. The captain's reply was 'Son! Come see me when you have had to fire your best friend. Then you will really understand what being a boss means'. This illustrates the difficulty of accepting responsibilities and of having to violate a social structure of which you are part.

5.5.6 Stage Coordinator

Systems projects are broken into stages of development according to a systems development life cycle. For large projects, it is desirable for each stage to have a coordinator (project leader) who reports to the project manager. For example, if the stage, or event, was conversion of accounting records from paper documents to an electronic medium, the person coordinating or leading it might be an accounting clerk reporting to the project manager. Thus the name – stage coordinator, project leader, conversion manager – is immaterial. The principle to remember is that for each event someone must be responsible for ensuring that it is done. The coordinator in the example illustrated could be the individual accounting clerk who actually does the work on a daily basis.

The stage coordinator plays an important role in the delivery process. It is important to realize that this may be perceived to be in direct conflict with the project manager's role. This is not so. A project manager is responsible for the whole project, whereas a stage coordinator is responsible to the project manager for delivery of an event or a subset of the end product. He or she has some of the same responsibilities as the project manager, but only for a stage or stages, and may be viewed as a junior project manager without the skills and experience in total project management. However, the stage of the project is managed and help is elicited from the project manager as required. The responsibilities of the coordinator are:

- To deliver deliverable(s) on time and according to generally accepted principles and obtain their acceptance.
- The proper execution of the project management process.
- Project planning and control for the stage being coordinated and its deliverables and team members.
- To keep the project manager and acceptor(s) informed of all relevant issues and for managing their expectations.
- Maintaining a personal commitment or making the lack of it visible to the project manager.

5.5.7 Project Team Member

It must be realized that individuals and not teams can be held accountable. How many individuals volunteer or are delegated to be part of a team at the office, but end up feeling it didn't really accomplish anything? Managers read team reports and wonder whom to blame when the work done was partly good and partly awful. To blame someone is a normal reaction, especially if fixing the bad parts will take weeks and you have to present the mess to management in a few days. However, blame should not be the prime focus. It is necessary to be more concerned with determining how to get the problem fixed and at what cost in time and money. This can happen when the wrong people are chosen for a team, or their tasks and responsibilities are not set out clearly enough, says Donald Brookes, Canadian director for the Harding Consulting Group.

It is important to establish commitment and accountability. An important thing to realize is that the character of each person is probably a combination of cognitive abilities and personality traits. Thus the team cannot be held accountable for a piece of work; only individuals can make a commitment to getting their piece done. Of course, collectively, the team can accept a plan and a project manager in the initial stages may think they are committed, but it is always individuals that must be held accountable for their product. When it is known that someone is responsible for something, we are judging this from a moral and pragmatic sense. The project manager, by understanding people, is therefore responsible for ensuring that each individual completes the appropriate task and that the sum of these tasks completes an event. If the team is properly managed and motivated, it can often accomplish infinitely more than the individuals on their own. However, much of their potential is wasted if appropriate structures are not set up and monitored through individual accountability.

A project team member can be a single individual with a narrow task, reporting directly to the project manager. If the team member is one of a group of individuals working on a task, then he or she would be responsible to the stage coordinator. In either case, team members are accountable for committing to one or the other and to the responsibilities assigned, or to making visible that their personal commitment has been dropped. The responsibilities of project team members are:

- To keep the stage coordinator or project manager informed of all relevant issues and getting help as required
- To plan their own work and manage their time in conjunction with the individual responsible for planning, i.e. making a contract
- To control their own work and demonstrate personal pride in achieving an individual goal and that of the team
- To keep user contacts, members of the acceptance team and others informed of all relevant issues
- The delivery and acceptance of deliverables
- To document results according to company standards
- To produce a quality deliverable relative to the resources used, i.e. value

A team member should want to feel pride of ownership. Naisbitt, the author of *Megatrends,* said in a book called *Reinventing the Corporation*: 'When you identify with your company's purpose, and when you experience ownership in a shared vision, you find yourself doing your life's work instead of just doing time'. Although he was writing about the whole corporation, the principle will hold true for project staff, i.e. they want to feel good about their deliverable(s).

It should go without saying that being a member of a team entails working hard, giving value for money and not being late for work or with deliverables. Should an employee, however, perform beyond that which is required? To do so may ensure that the willing team member is the one who is always called upon to help when things are going wrong. This may be acceptable if the project manager and the other team members showed their appreciation for this diligence, loyalty and helping hand. However, if the impression received is that the project manager treats the individual as someone whose feelings don't matter and that she can be 'used' at any time, then it is the team member's responsibility to change it. Obviously, being human, a person's motivation can easily be reduced, making it difficult to maintain the proper approach to all employees but especially to other team members encountered. This, if the team member allows it to happen, will ensure that commitment becomes suspect. If the team member decides it is not just her own perception that she is being taken advantage of, corrective action is called for. To correct the situation it is important to realize that it is unlikely that the team manager or other team members can be approached, as they will in all likelihood see it as an individual's particular perception. However, this should still be attempted, preferably before a long-term precedent has been established.

The writer knew of one case where the individual was always used. However, it was the person's own fault. The team member didn't ask for overtime because it was important to do the job within budget. He joked about being at work first and leaving last, but everybody took it as accepted practice because he was proud of the fact. It did not bother his co-workers or the project manager because they did not see the hours worked; they had long since gone to their social activities. Therefore, although he was used, it was his fault and he did not become sour because he realized it was self-imposed. However, if the situation deteriorates and becomes unbearable, corrective action is called for.

5.5.8 Resource Manager

This individual is the 'line' boss in the normal day-to-day organization (outside the project) of one or more of the project team members. Resource managers have personal administrative responsibility for members of their project teams. They are responsible for monitoring the performance of the resources provided to the project. They also manage the careers and training of all staff under their control, as well as providing an avenue for personal problem resolution outside the project line management. Some specific responsibilities are:

- Looking after the interests of staff in such areas as giving advice and guidance concerning their career development, education and training

- Allocating appropriate personnel to projects, in conjunction with the responsible and project managers
- Ensuring that performance reviews of team members are written. Consideration should be given to writing a contract with the project manager before project start-up. This would ensure that all members could be evaluated on how well they had done in meeting or not meeting the completion of their deliverable(s)
- Working with the project manager to ensure the personal commitment of team members.

5.5.9 Acceptor(s) (Quality Reviewers)

The acceptors (technical and business) are delegates of the responsible manager, and are fully accountable for the end product that is produced. They are responsible for ensuring that the end product meets the user's needs as specified and that it can be supported from a technical and user point of view. They represent the individuals or groups responsible for using, maintaining and operating the end product. They also represent the individuals or groups who could be affected, either directly or indirectly, by the installation of this project. Once accepted, they, and not the project manager, are responsible for any product deficiencies.

The acceptor responsible for the overall deliverable acts as the prime interface between the project manager and the users. In this capacity, he or she is responsible for keeping the relevant people informed of the project status, negotiating product changes with the project manager, and representing the interests of the product users and the product support organizations. For large projects, it is advisable to form an acceptance team. This will reduce the acceptor's workload and simplify the transfer of information and the decision-making process. In forming this group, the acceptor must define the principal areas affected by the product and obtain a representative from each area. This group would typically include representatives from each department upon which the end product is expected to have any significant effect. These individuals would have veto power, and therefore must have the authority to represent fully their respective areas. An acceptor is obligated to:

- accept the project deliverable
- accept the project schedule
- define user needs
- keep the acceptance team informed, committed and productive
- ensure that end-product changes and their impact upon delivery and acceptance are known and accepted
- keep their users informed regarding project progress

5.5.10 Acceptance Team Member

This individual is assigned by the resource manager to work on a specific stage or activity to ensure that the resource manager's requirements are met. A team member's responsibilities are to the acceptor and include committing to the responsibilities assigned, or making it visible that the personal commitment has been

Stage 1			
Deliverable	**Responsibility**	**Reviews**	**Sign-off**
Project plan	John Doe	Technical	
		Quality	
		User	
Requirements analysis report	Mary Smith	Technical	
		Quality	
		User	
Feasibility study	Puan Sharizah	Technical	
		Quality	
		User	
Management proposal	Mohammed Noor	Technical	
		Quality	
		User	

Fig. 5.4 A sign-off form.

dropped. As the acceptor is in effect the project manager for acceptance, the acceptor must be kept informed of all relevant issues. Thus, if the member needs help, the acceptor can provide it as required. As an individual, planning and controlling his or her own work, timing is essential. However, it may to some extent be dictated by the planner, project manager or other influences. Therefore it is appropriate when accepting the project schedule and the deliverables to ensure that the resource manager accepts the impact on the functional area from which the member is assigned. It is important to realize that keeping other acceptance team members informed of all relevant issues is mandatory for good working relationships to be formed.

An example of a sign-off form for each stage of the SDLC could be as presented in Fig. 5.4. Such a form could be completed for each stage (or deliverable).

5.5.11 Project Review Committee (PRC) Member

Project review committee members usually represent users, funders and providers of subject matter specialists for the project. Acceptors of major deliverables may also be members. The project review committee member's role is one of advisor to the responsible manager, who is the committee chairman, as well as to provide support, additional input and communication from the specialist area, for which the member is functionally responsible. The committee, as a group, has no direct project responsibilities, but to be successful each member of the committee must:

● keep functional area users informed

- help or give advice to the responsible manager, acceptor and project manager when requested
- review key procedural decisions
- obtain feedback concerning the user's perception of the project
- accept project and stage plans
- recommend acceptance or rejection of project or stage completion reports

5.6 Project Communication

The whole purpose of the project cycle is to facilitate project communication and ensure that the project is completed. The project model describes the individual roles and responsibilities of the principal characters. The project documents are formal vehicles that encourage the communication of the right kind of information between the right people at the right time.

5.6.1 Communication Between the Project Manager and Resource Managers

Good communication between the project manager and resource managers is crucial to the health of the project. The project manager is deliverable-oriented and must play the role of advocating the product's direct interests, regardless of other problems. The resource managers, on the other hand, are resource-oriented. They must make the best use of personnel by allocating them among projects, measuring their performance and helping them in their professional development. Sometimes, these two will conflict. The conflict, however, must remain healthy under the common loyalty to the organization's objectives and the mutual respecting of each other's roles. Wherever there is a conflict that they cannot resolve together, the problem must be brought to the attention of the responsible manager, or a higher authority. They must then each defend their positions by identifying the consequences. This is a healthy conflict that will ensure management awareness of the balance between resources and commitments.

5.6.2 Communication Between the Project Manager and the Acceptor

The duo of project manager and acceptor is the key to successful product definition and acceptance, ensuring that the development proceeds in an appropriate direction. These individuals have complementary responsibilities and must function as a team based on mutual cooperation. Their very existence separates the responsibilities for final determination of users' needs. Each individual, however, is 100% accountable to his or her own organization for both delivery and acceptance.

5.7 Summary

The titles used for project review committee, acceptors etc. are not standard or necessarily consistent in any one organization. Therefore they are given as a focus point and to stimulate thought when one is to be tasked, perhaps, with considering the organizational aspects of managing a project.

One difficulty, faced many times, is to appreciate the specific responsibilities of individuals involved in a project. This chapter has explained them in some detail, and thus they can be used as a checklist to ensure that each party knows what is expected. In any oversight, they can be used to delegate a responsibility that might not have been assigned. The chapter outlines an organization that has worked well for the author. Users like it because they participate, and through the communication channels they are always cognizant of what is happening. It must be recognized, however, that there is no one correct organization. In large organizations, there may be only project or functional organizations, or a combination of the two. In a small organization, multiple functions may be the responsibility of one individual. We have introduced the idea of teleworking, which will bring its own set of problems as it becomes more widespread. Harmony and being able to work in a multicultural environment among functional units have been highlighted as being imperative if a project is to be completed successfully. The next chapter will outline the first deliverable of the systems development life cycle, i.e. initiation, which some of the project players mentioned will help to produce.

6. *Project Initiation*

6.1 Introduction

In the preceding chapters we have covered the elements of a project management methodology; project management functions; project roles and responsibilities; and quality management. Thus we now have an awareness of what is necessary and involved in managing a project. This chapter takes us through the initiation of a project to get it started.

Proper identification of the project at the outset is the easiest thing to overlook, and yet lack of it is the hardest fault from which to recover. As explained previously, many projects have failed because of carelessness in this phase. Therefore, before initiation, consider whether the project results can be assimilated by the organization. Help employees prepare for change by anticipating why they might resist and by planning the best way to deal with the resistance.

6.2 Initiation

This activity is invoked when a need for a system solution, for example, a change to an operational or information problem, has been perceived as necessary by a functional user group. The senior manager should complete a systems development and operation profile, or mission statement form. This form is an essential systems project management methodology document to establish the project. The profile serves as a request for service and should be submitted to the organizational entity responsible for systems development. In most cases the need for a project is identified when someone, usually the user, recognizes that he and/or others could do their jobs more effectively if they had additional or different information, or followed different procedures. The purpose of the profile (Fig. 6.1), is to request that a project be considered for initiation. It makes the request to start the project identification process visible and gives the requester a vehicle to describe the benefits and reasons for the project. It also provides senior management with a thumbnail sketch of the project.

This form should be approved and signed by a responsible manager (usually the requester's line manager), who is someone affected by the request. If the request is expected to cross organizational boundaries others may also need to sign.

The individual responsible for systems development will start project initiation activities by assigning a resource or 'project manager', perhaps him- or herself. Some believe that the eventual project team should choose the project manager. This is not

System development and operation profile (mission statement)		
System name:		Date:
Office of primary interest and client name (sponsor):	Priority (check one) High [ ] Medium [ ] Low [ ]	
Client division:		
Start date (desired): Estimated completion date:		
Definition		
System objective (summary of information gathered from client) Attach to this form the information produced by the client		
Benefits to the organization (magnitude of improvement expected):		
Impact if not developed:		
Constraints:		
Integration/interfaces to other systems:		

Fig. 6.1 System development and operation profile.

desirable, because they are not accountable for the end product. The chosen project manager, in conjunction with the requester, should prepare a project initiation document. This document would identify functional requirements; initial estimates of cost; resource requirements; time required; size; operational problems; scope; complexity; proposed project manager (if not already appointed); proposed project review members; all areas affected; reason for the project; benefits; constraints; and policy issues. The project's relative priority should be articulated for the purposes of project start-up and an overall resource availability decision. Based on this preliminary impact assessment, the request should be accepted or rejected by the appropriate organizational authority.

When the project initiation document has been accepted by the appropriate authorities a project initiation request (Fig. 6.2) is completed and attached as the cover page to the initiation document. A preliminary project organization form should also be completed outlining the administration of the proposed project.

This form is an integral systems project management methodology document. Its purpose is to inform interested parties that a project has been requested. It makes the decision to use, or not to use, the systems project management methodology visible. It also makes visible the project manager's commitment to start the process necessary to produce a project plan. When it has been confirmed that approval has been obtained for a project to be undertaken, the responsible manager should complete the form and give it to the individual appointed to be the project manager, along with whatever supporting documentation exists. The project manager should review the situation and sign the document indicating his or her willingness to take on a personal commitment for the planning of the project.

Project initiation request		
Project name:	Project number:	Project manager:
Office of primary interest:	Project review committee (proposed members):	
Responsible manager (project review committee chairperson):		
Acceptor:		
Project circle: end product – acceptor – deliverer When the acceptor has signed the project completion form, the deliverable is understood to be finished The specifics of deliverables must be covered by completing the end product general description (below) and the delivery acceptance matrix (in project plan)		
End product general description (project objective): This section is a summary of any document produced by the client, which should be attached		
Project management approach		
Project management methodology to be used? Yes or no:		
Project manager acceptance (signature):	Date:	
Comments:		

Fig. 6.2 Project initiation request.

All four documents, namely the system development and operation profile (mission statement), initiation request, initiation document and project organization form, should be forwarded to the appropriate approval authority. Consider the advisability of computerizing the process, perhaps in a workgroup environment or routing through email. The purpose is to obtain a formal start-up of the project. For large organizations the authority may be an information management steering committee. In a small organization it may be actioned by simply passing it to an individual responsible for systems development. The appropriate person, or committee, should review the request and consider the resources required, the impact it will have on other projects and other existing priorities. After this review, and perhaps in consultation with the involved line management, the request should be approved, rejected or scheduled for additional work to clarify the request.

When the request has been authorized, the responsible manager should appoint an acceptor to act on her behalf. The primary skill of an acceptor is to be methodical. She must have an attitude that allows her to want to prove that the deliverable does not work. Thus a penchant for detail, if not perfection, coupled with the stamina to persevere and be hard-nosed, is mandatory. Without these, the results will be slipshod. Having illustrated some traits that may be considered negative, it is important to realize that the outward appearance is one of diplomacy.

After project acceptance, the project manager should reaffirm his personal commitment to the project. In addition, the individual responsible for systems development or the planning officer, should, if the organization has one, incorporate the details into the organization's information management systems plan.

The project manager works with the chosen acceptor to define specific, recognizable deliverables, and an acceptable end product. For many projects the end product can be identified by a simple description, such as that appearing on the project initiation document. In other cases, a more detailed problem analysis, as defined in the systems development life cycle, will be required to describe the end product. If this is required, then it must be recognized that the drawing-up of a business agreement to provide this particular deliverable is a separate preliminary task and is part of the initiation process before project planning.

Before any effective work on a project can commence, the three nodes of the project circle (end product–acceptor–deliverer), must be resolved, i.e. there should be an individual committed to deliver (project manager) a known end product (deliverable) to a known person (acceptor). Before the circle can be complete, however, the project must be specifically and visibly identified. This is done by completing the project initiation request. This makes visible the request to establish a project and to use, or not to use, the project management methodology. In the event of the project being accepted, this form remains as a visible document to show the active or inactive status of the project.

A project review committee meeting should be held to brief all interested parties and ensure a smooth start-up by: Confirming the Project Review Committee, project manager, and the acceptor.

The project identification tools (forms) described in this section enable all the above to occur in a consistent way for all projects. This ensures that appropriate projects are initiated and consideration given to their priority, complexity and resource requirements such that:

- A project can be considered by management through the submission of a complete system development and operation profile. This gives the user (requester) a vehicle to describe the benefits and reasons for the project and to request officially that the project be considered for start-up approval.
- A completed project initiation request form identifies the project and maintains the macro project status through to signed acceptance.

During the initiation and preliminary analysis, the first soft gross estimate is made. This estimate is made, perhaps by polling experienced people who have done a similar project, in order for a meaningful decision to be made. There may even be a database of historical data that could be useful or the estimate could be based upon one's own knowledge and experience. However, sufficient information may not be available to make detailed estimates until after the feasibility stage, when some idea of the design is determined. As the project progresses more information is known and estimates become firmer and more reliable. In addition to experience, polling and using historical data, there are several estimating techniques available to an analyst. Some are illustrated in the following sections.

6.3 Estimating and Costing

When a project is targeted for development, either during the initiation stage or later, there is a need for an estimate to be made on how long it will take and, by extension, *how much it will cost*. Therefore, although we consider estimating at this time it is an ongoing exercise.

The goal in estimating is to reduce costs, increase quality and service levels and give management a chance to confirm that it is committed to the project by approving the expenditures. This should be a continuous program in all companies, especially with globalization taking place; i.e. insular companies are unlikely to survive, and estimating will need to take into account cultural diversity and its impact on the estimating techniques used.

Calculating development times and costs for a project is generally unreliable. The variance between planned and actual costs often approaches an order of magnitude. This situation can be minimized by a proper understanding by the developers of key concept, namely ensuring that the end user understands the assumptions of the size of the project, the productivity of the project team and that the scope of the project is constant unless changed through change management. If these points can be agreed to, then if any of them subsequently changes the estimate has to be changed. Unfortunately, many end users take an estimate as being irrevocable and therein lies a problem: as the project moves along, estimates change because more information is known and the assumptions can be modified.

Estimating and subsequent measurement must be viewed as tools to be used to ensure that the organization's objectives are being met. For the purpose of this book the goals can be considered as:

- increasing the productivity of the information systems development teams and consequently reducing a project's delivery time
- increasing client satisfaction
- reducing support

6.3.1 Project Estimating

Although we have seen significant evolution within computing, the area of project estimating has not kept pace. Although computers hum along at millions of instructions a second, the speed of development of systems is still slow in comparison. IBM stated in 1990 in *Datamation* that programmers are averaging about 10 lines of code a day and applications are backed up by two to three years. Therefore, a good project estimate is essential to the successful development of quality information systems. Yet estimating the cost of a proposed system is often more difficult than creating the system itself. Many information systems projects address qualitative facets, such as 'What design?', 'What requirement?', 'What language?' and 'What methodology?'. However, there are many quantitative issues, such as 'How much time will it take?', 'How much should I budget?' and 'What is the risk of failure?'. There are many techniques for measuring these quantitative, issues but few are truly effective.

If industry standards could be applied easily, estimating would be a relatively simple process. However, although project costs are frequently overestimated, more often they are overrun. Consequently, in the evaluation of performance or payback the estimate is given little credence. That is why information systems initiatives are based less on rigorous cost–benefit comparison than on a perception of dire need at any cost.

Many estimates are based purely on experience. The more of this the project manager or analyst has had the closer the estimate should be to reality. This is partly because they are familiar with the activities that go to make up a full product deliverable. Applying lessons from the past can be used to provide information about the present. Some of these are initiation, meetings, training, form design, purchasing, coding, report writing and so on. A junior with minimal experience, on the other hand, could easily overlook a significant task. This is why an SDLC is important, as a check sheet at the very least. The importance of estimating is obvious. Without a clear appreciation of the costs of systems development, the executive does not have the information with which to assess a decision to invest in an information system. The effort related to developing a system could be related to project size, productivity and constancy of scope. The importance of constancy is critical. If the scope is not well established and understood by the end user, unplanned effort will likely be required during the implementation stage to 'make the system work'. Change control will ensure constancy after sign-off. This lends credence to methodologies such as the project management methodology, project control and the systems development life cycle, which can act as checklists. Therefore there must be a method to provide a consistent way to measure, portray and demonstrate the productivity of each application developed and its maintenance activity.

Paul F. Lazarsfeld, the Columbia University professor who developed the art of polling, used to tell his classes that whenever you attach a number to an idea you have learned something. You know more than you knew before. The number seems too large, too small or about right. You are already thinking in a more precise way (Senator Daniel Patrick Moynihan, *Newsletter*, 4 September 1981). If this is thought about for a moment one can see that it is true. For example, if a group of six people said that: 'next Saturday we are going to the beach' but did not know how far away the beach is, they could derive a reasonable estimate by consensus. This could be done by polling each individual in the group to give an estimate of the distance (assuming that they all have at least a reasonable idea of what it is). Say they gave respectively 10, 15, 20, 25, 30 and 35 miles; we could then say that 35 is too large and 10 is too small, but 20–25 seems about right. Thus taking an average we could say that it is approximately 22 miles and that it should take less than one hour to get to the beach, i.e. we have thought in a precise way and will probably find our estimate fairly close.

6.4 Estimating Concepts

It is impossible in this book to write a treatise on concepts. However, it is considered useful to at least explain some principles. We will explain three topics:

- an estimate
- a project
- a relation of the Software Engineering Institute's Capability Maturity Model

6.4.1 An Estimate

An estimate is a package of information that describes the anticipated potential resource requirements for a particular project given specific characteristics and attributes. The estimate is one possible scenario among many scenarios that make up the solution set of possibilities and is bounded by project risks, constraints and assumptions.

6.4.2 A Project

A project is any effort that has a plan and deliverables that are constrained by schedule commitments, resource requirements and budget limitations; and can be delineated from other concurrent activities.

Because project estimates are usually derived before the creation or identification of many defining characteristics, and because the purpose of the estimating process itself is to determine or approximate these characteristics, we have broadened the notion of a project to consider the essential characteristics and attributes of a project.

A project is considered to be any organizational undertaking that will require allocation of resources (people, time and money). A project may be seen to be a contiguous set of activities performed to satisfy the project's requirements.

6.4.3 Relation of the Software Engineering Institute's Capability Maturity Model

The Software Engineering Institute (SEI), a federally funded research and development organization at Carnegie Mellon University, has developed a model of organizational maturity for software organizations, called the Capability Maturity Model. The maturation of the software processes within an organization, based upon this model, will improve the predictability and controllability of projects within the organization. This model has five maturity levels:

- Level 1: Initial
  Characterized by unpredictable cost, schedule and quality. This is where *ad hoc* processes are used to perform the work and where variations in quality and schedule are large. These processes include the means by which estimates are created.
- Level 2: Repeatable
  Characterized by variable cost, schedule and quality.
  The focus of Level 2 is to lay a foundation for future improvements and focus on leadership issues, including estimating.

- Level 3: Defined
  Characterized by reliable cost and schedule, but unpredictable quality.
- Level 4: Managed
  Characterized by reasonable statistical control over quality.
- Level 5: Optimizing
  Characterized by a quantitative basis for process improvement and automation.

6.5 Estimating Principles

Three principles influence the approach and rigour of the estimate. Project managers updating estimates should apply them. They are:

1 Apply the correct amount of resources to create and refine the estimate.
2 The estimate of the resources required for a given scenario cannot be arbitrarily changed.
3 Re-estimate often, even if the deadline cannot be changed.

The foregoing principles are shown in Fig. 6.3.

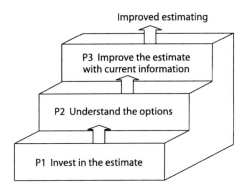

Fig. 6.3 Estimating principles.

Principle 1: Apply the Correct Amount of Resources to Create and Refine the Estimate

Project leaders and vendors must agree in advance on the level of detail and scope of the estimate. The following guidelines help determine the level of detail:

- The magnitude of the project.
- The risk of an inaccurate estimate. Greater risk should equate to greater rigour in creating the estimate.
- Project uncertainties. Does the project present new or untried tools, techniques, business situations or processes? The less that is known about what can be

expected in executing the project, the more important it becomes to apply sound estimating techniques.

Principle 2: The Estimate of the Resources Required for a Given Scenario Cannot be Arbitrarily Changed

An estimate consists of a range of possible outcomes, based on a specific set of input parameters. In the case of a systems engineering project, the possible outcomes may include such elements as the number of persons required to fulfil project obligations, the size of software in delivered function points (FP) produced by the project team and the calendar time required to complete the project. Note that each of these elements, or project resources, will be provided as a range of possible values. These value ranges can vary with the precision that is required to determine how likely a particular set of values is to occur.

Issues that can affect the precision required of the estimate can include the following:

- Inherent risk of the project
- Reliability of the information used to create the estimate
- How risk-averse the stakeholders are
- Effectiveness of the estimating process

Principle 3: Re-estimate Often, Even if the Deadline Cannot be Changed

Projects evolve over time and more information becomes available. This information will either confirm or refute assumptions made in the original estimate. Even though the organization, based upon the estimates in this document may make commitments, it is vital to project managers and others that accurate estimates are kept of remaining work. This will allow proper business decisions to be made based on current information.

6.6 Constraints

Constraints are limitations imposed on the project. Some requirements reflect decisions, perhaps beyond the control of the organization. For example, if a document management system is accepted for a generic office environment, then it may be imposed on (say) the human resource management system because of economies of scale and a reduction in training costs etc. Also, when the generic office environment is implemented, there will be constraints on freedom of design and delivery.

A constraint can also be imposed based upon an assumption. For example, the design of an improvement to an existing application could be constrained by the assumption that existing products must be used. All assumptions should be clearly documented. Thus, if an assumption is found to be incorrect, the estimate can be reevaluated.

Constraints can be organized according to the type of limitation. Listed below are categories that can be used when updating the estimates. Standards should always be referred to because they may act as constraints to a solution.

- *Technical*
  Requirements may dictate technical decisions, such as the amount of historical data to be maintained or the use of CD-ROM storage.
- *Quality/reliability*
  The organization may have predefined parameters for system operation, such as the amount of system downtime per week.
- *Required methodology*
  The organization may require that a specific methodology be used during a project, such as a specific SDLC.
- *Time/schedule*
  Project completion may be required by a specific date, such as a year-end in a financial system.
- *Resources*
  Specific resources may be required.
- *Regulatory*
  The government may impose regulatory rules.
- *Internal*
  Management may impose specific constraints.

6.7 Risks

Risks are factors that could have an impact on the estimates.

6.7.1 Risk Categories

The following are areas involving risk:

- *Stability of vendors*
  Project managers should ensure that the vendors on any project maintain project leaders etc., as this can increase risk.
- *Stability of requirements*
  If the requirements or scope of projects specified in the estimate document change, then risk can increase.
- *Stability of line management*
  If designated project champions change, then this can increase risk.

6.7.2 Degree of Innovation or Newness of Technology

Some projects are innovative, and this will increase risk especially as time may not permit evaluation.

6.8 Budget Cost Estimates

6.8.1 Methodology

The prediction technique is the basis for deriving the budget estimates. In the prediction method, consideration is given to the pattern of past behaviour of data points, assuming a constant environment. For example, a prediction can be of a likely next occurrence, given a series of events. In the series 2, 4, 6, x, we would expect x to take the value '8' given the previous pattern/experience considered. In this case, the application of the prediction technique is the projected application/project size and cost based on projects of similar size and cost from previous patterns or similar experience. Some projects can be considered to have some predictability for estimating purposes because their underlying technology is mature and can be measured against other similar projects.

A costing hierarchy framework (Fig. 6.4), could be defined as a standard approach in developing the cost estimates for, say, a three-team application as illustrated in the figure.

To derive the cost estimates for the total project (summary), three basic questions should be answered for each team's application:

● How much does it cost to deploy the system and to operate the system yearly?
● What is the development/deployment schedule for the applications?
● What is the yearly allocation of the cost?

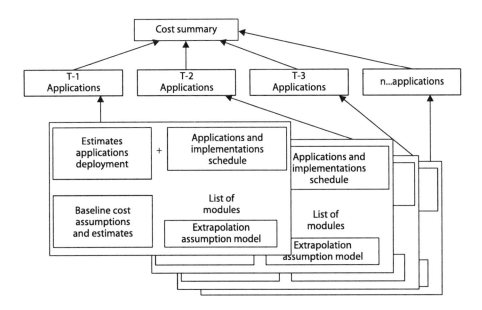

Fig. 6.4 A costing hierarchy framework.

6.8.2 Estimating Cost Process

1 Define the budget summary format that will identify:
   (a) the budget requirement for the applications projects outsourced; or
   (b) management support and non-application-specific projects.
   These estimates will be shown by year and represented in constant money. For the vendors' costs, separate capital and operating expenditure estimates.
2 Baseline/consolidate the list of applications/suite of applications that will be deployed during a period.
3 Develop a deployment schedule for each application or suite of applications, showing:
   (a) What application/suite of applications is to be deployed to which client and when
   (b) When the deployment activities end and when the systems go live
4 Define a cost element structure (CES) which identifies the list of cost elements and sub-elements to be estimated.
5 Using the CES, calculate the cost for each application/suite of applications: the one-time cost to design/construct/test the application systems and the yearly cost to maintain and operate the system after it goes live.
6 Calculate an average capital expenditure for one application/suite of applications per organizational unit.
7 Calculate the total capital expenditure costs by multiplying the cost derived in Step 5 by the number of clients assumed to receive the application.
8 Calculate average yearly operating expenditures for one application/suite of applications.
9 Calculate the total operating expenditure cost by multiplying the average yearly operating expenditure derived in Step 8.
10 Combine the application cost estimates and the summary budget estimates.

6.8.3 Assumptions

An assumption is defined as a statement accepted or supposed to be true without proof or demonstration. In estimating cost, document any assumptions that have been made upon which the estimators have based their estimate.
   Some categories of assumptions addressed here are:

- *Expiration of estimate*
  The client may assume that the estimate does not require re-estimating, even though the estimates may expire before the end of the project.
- *Staffing issues*
  The estimators may have assumed a level of expertise to be higher than that available.
- *Resources and resource availability*
  The estimators may assume the availability of project management and equipment, if required.

- *Customer requirement stability*
  It may be assumed that the requirements are stable, at least in the short term.
- *System architecture*
  The assumption may be that the architecture in place will remain but that new applications can build upon it as necessary.
- *Documentation*
  The team providing the solution will provide all system and user documentation and training materials.
- *Project complexity*
  If the environment is new, a high complexity view should be taken in deriving estimates. Thus estimates could be high.
- *Roles and responsibilities*
  Roles and responsibilities, if not clearly defined for the project, would add to its complexity.
- *Third-party vendors*
  An incorrect number of software licences may require that the estimates be recalculated after the first unit has been implemented.
- *Deliverables*
  Deliverables may not have been specified because a requirements analysis has not been done. Therefore estimates may be soft and based upon the estimator's experience.
- *Application vendors*
  Project/pilot systems development/deployment could be performed by vendors, with the vendors providing their external resources. Thus, one should realize that the vendors' costs include profits.
- *Systems operations*
  Determine who will be responsible for the operations of the systems upon completion of implementation.
- *Network services*
  Network connectivity and services may be provided by outsourcing for inter-unit connectivity.
- *Application-specific*
  These assumptions cover both the capital expenditures and operating expenditure items.
- *Enterprise-wide*
  These assumptions would cover the general costs that are non-application-specific, such as vendor implementation, non-application-specific training (computer literacy) and other unidentified projects.

6.8.4 Principles and Techniques of Estimating

Management decisions concerning the start or continuation of a project or a change in its scope or direction will be based somewhat on estimates, although legislation could force the start of a project irrespective of costs. In this case, estimates are used to give management a feel for the magnitude of the assignment. All projects should therefore be broken down into stages and phases or steps etc., so that as accurate an estimate as possible can be obtained. The process for estimating is not an automatic one. Estimating largely depends on the knowledge, experience and judgement of the individual(s) making the estimate. The danger of using formal techniques is that the results can appear more accurate than they are.

As projects have their own peculiarities and constraints it is appropriate that experience should be one of the most commonly used components as a basis for initial estimates. However, the activities of project team members are affected by their skill levels. Such estimates can be cross-checked against formal methodologies. A useful approximate guide is listed below (rules of thumb). Organizations with some historical data can quickly derive their own table and use this for the first soft planning estimates.

Some general principles that can be used for estimating are:

- Relate experiences to the current project.
- Break a project into small parts, such as 10 days or fewer, so that experiences can be more easily applied.
- Keep and subsequently use historical records of projects for future use and comparative analysis.
- Use a standard methodology so that transfer of values is valid.
- Review and modify estimates continually throughout the project so that they become firmer and firmer as the project unfolds.
- Break a large project into a set of sub-projects with as small a duration as possible, e.g. six months or less. These could then be further broken down into small parts, as in the second item in this list.
- Use a consensus approach (sometimes called the Delphi method) to calculate an average based upon variable input from the project team. Consider using the Joint Application Development approach to get the team together to participate.

6.8.5 Estimating Training

Underestimating the training required is a common problem. A training plan is essential and should be costed at the time project estimates are made. This is often overlooked. For example, consider the true cost of training 1000 employees in five regions, i.e. on average 200 per region. Assume, or from some method, calculate that training will take two half days in groups of 10 and is to be given by an external training company. The true cost would consist of 100 days of the trainer's time, plus staff's lost productivity, possible travel and materials costs, and perhaps the development of one's own customized course. Obviously significant costs are involved and should not be overlooked. An example of a six-step basic methodology for training follows; each step should be estimated and costed.

1 *Objective* – establish an overall training strategy. For example, is training to be embedded in the system? Will it be classroom-based? Will it be computer-based training? Video? At this time the terminal and sub-terminal objectives, scope and staff to be trained are considered.

2 *Analysis* – identify job responsibilities, required skills and knowledge based on the technology being implemented. Determine the current skill levels and identify the difference between the level required and the current level; select the best delivery method based on audience type. Establish a training curriculum and detail the program and course objectives. Develop evaluation processes and techniques.

3 *Design* – details of the training program design are formalized and custom courses designed.

4 *Development* – customized courses need to be developed and beta tested.

5 *Delivery* – determine whether off-the-shelf standard training or customized training programs need to be scheduled and delivered.

6 *Evaluation* – ensure that response mechanisms are arranged and monitored to evaluate the success of the training programs and courses.

6.8.6 Learning Curve

One method of determining how long something will take to produce and the cost per unit of output is the learning curve. The total number of person-hours to produce a given quantity of units is sometimes needed in advance to bid on a contract, to determine a completion date or to be used as a planning tool. The learning curve is a common method in industry, also known as the airframe curve, because studies of aircraft companies suggested that the method produces consistent results that can be developed into standards. The theory is that individuals learn from experience by repeating the same operation a number of times. The more times the operation is repeated, the more efficient the person becomes. The net result is that the time taken to perform an operation is reduced. We all know intuitively that this is true. Companies therefore habitually use what is commonly referred to as the 80% model. However, a company it can derive its own model from empirical data gathered from its own experience. What the 80% model suggests is that there is a 20% improvement each time production doubles. That is, individuals tend to require less time to perform a task successfully after they have practised it a number of times. As the limit of efficiency is approached, the amount of time to produce will stabilize. In this text we are not interested in producing production units, but rather in determining the amount of time to perform a number of tasks, such as computer operations or transactions in an information processing environment.

A common problem associated with project scheduling is to fail to take into account the amount of effort required to develop training plans, courseware and implementation. The problem of implementation is further compounded by the fact that very little is retained from the first course. Therefore, a learning curve approach to implementation to find the true effort required to train individuals over a period of time may be valid. For example, to determine how much data can be captured before a plateau is found, consider using a learning curve. This assumes that learning is fairly rapid at first but then levels off, at which point the organization would know how much training an individual needed before becoming proficient. The number of transactions than an individual is able to capture at the plateau would then become the performance standard for data entry. However, if the transaction rate is used as a performance figure, then the question of acceptable error rates must be considered. When this figure is known a value can be given to the cost of training. For example, if it was found that it took 5 days' training to reach an acceptable level (plateau) and that 1000 individuals must be trained, and that 10 people can be trained at any one session, then it is easy to see that 1000/10 × 5 = 500 days of training would be required. This would tell management how much lost productivity time would be required to train the individuals. The final figure on the curve could be an ongoing value that can be used to determine performance; for example, if the plateau was 5 minutes per transaction, then management would know that one person could do approximately 100 per day.

Two models are presented to demonstrate the techniques of the family of tools known as learning curves:

- *Model 1 – Constant learning*
  In this model, the assumption is made that the increase in efficiency (i.e. the learning effect) is constant.

  This means that each time the operation is repeated the improvement in time over the previous operation is constant.

  This assumption suggests that there is no limit to the improvement in efficiency. However, there are some real practical limits, such as a negotiated working agreement not to work beyond certain limits of productivity.

- *Model 2 – Accelerated learning*
  In this model, the assumption is made that the increase in efficiency (i.e. the learning effect) is more rapid at first and then tends to slow down as a limit in improved performance is reached.

  This model is perhaps the most documented model, in that the aircraft industry found, over many monitored production runs, there was a 20% improvement every time the production doubles. For this reason, this particular curve is known as the '80% airframe curve'. This particular model will be the subject matter in our treatment of Model 2.

We shall examine the usefulness of the learning curves at the following levels:

- Model 1 with examples
- Model 2 with examples
- Comparative tables for Models 1 and 2

The examples will be directed towards determining the time taken to train an employee and establish a rate of operations, per day, based on the improvement in productivity that results from the training.

6.8.7 Model 1 – Constant Learning

Assume that the increase in efficiency (i.e. the learning effect) is constant. This means that each time the operation is repeated the improvement in time over the previous operation is constant.

Figure 6.5 depicts the linear constant learning model.

Given the assumption of a straight line relationship:

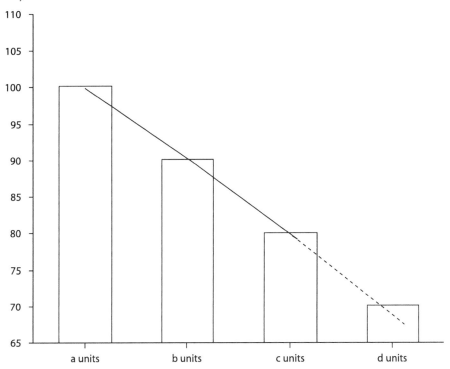

Fig. 6.5 The linear constant learning model.

$$y = b - ax$$

where a = slope, $b = c + a$, n = operations, the time taken to perform the first operation = $c + a/2$ and the time taken to produce the second operation = $c - a/2$.

The time taken to perform all the operations can be found from:

$$\int_0^n [(c+a) - ax]dx = (c+a)n - \frac{an^2}{2}$$

Example

An organization is preparing to introduce a new office automation product and wants to establish the correct workshop training programme for its employees. The organization has found that in the past a mixture of presentations, demonstrations and hands-on training has proved the most effective. Such a mixture involves each feature being presented, demonstrated and then exercised by the employee under training.

Assumptions

Number of product features = 45
Initial training time per feature = 3 minutes

Percentage improvement after each operation = 5% of initial training time
Initial training time for all features = 135 minutes
Number of times feature is exercised = 10

$c = 135$ minutes

$a = 6.75$ minutes

$n = 10$

time taken $= (135 + 6.75)10 - 6.75(10)^2/2$

$\qquad\qquad = 1080$ minutes

$\qquad\qquad = 18$ hours

$\qquad\qquad = 2.40$ days

It can be determined that a two-and-a-half day training programme would meet the needs for the new office automation product.

Several variations can be included in this approach. For instance, the 45 features could have been classified as easy, intermediate and complex, and the resulting training programme would be the sum of the times determined by using different percentage improvement figures for the easy, intermediate and complex features.

You may also be interested in the improvement in productivity for each employee. This can be determined by the following approach. For the first time the product is tested:

$y = 135$ minutes

(this is one of the assumptions). For the tenth time the product is tested:

$y = (135 + 6.75) - (6.75 \times 10)$

$\quad = 74.25$ minutes

The improvement in productivity factor is:

$74.25/135 = 0.55$

The improvement in productivity per feature tested is:

$3 \times 0.55 = 1.65$ minutes

This results in a trained employee being able to perform the following number of feature operations per day, assuming that the employee is only available to operate the features for 85% of the day:

7.5 hours $\times 0.85 \times 60$ minutes$/1.65$ minutes $= 231.8$ feature operations per day

The figures of 2.5 days for training and the resulting ability to perform 232 operations per day provide the correct level of training and resourcing for their operations.

The next model will examine the same assumption against the situation in which the employees learn more quickly at first.

6.8.8 Model 2 – Accelerated Learning

Assume that the increase in efficiency (i.e. the learning effect) is more rapid at first and then tends to slow down as a limit in improved performance is reached. Figure 6.6 depicts the accelerated learning model.

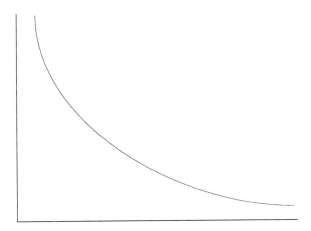

Fig. 6.6 The accelerated learning model.

Given the assumption of a power function relationship:

$$y = ax^b$$

the time taken to perform all of the operations can be found from:

$$\int_0^n ax^b\,dx = \frac{an^{b+1}}{b+1}$$

where a = time of first test, b = improvement rate and n = number of tests.

This function can be transformed into a straight-line relationship to simplify the computational process:

$$y = ax^b$$
$$\log y = \log a + b(\log x)$$

where a = time of first test, b = improvement rate and n = number of tests.

Of interest for both equations is the value of b. Based on research, the organization has chosen to utilize the '80% Airframe Curve', which states that there is a 20% improvement as production doubles. Therefore, expressed as a ratio we have:

$$2^b = 0.8$$
$$b\log 2 = \log 0.8$$
$$b = \log 0.8/\log 2$$
$$= -0.097/0.301$$
$$= -0.322$$

Example

The situation is exactly the same as used in Model 1.

Assumptions

Number of product features = 45
Initial training time per feature = 3 minutes
Percentage improvement after each operation = 20%
Initial training time for all features = 135 minutes
Number of times feature is exercised = 10

$a = 135$ minutes

$b = -0.322$

$n = 10$

Time taken to perform all tests:

$$\frac{an^{b+1}}{b+1} = \frac{135(10)^{(-0.322+1)}}{(-0.322+1)}$$

$$= 948 \text{ minutes}$$

$$= 15.81 \text{ hours}$$

$$= 2.11 \text{ days}$$

The organization was able to determine that a two-day training programme would meet its needs for the new office automation product.

Several variations can be included in this approach. For instance, the 45 features could have been classified as easy, intermediate and complex, and the resulting training programme would be the sum of the times determined by using different percentage improvement figures for the easy, intermediate and complex features.

Time taken for the tenth test:

$$y = ax^b$$

where $a = 135$ minutes, $b = -0.322$ and $n = 10$, gives

$$\log y = \log a + b(\log n)$$

$$= 2.130 + (-0.322)1.000$$

$$= 2.130 - 0.322$$

$$= 1.808$$

$$\therefore y = 64.269$$

The improvement in productivity factor is:

$$64.269/135 = 0.476$$

The improvement in productivity per feature tested is:

$$3 \times 0.476 = 1.428 \text{ minutes}$$

Table 6.1 Comparative table for Models 1 and 2

Number of times features are exercised	Model 1: Constant learning		Model 2: Accelerated learning	
	Time (min)	Percentage improvement	Time (min)	Percentage improvement
1	135.000	–	135.000	–
2	128.250	5.000	107.995	20.004
3	121.500	5.263	94.777	12.239
4	114.750	5.556	86.391	8.848
5	108.000	5.882	80.402	6.932
6	101.250	6.250	75.817	5.703
7	95.500	6.667	72.146	4.842
8	87.750	7.143	69.110	4.208
9	81.000	7.692	66.538	3.722
10	74.250	8.333	64.318	3.336

This results in a trained employee being able to perform the following number of feature operations per day, assuming that the employee is only available to operate the features for 85% of the day:

7.5 hours × 0.85 × 60 minutes/1.428 minutes = 267.86 feature operations per day

The figure of 2 days for training and the resulting ability to perform 268 operations per day provide the correct level of training and resourcing for the company's operations.

The learning curves illustration concludes by presenting a set of comparative tables (Tables 6.1 and 6.2) for Models 1 and 2.

6.8.9 Rules of Thumb

A typical situation is where a manager is preparing a budget and needs a figure for planning purposes. Experience suggests that the figure is anywhere between x and y. This, however, will not satisfy the manager, who wants more precision. So you say, 'Well, we can probably do it for z'. The manager thanks you, and you have now created an albatross for yourself. Therefore, it would have been better to have explained that any figure at this time would be based on the assumptions mentioned earlier. Then you would need to explain the assumptions and obtain input that is more definitive. For example, if developing a tracking system you could say the estimate is based on the size of two input documents and on three functions (scheduling, statistics and case information), and produces six reports. The development approach would be explained and productivity can be estimated (it will take an elapsed time of six months and will cost so much). Having done this, a meeting should be convened of

Table 6.2 Comparative table for Models 1 and 2

Observed Result	Model 1: Constant learning	Model 2: Accelerated learning
Training time required	2.5 days	2.0 days
Initial time per feature	3.000 mins	3.000 mins
Improvement factor	0.550	0.476
Final time per feature	1.650 mins	1.428 mins
Number of operations per day based on 85% availability $(7.5 \times 0.85 \times 60 = 382.5 \text{ min})$	232	268
Persons for 1000 ops/day	04.31	3.73
Persons for 2000 ops/day	08.62	7.46
Persons for 3000 ops/day	12.93	11.19
Persons for 4000 ops/day	17.24	14.93
Persons for 5000 ops/day	21.55	18.66

the project review committee, where the estimate would be presented and the assumptions explained. Thus, as the project moves along and changes are required, the original estimate can be used as a baseline to explain that more work equals more time and money; that is, if the scope of the project changes, then so does the estimate. To help with these estimates, the following commonly used rules of thumb have been found to be applicable for many projects. Others can be found in published works, or your own organization may have some standards.

Some measures that are used are size-orientated measures (e.g. lines of code per person month) and ratios. Table 6.3 shows the ratios for one traditional systems life cycle.

It is important to realize that deviations from the values are common. For example, if a rush is made to start coding, this generally decreases the design component time but extends the implementation time because of the poor quality of coding. In addition, the iterative approach can lead to extended design time because agreement on deliverables is difficult (impossible?) to obtain. Anyone who has worked in an iterative or prototype environment will recognize this fact. However, using the joint application design technique has been found to contribute to the quality of design by improving the front-end deliverables and thus reducing the time spent on defect removal. The effect is illustrated in Fig. 6.7, which shows that JAD can produce the final deliverable 50% sooner than by rushing to code or using iterative methods.

With the use of CASE tools, experience has shown that planning, analysis and design costs increase, but those for coding, testing and implementation decrease. However, CASE tools are evolving, and it is to be seen what new ratios can be developed. Some experience suggests productivity improvements of 50%. Thus, we will see percentages increase for logic development and decrease for others. This is illustrated in Fig. 6.8 (the CASE tunnel effect), which shows a break-even point at about the design stage, i.e. when through the tunnel there is a case for CASE. Then there is OOP (object-oriented programming), which will save considerable time in the development stage. There will be libraries of objects already coded and reusable in other programs. Therefore, rules and logic will be constant.

Table 6.3 Ratios of elapsed time and expenditure in each project stage

Systems development life cycle phase	Elapsed time (%)	Cost (%)
Initiation and preliminary analysis	5	2
Feasibility – analysis	10	5
Prepare logical data flow diagrams (allow half day per page of LDFD)		
Prepare requirements specifications (allow 1–5 days)		
Prepare discussion of problem areas and their costs (allow 1–5 days)		
Develop detailed functional specifications:		
Review existing documentation, prepare or revise logical data flow diagrams (allow one day per LPFD plus half day per LDFD for walkthroughs)		
Prepare function hierarchy diagrams (allow one day per FHD, plus one day for walkthrough)		
Prepare description of functions (allow half day for each level above the lowest level, one day for each lowest level function plus half day for a walkthrough)		
Indexing and sign-offs (allow one day)		
Design	25	18
Development	40	45
Logic development 35%		
Coding 25%		
Debugging and testing 35%		
Documentation 5%		
Implementation (includes defect removal)	20	30

6.8.10 Estimating Test Times

One method is to use past estimates from similar projects. Theoretical estimating may be used to supplement a well-maintained history that is analyzed and made available. One reason for this is that the history reflects the culture and mind-set of the employees. Of course, it may be argued that employees leave. This is true, but usually the culture continues and new employees generally follow the way things have been done in the past. In fact, if changes are made it is usually for the better, so that the estimate is generally on the high side.

6.8.11 Error Removal Cost

Errors are extremely expensive. They become more expensive at an accelerating rate across the systems development life cycle. Therefore, tools and techniques that prevent, detect and eliminate errors early in the SDLC are required. 'Front-end loading' is often used to describe systems done with deliberate, thorough, up-front definition and analysis work with the intent of realizing savings in later phases.

Management must realize that there is never enough time to do it right, but there is always enough time to do it over.

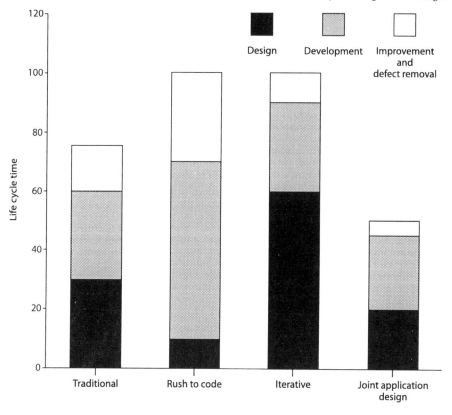

Fig. 6.7 SDLC approaches.

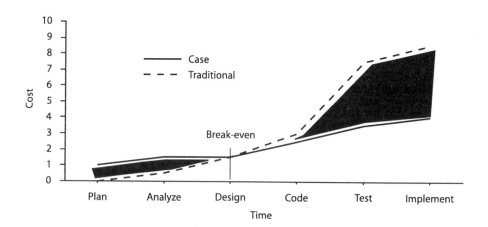

Fig. 6.8 The CASE tunnel effect.

Table 6.4 Cost of correcting errors.

SDLC phase	Unit cost
Initiation	1
Feasibility	2
Design	5
Development	10
Alpha testing	15
Beta testing	25
System testing	50
Post-implementation	100

The principle is to spend the money on tools and techniques that avoid the need to do it over, i.e. catch errors early while they are least costly to correct. There are numerous references to the costs involved. The classic on software economics is *Software Engineering Economics* (Boehm, 1981). Another is *Software Reliability: Achievement and Assessment* by B. Littlewood, published by Blackwell Scientific Publications.

If a criterion for test completion works it should be made a standard so that other developers in the organization can benefit.

As pointed out previously, errors that are found late in the development stage cost more to remove than those found in the early stages. Table 6.4 depicts the effect.

6.8.12 Formulas

Successful systems development requires the confidence and participation of the client, recipient or user. A good project estimate should be credible, based on rational assumptions and formed from a consensus of stakeholders. These characteristics are inherent in function point analysis techniques, developed by Al Albrecht of IBM in 1974, primarily as an after-the-fact productivity measurement for its information systems service organization. The analysis determines the relative size of a system. The objective was to develop a relative measure of function value delivered (function points/person months) independent of the technology or approach used. Using this technique gives the ability to develop accurate estimates of future work. Personal computer software is available to track the flow and quality of projects by analyzing progress on key function points. According to Applied Business Technology Corp., their product *Metrics Manager* lets managers establish a baseline for their quality and productivity variables and forecasts. This product is based on the use of function points. Proponents claim that functionality is a more accurate measurement of scale than simply counting lines of code. Some variables used are time to completion, programmer experience, person months needed, estimated costs, actual costs, defects reported and customer satisfaction. It may be found that one type of application progressed at 20 function points per month and another type at 25. Such values can be used to measure and quantify quality and then plan to improve it.

IBM found that the basic value of an application function is proportional to the number of external inputs, outputs, inquiries, interfaces and master files delivered in the development project. Collectively called 'data control types or function types', each is assigned a weighted value for simple, average and complex cases. The result is a set of dimensionless numbers, defined as function points, which provide a relative measure of function value to be delivered.

In addition, there are factors affecting the size and complexity of the target systems, called 'general application attributes or processing complexity factors'. These can range from data communications and distributed processing to reusability and ease of installation. Some or all of these characteristics may be present in any given system. It is therefore necessary to quantify the degree of influence that each of the factors is expected to have on the system according to a scale.

The first requirement in this approach to estimating is a reasonably accurate model of the target environment, and an examination of the target system itself. If an estimate is required for the project before this can be done, then the average delivery rate for the department or unit can be used. However, it should always be kept in mind that each project is unique and those delivery rates for the project being estimated will be the most accurate. If using comparisons to make estimates, it is essential that apples be compared to apples. This is to say that the delivery rate of a personal microcomputer application should not be used to estimate a mainframe or server application.

The next step is to involve stakeholders in a joint application design (JAD) session to settle structural issues and to identify the transactions by type, such as inquiry, add, modify and update. It is appropriate to involve the financial group if they are not already included.

The next element is an estimate of the person-time required to code and test simple examples of the three to five data control types. This estimate is the basis for a standard and should ideally evolve from a consensus of the entire information systems development team.

Using the values identified for the basic elements, and some simple mathematical operations, a total time required to develop a system, from specifications to working programs, can be calculated.

The processing complexity adjustment (PCA) in person-days is used to estimate development of the system from specifications. This includes coding and testing the programs as specified, but does not include analysis, design and implementation. To include these it is necessary to determine the relationship between the development stage and other parts of the systems development life cycle. An examination of the SDLC in this book and others indicates that although the conventions and descriptions in each stage may differ, the objectives and activities in the model are generally the same, albeit having to combine some stages to make the model conform to a traditional one. Therefore a relative sizing between the stages can be derived. On a scale of 1 to 10, the development stage, as the standard, is always 10, while the proportions of the other stages may vary from project to project.

The first stage, initiation, includes definition of functional requirements, analysis, planning and a model of the system. This lays a strong foundation for the other stages in the SDLC.

The second stage, feasibility, includes critical success factors, network analysis, capacity requirements and a conceptual design.

The third stage, design, takes the feasibility study and the functional requirements and designs a system. The activities of the design stage that would be included are: detailed specifications, change procedures and quality assurance.

The above three stages are sometimes combined into one, i.e. design.

The fourth stage, development, is when the wheels hit the road. The actual programs are written and the system is tested. The results of the prior stages are now seen.

The fifth stage, implementation and defect correction, concerns itself with training, testing, conversion and parallel operation. During the initial planning, a cutover time should be determined. This can be a critical success factor where timing is of the essence, such as in financial systems.

The sixth stage, post-implementation review, is an independent review from the developers and assesses whether the specifications have been met. Also included is a review of costs.

It is possible to extrapolate the processing complexity adjustment (PCA) to cover the analysis, design and implementation stages by setting its value to 10 and calculating time values for the first three stages based upon the relative proportions of each stage.

Since the time involved in the two stages of development and implementation can be more accurately defined as a function of the total project time than of the development time, each should be calculated in proportion to the total of the first four stages at 12.5% and 2% respectively.

In large systems, all totals should be adjusted for complexity and constraints specific to the system and the environment. A constraint may be that management cannot authorize progress until a deliverable has been signed off. This might be an average of six weeks, in which case this constraint must be built in. To progress while awaiting sign-off is a judgement that the project manager should make, i.e. no project should be process-bound.

The initial project estimate is not final. It must be adjusted to match the 'as built' rather than the 'as planned' situation. There is only one certain feature in a project and that is: *there will be changes*. A change may vary from simply changing a word in an error statement to changing a complex algorithm. Therefore there must be a change control procedure in place. It is also appropriate to adjust the productivity measurement. How to do this is contained in the 14 standard characteristics of application environments that have significant influence on the design, development and testing of systems. Each of these characteristics is assigned a rating on a scale of 0 to 5. The total of the assigned influence ratings is used to establish the total degree of influence (TDI) or complexity factor (CF) adjustment. Automated tools may also help in determining a CF. An example of a completed CF table is shown in Table 6.5.

The total degree of influence (TDI) will range between 0 and 70 (14 × 5), with a midpoint or theoretical average of 35. The TDI is used to calculate the adjusted final function point count; see the example below. This calculation can be applied either to each stage or to the total project estimate before the SDLC stage proportioning.

It remains now to distribute the time estimate over the skill and experience levels of the team members and factor for contingency, overhead and time-paid-not-worked to arrive at an estimated total and approximate calendar time.

Table 6.5 Processing complexity factors

Factor	Value
1 Data communications	5
2 Distributed data/processing	2
3 Performance objectives	3
4 Tight configuration	2
5 High transaction rate	3
6 On-line inquiry/data entry	5
7 End user efficiency	3
8 On-line update	5
9 Complex processing	1
10 Code reusability	0
11 Conversion/installation ease	2
12 Operational ease	1
13 Multiple site installation	1
14 Facilitate change	4
Total degree of influence (TDI) or complexity factor (CF)	37

Before accepting a change into a system, its impact on the project, be it financial or schedule-related, should be assessed. To assess the impact of change standard criteria are necessary; otherwise each change can be assessed from different perspectives. Function point analysis makes criteria explicit and quantifiable.

In assessing the impact the following questions should be asked and resolved:

- Does the change add, delete or modify data control elements? Which elements are affected? Does the change, increase or decrease the complexity of the system?
- Does the change affect any of the 14 complexity factors? Which factors change and by how much?

On completion of the analysis, the effect (positive or negative) on the current project schedule can be calculated.

Productivity is measured against the project work plan with a work breakdown structure. All projects should have a project control system and these are components of such a system. Each activity is related to one or more data control elements. Using the relative values in the estimating process, a value measured in function points is determined for each activity. Totalling and reconciling the function points in all phases produces a single unit value in time for a function point. This is done by reducing the estimate of the project by the amount of time-paid-not-worked and dividing the result by the total number of function points.

Progress in completing the project is accumulated as percentage completed or percentage remaining by task. This is converted into function points completed and, using the unit time value, into earned time. Earned time over actual time is the productivity level. This can be determined for the team, the individual or the project stage. A good project estimate assists in sound budgeting and scheduling. These form the basis on which progress and performance is measured.

6.8.13 An Example of Function Point Analysis

Background: An asset management system is now in production. The user now wishes to change the system to add the following on-line menu-driven components:

- demand for reports – display of asset parts
- display of asset description – maintenance

Figure 6.9 is a simplified on-line system schematic to illustrate the functions. The process to determine function points is as follows:

Activity 1: Identify all functions required.

Activity 2: Classify the functions into:

Outputs   = OT
Inquiries   = QT
Inputs   = IT
Files   = FT
Interfaces = EI

Activity 3: From the appropriate function type matrix (examples below: Tables 6.6–6.9), decide the functions' levels of complexity, i.e. whether they are simple, average or complex.

Enter the value 1 in the appropriate column of the detail sheet.

Sum the values in the columns.

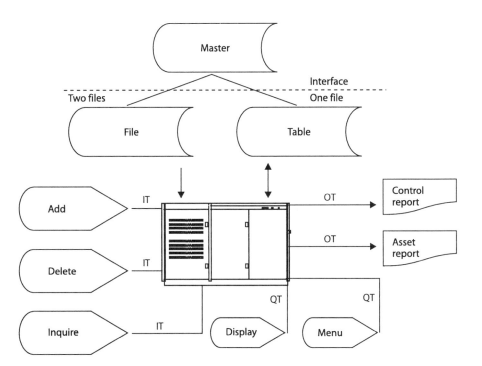

Fig. 6.9 An example of an on-line system illustrating inputs/outputs – function types.

Table 6.6 Function type matrix: form outputs

Files referenced	Data items referenced		
	1–5	6–19	>19
0–1	S (4)	S (4)	A (5)
2–3	S (4)	A (5)	C (7)
>3	A (5)	C (7)	C (7)

Table 6.7 Function type matrix: form inputs

Files referenced	Data items referenced		
	1–4	5–16	>16
0–1	S (3)	S (3)	A (4)
2	S (3)	A (4)	C (6)
>2	A (4)	C (6)	C (6)

Table 6.8 Function type matrix: form files

Logical records formats	Data items referenced		
	1–19	20–60	>60
1	S (7)	S (7)	A (10)
2–6	S (7)	A (10)	C (15)
>6	A (10)	C (10)	C (15)

Table 6.9 Function type matrix: form interfaces

Logical records formats	Data items referenced		
	1–19	20–60	>60
1	S (5)	S (5)	A (7)
2–6	S (5)	A (7)	C (10)
>6	A (7)	C (10)	C (10)

Note: for the function type 'inquiry', select the more complex of input or output.

Activity 4: Complete the appropriate column in the details sheets (Tables 6.10–6.14) using values from Tables 6.6–6.9.

Activity 5: Transfer the Total values on the detail sheets to a summary sheet (Table 6.15).

Calculate the unadjusted function points by multiplying the factor by the number of inputs, etc.

By summing the function points, we derive a value known as the unadjusted function points.

Activity 6: The final function point count (FFPC) is determined by the following formulae:

$$FFPC = PCA \times \text{Unadjusted function points}$$

Table 6.10 Detail sheet: outputs

Function type: Outputs

Application: Asset management

Description	Simple	Average	Complex
Asset reports:			
Detail report (2 files and 10 data items)		1	
Summary report (1 file and 2 data items)	1		
Control reports:			
Detail report (3 files and 6 data items)		1	
Summary report (2 files & 5 data items)	1		
Totals	2	2	

Table 6.11 Detail sheet: inquiries

Function type: Inquiries

Application: Asset management

Description	Simple	Average	Complex
Master menu (0 files and 1 data item)	1		
Item description display (1 file and 1 data item)	1		
Item quantity display (2 files and 4 data items)	1		
Deletion of part	1		
Totals	4		

Table 6.12 Detail sheet: inputs

Function type: Inputs

Application: Asset management

Description	Simple	Average	Complex
Add (1 file and 2 data items)	1		
Delete (2 files and 4 data items)	1		
Report request (1 file and 2 data items)	1		
Totals	3		

PCA = Processing complexity adjustment = $(0.01 \times \text{TDI}) + 0.65$

i.e. for our example:

PCA = $(0.01 \times 37) + 0.65 = 1.02$

Therefore

FFPC = $1.02 \times 70 = 71.4$

The total degree of influence is derived from the 14 complexity factors and can only increase or decrease the function point count by a maximum of 35%. The

Table 6.13 Detail sheet: files

Function type: Files			
Application: Asset management			
Description	Simple	Average	Complex
Equipment (1 relationship and 2 data items)	1		
Selected equipment file (2 logical files):			
Description (1 relationship and 5 data items)	1		
Location (1 relationship and 6 data items)	1		
Totals	3		

Table 6.14 Detail sheet: interfaces

Function type: Interfaces			
Application: Asset management			
Description	Simple	Average	Complex
Equipment master to selected items (2 files):			
Description (1 relationship and 5 data items)	1		
Location (1 relationship and 6 data items)	1		
Totals	2		

minimum possible value of TDI is zero. A rating for each of the 14 complexity factors would give a PCA of 0.65. The adjusted function point count would then be 35% smaller than the unadjusted function point count.

The maximum possible value of TDI is 70, i.e. 5 × 14, which would give a PCA of 1.35. The unadjusted function point count would then be 35% lower than the unadjusted function point count.

The method is not easy to apply, as the analyses needed to derive logical transactions need experienced staff, although consultants can help to train internal staff. There is also a need for subjectivity in certain cases. The application illustrated is a business application, and this is its most common use. Because of the complexity of scientific or technical application, the method may not be appropriate.

The weaknesses of the Albrecht method can be overcome, according to Charles R. Symons, by adjustments to the counting method. This method is based upon rules that have evolved and are continuing to evolve. *Computing Reviews* comments on a book *Applied Software Measurement – Assuring Productivity and Quality* (Caper Jones, 1991) as a milestone in the maturity of function point analysis and the exposure of measurement strategies. The results and profiles in the book are based on real experiences across a wide range of companies. Ed Yourdon writes that this is a bible on software metrics. In *Case Trends*, Robert K. Wysecki says that it is required reading for every student and practitioner of software measurement. All in all, it is a complete guide to the latest methods for accurately measuring quality. The book discusses all the major variations in functional metrics, including De Marco 'Bang'

Table 6.15 Summary sheet

Application date:					
Function type	Number	Complexity	Factor	Calculation	
Outputs	2	Simple	4	8	
	2	Average	5	10	
		Complex	7		
	Calculation total:				18
Function type	Number	Complexity	Factor	Calculation	
Inquiries	4	Simple	3	12	
		Average			
		Complex			
	Calculation total:				12
Function type	Number	Complexity	Factor	Calculation	
Inputs	3	Simple	3	9	
		Average	4		
		Complex	6		
	Calculation total:				9
Function type	Number	Complexity	Factor	Calculation	
Files	3	Simple	7	21	
		Average	10		
		Complex	13		
	Calculation total:				21
Function type	Number	Complexity	Factor	Calculation	
Interfaces	2	Simple	5	10	
		Average	7		
		Complex	10		
	Calculation total:				10
Total unadjusted function points:					70

Metrics, Feature Points, the British Mark II Function Point Method and much more. There is also an example of a fully measured project that can be used as a model for the serious estimator.

6.8.14 Updating the Function Point Base

If a function method is used in an organization then the base counts must be kept current, because they are the basis for all subsequent productivity measurements. To establish a base, existing systems can be counted. For example, assume that our asset management system, which was implemented four years ago, has new versions introduced biannually. At these new releases new functions are added and sometimes deleted. By using the base count developers can measure:

- Productivity or delivery rate for the initial system. This is the number of function points delivered divided by the number of work months. By establishing a goal for a certain rate, managers can perform comparative analyses among different systems.

● The change rate for the enhancement after implementation. This measures the work effort in days or hours. The same unit of time must be used when using the change rate for consistency in analysis.

● The support rate required for maintaining the system. This is used to determine the amount of work expended by maintenance staff.

For example: assume that the base count of our asset management system for development was 2400 function points, which represented 128 work months (WM), i.e. a delivery rate of 18.75 function points per WM. The following example illustrates the biannual productivity rate.

For the first biannual update, 20 function points were added, 12 deleted and 15 changed, for a total of 47 and a new base of 2400 + (20 added – 12 deleted) = 2408 FPs. This figure also represents the support rate.

Work effort was 4 WMs. Therefore the change rate is 47/4 = 11.75 FP/WM.

At the second update 24 FPs were added and 75 FPs were changed and the work effort expended was 4.5 WMs. In this case the change rate is 24/4.5 = 5.33 FP/WM. The FP base is now 2408 + 24 = 2432 FPs.

To determine the productivity gain it is necessary to determine the difference between the current rates of delivery and the established baseline rate. Of course, it is also just as important to understand why rates are changing or why there are different rates between projects. This could become important when choosing CASE tools, i.e. has their introduction made projects more productive?

For development, analysts should make the first estimate during project planning and change it iteratively until the count is complete at the design stage. To have a figure to start with at the planning stage, use an estimated function point size and divide it by the current delivery rate, i.e. assuming that the estimate is 2400 FPs and the current delivery rate is 24, then the work months of effort required to develop the system is 100.

Enhancements again use the function point method, but of course the effort will be a smaller number. For example, using our asset management system of 5.33 FP/WMs and assuming that the function point count for the changes required is 130, the amount of effort required is 24 (rounded) work months of effort.

To estimate staffing requirements for support, first take the total function points required, e.g. 12 480 and then divide this by the total FPs, e.g. 1000, per work month for a required total of 12.5 work months of support.

6.9 Joint Application Design (JAD) – Joint Application Requirements (JAR)

The traditional approach to designing a new product or system, or defining a required modification to a previously installed system, or in determining how long a project would take, was for a member of the project team to start with a series of memos and meetings with various user groups to gain a flavour of their needs and requirements. Following this generally lengthy process, either a draft of the external design or the business specifications, with estimates, were prepared and sent to the users for review. These specifications reflected what the analyst interpreted the users' needs to be. Requested changes were returned to the project team, more memos and meetings passed, and a second draft presented. This iterative process continued until specifications were signed off.

The joint application design (JAD) or joint application requirements (JAR) approach, does not require 'interpretation' of requirements because the users are directly involved in the development of the requirements and specifications. By using it, users are provided with a way to involve themselves in the project, thus increasing the quality of project deliverables and decreasing the time required to obtain the deliverables. It is an interactive design methodology providing a forum in which users and operations and systems staff meet to define the requirements for new or enhanced systems.

The approach encourages corporate consensus with all participants bringing their own experiences and vision to the table. Through its use, a mechanism is provided for managing the politics of a project and increasing the commitment of all parties. It is, further, an opportunity to get the business requirements and systems specifications right the first time. In so doing, the organization's information needs are served better and more quickly.

The key word is consensus. A session is a meeting of peers: no matter what an individual's level in the organization may be, in the JAD/JAR they are participants, and each has an equal say. A JAD session led by an external consultant is useful to detect intimidation, and the consultant, as an impartial facilitator, can move quickly to diffuse it.

6.9.1 JAD Communication

A critical success factor in a JAD depends on the facilitator's and participants' abilities to communicate effectively. To be successful it is important to become a first-class presenter. It is necessary to be able to present ideas in as short a time as possible. Milo O. Frank, one of America's foremost business communication consultants, has discovered that the message participants send is at the heart of every effective participant. Thus, before individuals get together in a session, it may be worthwhile to explain how the session will be conducted, e.g. a set number of minutes per idea or questions with clarification. This will help participants to focus on their points and help them get them across. Readers should practice this idea by selecting a subject and explaining it in 30 seconds. It will be found that a lot of ground can be covered.

All participants, including the facilitator, should realize that words account for a small part of the total message they convey to each other. The rest comes from style, use of voice and body language and other forms of non-verbal communication. The facilitator and participants must be able to summarize a worthwhile message and be ready to communicate. They should also realize that it is essential to relate the message to something of interest, otherwise the audience's attention will wander. In order to obtain acceptance, it is important also to get immediate feedback to determine whether the audience grasps and accepts the ideas or requirements presented. If they do not grasp the concepts, a poor job is being done in communicating. In addition, in any communication the tone of voice must be without emotion, as argumentation interferes with the message. Any comments should be clear and concise. Keep persuasion to the end. Only when confident that the audience understands should the focus be on getting them to accept the point of view.

In most JAD sessions there will not be any need to change agreed-upon points. However, there may be times when, from experience, an individual may know that an incorrect decision has been made or is being made. In such a case, it may be preferable to keep the point to the end before trying to make a persuasive case to the participants. When the time is opportune, be specific and confident, explain the reason for the disagreement, and focus on getting the audience to accept a new point of view.

In communication, facilitators are finding that there is more to JAD than flip charts, coffee, tea and muffins. We now have electronic meeting systems (EMS). Under this scenario, every participant in the session has a workstation. Thus, they can participate both verbally and electronically. The electronic method equalizes participation – the loudest voice is quietened and the shy are encouraged. This creates a level playing field. In addition, much of the dialogue can be anonymous. It is also not necessary to attend the session full-time. Tasks can be sent to all participants' home workstations and they can work at their own speed on the topics in which they have a personal stake. This may be called groupwork or collaborative computing. The advantage of this approach is that it helps to solve the inefficient meeting problem. One of the popular computerized tools is electronic brainstorming, in which electronic files replace the sheets of paper that are circulated among meeting participants as they generate and comment on anonymous ideas that were previously written on these 'sheets of paper'. The downside given by some detractors is that this method hurts the 'group dynamics' of a meeting, i.e. the special atmosphere that one sees whenever people are together. It will be the facilitator's choice: some will keep to markers and flip charts; some will use EMS exclusively; and others will use a combination.

6.10 Cost Estimating

Input from the estimates forms the basis of the estimated financial implications. The figures are usually put together with limited knowledge and derived from a mix of intuition, experience and a consensus of professionals. It must be realized, however, that at the beginning of a project the estimates are, through necessity, very soft. If they are updated regularly throughout the project duration, they can become firmer as practical experience is gained.

6.10.1 Cost Elements

Two types of expenditure are of concern in examining the financial impact of a project, namely one-time expenditures, and on-going operating and maintenance expenditures. Values should be derived and assigned to each line object.

Development and one-time capital expenditures include the following:

- System development costs are mainly those expenditures incurred for work terms, consulting and system development services.
- Equipment and software acquisition cover the purchase prices of hardware and software.

On-going operating and maintenance (O&M) expenditures include:

- Data communications – charges incurred for the use of data communications facilities and services.
- Support centre operations – expenses incurred in operating the centre and access to an external database.
- System maintenance, i.e. the costs for internal and external staff resources to perform system maintenance activities.
- System support, i.e. the costs for internal and external staff resources to perform system support activities, such as the development and/or delivery of training courses.
- Management and administration – expenses incurred in connection with management and administrative activities, for example, consulting expenses to assist in implementing office automation.
- Equipment maintenance and software upgrade costs.

These costs can be entered into a computerized project plan along with the hourly costs, and the total estimated cost of a project derived.

6.11 Project Risk

The measurement of *risk* can start at any time – the sooner the better, even before the project has been formally started. One reason this is so is that the project manager can decide whether the project is wanted.

6.11.1 Risk Management Plan

Risk assessment and management (Fig. 6.10) enable early mitigation of the impact of threats to the success of a project. The purpose of the risk management plan is to identify, assess and manage possible risks to the success of the project in meeting its cost, time scope and quality targets. The risk management plan and its implementation will primarily be the responsibility of the project director, with support from the project administration and support team and the business implementation team.

6.11.2 Risk Assessment

Project development is vulnerable to such risks as schedule or budget overruns, systems that do not live up to user expectations, and wasteful project spending. Even if managers apply all their experience and knowledge in overcoming particular

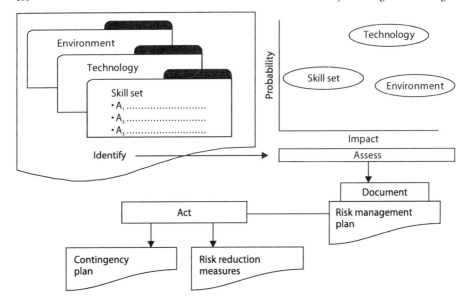

Fig. 6.10 The risk management process.

problems, however, the project may still fail because of pitfalls inherent in the systems effort itself.

At least three factors contribute to project risk:

● Project size
● Users' and designers' level of familiarity with the technology employed
● System structure

These factors can be measured to determine the degree of risk inherent in a planned project. We examine the factors and create a risk profile.

Understanding the project risks will help the manager's credibility and should prevent unpleasant surprises later in the project. In addition, identifying and discussing the risks will enable all parties to become better-informed decision makers.

You should not be reluctant to discuss the issue of risk. It is assumed that the client would prefer to be aware of the risks and understand the potential impact on the project. Thus the project manager should address the issue rather than be considered negligent.

Any new venture involves risk. While the estimating and planning processes normally provide a contingency fund and float to cope with unexpected problems that arise, it pays to prevent problems in the first place. It also pays to concentrate the prevention effort in those areas where the risk is highest and the impact greatest.

Risk assessment and management begin by identifying the threats to project success. Each threat is then categorized based on the probability of the event occurring and its effect should the event occur. A broad spectrum of threats must be assessed from both internal and external sources. Many threats are outside the project manager's direct control, but all threats should be assigned to a risk owner responsible for monitoring and reporting changes etc. However, the majority of threats arise from uncertainty, which is due in most cases to lack of information. These can be reduced by better information, communication and controls.

A risk management plan should be prepared as early as possible by the project manager. The plan should be maintained as work proceeds and covers the following important areas:

- Types and identification of threat
- Probability of particular events occurring and impact if each does occur
- Contingency plans
- Risk reduction actions
- Roles and responsibilities in risk management

6.11.3 Key Points

- Risk management reduces the likelihood of threats and may constrain their potential impact.
- Start the process as early as possible and reassess risks throughout the project.
- Prevention is better than cure.
- Define threats and counter measures in a risk management plan.
- Develop contingency plans to meet unavoidable threats.
- Concentrate on threats where the risk is highest and the impact greatest.

A risk assessment form (Fig. 6.11), could be used as the basis of the project manager's ongoing risk management efforts.

6.11.4 Risk Checklist

For a project the following primary risk factors should be evaluated and a questionnaire designed to gather and quantify the data about these factors:

In carrying out a risk assessment on a project, it is useful to refer to the work breakdown structure to identify the elements potentially under threat. These threats can be:

- Internal to the project
  - Incomplete definition of scope, e.g. size; this should be measured in worker time, calendar time, cost, number of departments affected and geography.
  - Poor (or lack of) end-to-end planning
  - Lack of appropriate resources or skills
  - Structure: this is measured in terms of the precision used to define system objectives and output, the number and complexity of necessary procedural changes, and the attitude and commitment of the users to the system.
  - Internal adjustment necessitated by the influence of external issues/changes

Project:		Project manager:		Category:				
Potential threat	Impact (note 1)	Probability (note 2)	Impact × probability	For 'high risks' (note 3)				
				Actions to prevent	By whom/ when	Contingency plan	By whom/ when	

Note 1   Impact: rank 1–5, where 1 = low effect on objectives, 5 = high effect
Note 2   Probability: rank 1–5, where 1 = low probability, 5 = high probability
Note 3   Score (impact × probability): 1–4 = low risk (ignore); 5–15 = medium risk (be aware and monitor); 16–25 = high risk (identify actions and contingency plans)

Fig. 6.11 Risk assessment form.

- External to the project
  - Legislation
  - Competitor action
  - Unpreparedness or uncooperativeness of partner organizations (e.g. government agencies, suppliers)
  - Corporate policy (in this case, parent corporation or shareholder policy)
  - Changes in environment:
    political
    economic
    social
- Technological
  This should be measured in terms of the project team's familiarity with the hardware, software applications, and standards and procedures, taking into account:
  - General risks
  - Leading edge technology (will it work?)
  - Tight time-scale
  - High dependence upon external suppliers or resources
  - Change in culture and behaviours required
  - Personality clashes (within or outside the project team)
  - Loss of key personnel
  - Accommodation
  - User or customer capacity to absorb change anticipated
  - Union or staff resistance
  - Lack of co-location of the project team

6.11.5 Risk Reduction

Some general risk reduction measures include:

- Define the project fully and carefully from the start. Address this through careful planning, discussions with the client and relevant agencies, and specific project management initiatives.
- Plan the project end-to-end, noting and gaining agreement to the essential decision points and dates. Use the specified project milestones as a guide, and follow the implementation plan, with periodic reviews by important team members and schedulers to ensure that the project is on track.
- Bring decision points as far forward (early) as possible. Make an effort to bring forward decision points by planning for the implementation of the project even prior to the finalization of any agreement.
- Have an effective project director, project team managers and team. Have specific plans to place experienced staff from inside and an outside consulting firm with project management expertise in key leadership positions on the project.
- Ensure that all initiatives affecting partner organizations are visible while the project is under way. Keep in close contact with the organizations through liaison groups and also through the presence of users on the project's steering committee, in order to keep a close eye on any other initiatives affecting implementation of the project.
- Ensure that the project director and project team managers make time to stand back from the project regularly (e.g. at the end of each month) to review progress, the issues and the focus of effort. Build procedures into the project management plan calling for periodic project progress reviews, with appropriate corrective action to be taken as needed if project runs into obstacles.
- Strong coordination with partner organizations. Achieve this through an external liaison team, which will assign specific staff solely to the management of relationships.

6.11.6 Risk Management Experience

Risk management is crucial in controlling overruns of both project cost and project time frame. If an organization is using external resources, it should use as one of its selection criteria the risk management experience of the vendor. Vendors and/or project managers should have extensive experience in managing risk in multi-organizational technology implementation projects, and would therefore bring this experience to bear in implementing a project.

The vendor/project manager should recognize that effective risk management is key to the successful, cost-effective and timely implementation of the project, particularly if the time frame between initiating and implementation is short, and if there is a reliance on the cooperation of government agencies and suppliers in technical, operational and commercial aspects of the system.

6.12 Summary

In outlining the initiation of a project, we have been exposed to the start-up process for a project, with an emphasis on ensuring that the three nodes of the project circle are complete. To estimate resources and the size of the project, some methods of metrics have been explained, with a detailed explanation of function point analysis. The chapter is completed with an outline of the merits of using a joint application design approach to obtain consensus on the different components for delivering products.

Initiation is a very important part of any project, as it describes the responsibility, scope and estimated costs of the project. To reiterate: not doing this component correctly is one of the hardest faults from which to recover.

We have outlined risk management, which many managers simply ignore as something inherent in any project. Although this may be true, the actual exercise will make you cognizant of the risks and, if you are the project manager, by accepting the project you are accepting the risks.

When a project has been accepted, the next step is to plan for its completion. Thus the next chapter will outline the process for planning development of an approved project.

7. Tools of Project Management

7.1 Introduction

Planning is too ubiquitous to require justification, but what is project planning? It can be considered as the planning of a project by breaking the objective down into manageable events and tasks; scheduling them; and assigning resources to complete the events (deliverables). Subsequently the components of the project need to be managed and the results evaluated.

Planning consists of strategic and tactical aspects. Strategic planning defines the objective, evaluation of macro issues and deciding where you want to be in a given period. Tactical planning takes the strategic plan and develops a detailed road map of how the results will be achieved. The details focused on are: 'Who does what?'; 'How long will it take?'; 'In what sequence will the activities be undertaken?'; and 'What will the cost be?'. This ensures that all individuals having an interest in the outcome of a project are provided with a common direction and a frame of reference within which they are empowered to make decisions.

We have explained in previous chapters some of the problems associated with managing projects; the philosophy behind a project management methodology; an organizational entity for project development; the linking of a project management methodology and a systems development life cycle; project roles and responsibilities; quality management; risk management; and some techniques for estimating how long a deliverable will take to be finished. We have seen how people and their commitment are essential in producing quality deliverables. Our attention now turns to the building blocks on which good project management is predicated and how the project manager can plan the environment, namely:

- Project and stage planning activities
- Description of a project or stage plan
- Skeleton plan

The structure of the book is now becoming more precise (rigid), to the extent that there are strict rules for the planning and control of projects which give them a frame of reference. Examples of the use of standard forms are given. Without explaining these, and why they are in some cases essential, there would be a lack of focus. Using the tools outlined, or some variation of them, enables a project manager and the team to complete stages in a logical and sequential manner, keep management informed and deliver an acceptable product. As pointed out earlier, consider automating the forms and documentation processes, and update an automated project directory using groupware and document management tools.

Experienced project managers may not need to read this chapter, especially if they have a standard methodology in place and it meets their need. However, it can be used as a checklist and will help readers to appreciate the importance of planning. Further, it provides an exposure to managing projects utilizing the Web.

7.2 Project and Stage Planning Activities

This chapter outlines the project and stage planning activities, i.e. information that is necessary for the acceptance of a personal commitment. Project and stage planning both deal with the beginning – not necessarily the beginning of a project, but rather the beginning of a personal commitment. 'The beginning is the most important part of the work' – Plato.

The purpose of the plan is to provide a formal vehicle for the project manager to accept or reject responsibility for the project by either making a commitment or rejecting the project. This latter decision is difficult when one has responsibilities. When accepted it ensures that the project manager, acceptor, responsible manager and resource manager – in fact, all signatories – by signing have signified their agreement on the scope and objectives of the project. The mere signing will establish the relationship between people, their commitments for deliverables and the activities anticipated that lead to a common goal, i.e. the end product. After acceptance, it will be possible to establish the start of the on-going planning cycle upon which control of the project is based. Finally, it will maximize the likelihood that management will accept the project as valid and assign the resources required. Thus invalid rejected projects are known before they get too far.

The basic project plan is made up mostly by completing a set of standard forms that are brought together under the umbrella of the skeleton plan. This enables the project manager to construct a simple plan that answers all of the questions posed below. These must be asked at the start of a project or stage in order for the manager to realize what is being committed to when project responsibility is accepted.

- Who will be affected by the plan? Determine this by carefully making a list of all the functional units and the individuals whose jobs may change, whose reporting relationships may change and whose empires may expand or contract, and identify those who can exercise influence. This analysis is very important in subsequently communicating project status and lobbying for support and the acceptance of ideas. Nurturing these people can be invaluable when the project starts to meander off-course.

- What format should the plan follow? Using the skeleton plan illustrated in this chapter will, if followed, ensure that all areas have been covered and all questions answered.

- How will it be known when the project is finished? Filling in a project or stage completion form and distributing it will visibly declare to recipients the acceptance of responsibility by the acceptor for the deliverable completed. It will also provide a precise definition of the product as the visible and recognizable completion goal. You might think that simply looking at the deliverable and seeing (and perhaps touching) it makes it visible. It is true that a deliverable either exists or it doesn't, but this is too simplistic an approach because it lends itself to 'smoke and mirrors' deception if a presentation is given by a polished presenter. All deliverables should be signed off as meeting specifications. If the deliverable is accepted with less, then it should be so noted. Different perceptions come into play when an individual is asked to approve something. The author was involved in a sign-off of a systems review. I looked at content, i.e. were the recommendations better than the existing situation? The acceptor looked at words such as 'discrepancies' and decided that there were no discrepancies, just issues to be resolved, and therefore would not sign-off until the word had been changed. If an individual is responsible for accepting the deliverable and has signed the form, then the signer is more likely to ensure that the deliverable is what is specified and that appropriate testing etc. has been done.

- What is going to help determine what is required to complete the plan? A deliverable acceptance matrix will help in identifying the deliverables required from the project or stage and to identify both the acceptor and deliverer. The matrix also describes the end product or a precise definition of the acceptor's and other principal characters' responsibilities to the product, and helps make the remainder of the plan much easier to complete.

- How should the project team be organized and who will help when problems occur? Some of the principles in this book will help in deciding how best to organize. There is no one best way. However, completing the project organization form will ensure that you formally address the issue and that:
  - all the principal characters are specified and made visible;
  - descriptions of their responsibilities are outlined;
  - the project's responsibility lines, together with the avenues for sharing project responsibility, are specified

- What activities are likely to be required? These can be described on a project activity (task) planning schedule (automated or manual). This is a working document used to document and estimate all the likely activities required to produce all deliverables. It needs to be maintained on an ongoing basis.

- What resources are likely to be required for each activity? An activity resource estimates form, when completed, produces a working document of estimates for all resources for each activity required to produce all deliverables.

- How are resources applied to the activities to get an estimated schedule? Estimating and fitting resources against the activities on the work plan and resource schedule will enable a schedule to be derived.

- How will sufficient project control and adequate communication be ensured throughout the project? To control a project it is necessary to have a project control plan form. This identifies the standard communication channels, ensuring that all avenues for sharing responsibility remain open, and identifies all other tools to ensure the project manager's control of the project. To reiterate: listing those affected by the plan is an important step.

- How is it ensured that the project players agree with and are committed to the plan and that resources get committed to the project? This is accomplished by completing and having approved a plan acceptance. Through this action the project manager will:

> *make visible to management the commitments made to provide the resources estimated as necessary for project success. It signifies that all signatories have committed to providing the resources. This helps to protect the project manager from invisible passive acceptance of the plan, which would make it extremely difficult to get the project staffed properly and in a timely fashion.*

In answering the above questions, the project manager establishes a clear relationship between individuals and deliverables and is therefore prepared for whatever may happen. The manager now has the mechanisms and, more importantly, the confidence to keep on top of all the deliverables and activities.

A project organization chart (Fig. 7.1), or an equivalent chart, is an integral component of project management. It answers the question 'How should the project team be organized and who will help when the project is in trouble?'. It also ensures that the key nodes of the project model are known and visible and that the avenues for

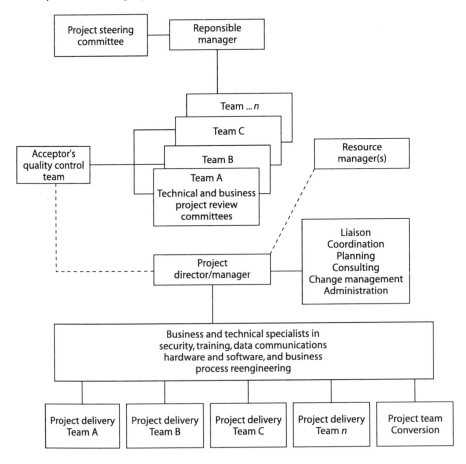

Fig. 7.1 Project organization chart.

sharing responsibility upwards (responsible manager), downwards (delivery team), and sideways (acceptor) are identified. It also ensures that there is an unbroken responsibility line to the top of the organization. This form should be completed by the project manager after discussions with the resource managers, the responsible manager and the acceptor to identify the individuals required, and it should be included in the plan.

7.2.1 Project and Stage Planning (Checklist)

The same approach to planning should be used for the planning of the project as a whole or of any given stage of development. Differences will occur in the level of detail (number of deliverables, activities, resource specifications etc.) needed for each. In the project plan, the level of detail need only go down to the stages or major deliverables to be produced; resources and time frames may be summarized. In the stage plan, sub-deliverables and more detailed descriptions of activities and resource requirements will be necessary. The approach, however, remains the same for both. It should be noted that this section assumes that the project manager will prepare the plan. However, in the case of a stage plan this responsibility may be delegated to the appropriate stage coordinator. Most computer project planning software enables lower levels of detail to be hidden. Therefore a manager may only be interested in the highest milestone level, whereas a supervisor would undoubtedly want to know about the task level.

The purpose of the plan is to determine the best way to complete a project on time and within budget. To do this it is necessary at the start of planning to follow some basic steps, namely:

1 Define the project objective.
2 Segment the work into phases.
3 Divide the phases into tasks (activities).
4 Assign resources to each task.
5 Estimate how much time each task requires.
6 Arrange the tasks in a logical sequence, e.g. you cannot develop until you have designed.
7 Schedule the tasks.
8 Communicate and review the plan with the affected parties.
9 Ensure that an acceptor has been assigned. If not, get one from the responsible manager.
10 Obtain agreement from the acceptor on product completion definition by referencing the project or stage completion form.
11 Complete the deliverable acceptance matrix in conjunction with the acceptor.
12 Solicit commitment from team members for producing the deliverables.
13 Solicit commitments for acceptance of deliverables
14 Identify with the manager, acceptor or deliverable acceptors the standard (format and level of detail) to which the deliverable will be produced.
15 Complete the project organization form and identify the delivery team structure.

16 Determine and document individual and organizational responsibilities.

17 Identify and review with the acceptor the activities that it is anticipated will be required to complete the job, and their relationship with one another. Do not yet estimate duration.

18 Determine the resources required for each activity identified in Step 17 using the activity resource estimates form.

19 Schedule the resource allocation (apply resources of Step 18 to the activities in Step 17 over the time frame) on the work plan and resource schedule.

20 Re-examine and revise, if necessary, Steps 17, 18 and 19.

21 Schedule activities on the activity planning schedule.

22 Identify all communication channels (avenues for sharing responsibility) that must be kept open during the project, and the tools for doing so, on the project control plan form.

23 Complete the plan acceptance form, filling in all names, and submit for approval.

24 Prepare a first draft of the plan, bringing together all the tools according to the format of the skeleton plan. Do not attempt to resolve all the questions or fill in all the blanks on this draft.

25 Send the first draft of the plan to the acceptor, responsible manager, resource manager and project review committee.

26 Modify the draft plan by making agreed upon changes.

27 Obtain acceptance of the plan from the acceptor, responsible manager, project review committee members and all resource managers providing resources to the project.

28 Prepare the project committee members' briefing books and distribute them to project review committee members.

29 Brief the project review committee on the project management methodology and on roles and responsibilities.

7.2.2 Skeleton Plan

This is a necessary systems project management methodology document for both the overall project and each stage. The purpose of the skeleton plan is to answer the question 'What format should my plan follow?'. The plan should define:

- a specific end product
- the resources and support required to deliver the product
- the responsibilities of everyone involved in the project, and the conditions and mechanisms for sharing responsibility
- a schedule (assume start date and amend if necessary) of anticipated project activities, and resource estimates for each, to support the stated resource requirements
- the methods for controlling the delivery of the end product

The plan documents the project manager's personal commitment. Its preparation, therefore, must be the responsibility of the project manager, who will usually prepare a draft plan. Normally, the help of the acceptor and the responsible manager and team members, if they are known at this stage, will be enlisted to complete this. When completed, the responsible manager approves the draft plan. When the draft is approved, preparation of the final document is commenced and coordinated by the project manager with the help of the project team members. The responsible manager eventually accepts the final plan document. Subsequently it must be approved by the acceptor; by all individuals scheduled to make a significant contribution of resources to the project on either the delivery or the acceptance teams; and by the members of the project review committee.

In all cases, approval is required from the resource managers and the direct supervisor, in the normal line organization, of each individual expected to contribute any significant amount of time to the project.

The plan as a minimum should consist of the following eight sections.

Section 1.0: Introduction and Background

The events that led to the beginning of the project plan should be described. This section may contain an overview of the problem to be solved and/or refer to a document that specifies *what* has to be done. Significant points from a request for proposal, proposal contract and/or deliverables from other projects or stages should also be considered for inclusion.

Section 2.0: Plan for Project Completion

The end product (deliverable) of the project or stage should be defined precisely, as well as the particular deliverables making up the end product. It should contain the following sub-sections.

Sub-Section 2.1: End Product

This should identify the signed project completion form as being the authority for *the* end product. As such, it should display the unsigned form, showing who must sign it (acceptor); it should also identify who is going to deliver it (project manager). This document is described in this book. This sub-section answers the question 'How will it be known when the project is finished?'.

Sub-Section 2.2: Deliverables

Deliverables should be outlined that will support the end product in terms of what it is, who will accept it, who will deliver it, whether a deliverable acceptance form will have to be signed and who will recommend acceptance. This should be documented on the deliverable acceptance matrix form described in this book. Also displayed should be a sample of the deliverable acceptance forms.

This sub-section answers the question 'Who is going to help determine what is required to complete the project?'.

Sub-Section 2.3: Standards

Standards provide a more detailed description of the documentation and other standards to which the deliverables will be produced. This will help both the deliverer and acceptor of each deliverable to recognize when the job has been completed.

Section 3.0: Project Organization and Responsibilities

A project organization chart should be derived. There should also be an explanation of the roles and responsibilities of each person indicated on the chart. Therefore the avenues for sharing responsibility with the responsible manager, the acceptor and the project team will be well defined. This will form the basis for proper project control.

When completed, this section answers the question 'How should the project team be organized and who will help when the project gets into trouble?'.

Section 4.0: Activity Schedule

This section describes the current tasks that it is anticipated will be required for the delivery of the project and for the deliverables. It also identifies the estimated start and end dates, as well as the individual to whom the assignment has been assigned. This may be documented on the automated (PERT–CPM) activity planning schedule or on a manual form (This will be explained later in the chapter). This section answers the question 'What activities will likely be required?'.

Section 5.0: Work Plan and Resource Schedule

Resource estimates are identified and scheduled for the tasks shown in Section 4.0. Again some form of PERT–CPM may be used. It is divided into the following sub-sections.

Sub-Section 5.1: Activity Resource Estimates

This sub-section contains information identifying each task identified in the activity schedule (Section 4.0). These forms are work sheets and may be appended or omitted.

When completed, this section answers the question 'What resources are likely to be required to complete each activity?'.

Sub-Section 5.2: Work Plan and Resource Schedule

This sub-section applies the resource requirements by task from Section 5.1 of the plan to all individuals involved in that activity on both the delivery and acceptance sides of the organization, and distributes them by month, providing a monthly resource schedule per individual.

A work plan answers the question 'How can the resources be applied to the endeavour to get an estimated schedule?'. These forms are work sheets and may be appended or omitted.

Section 6.0: Summary of Time and Cost

Sections 4.0 and 5.0 of the plan should be summarized for all resources required by and affected by the project. This includes the time of managers, the costs of personnel to be trained (include lost productivity time) and the time needed for testing. It should contain the following sub-sections.

Sub-Section 6.1: Summary of Time

(From Section 4.0 of the plan.) No specific form is used, as it is determined by the input/output requirements of the tool being used or the organization's time utilization system.

Sub-Section 6.2: Summary of Costs

(From Section 5.0 of the plan.) No specific form is used; it is a function of the tool being used or what is required by the cost accounting unit.

Section 7.0: Project Control

This section answers the question 'How will sufficient project control and adequate communication be ensured throughout the project?'. Controlling is considered by many to be the most basic role of management. A project manager who can control the management of a project will end up with the result being a 'thoroughbred' and not a 'camel'. Control is a monitoring tool and does not imply autocratic dispensation of authority.

The methods and tools that the project manager will use to control the project should be described. As such, this section must describe each 'avenue for sharing responsibility' or communication channel that must be kept open by the project manager to maintain his or her own, as well as others', personal commitment to completion. As a minimum, this must include the following avenues:

project manager ↔ responsible manager
project manager ↔ acceptor
project manager ↔ project team member

In addition, the following may be included:

project manager ↔ resources manager
project manager ↔ himself (storage of relevant information)
project manager ↔ PRC member

The lines of communication are illustrated in Fig. 7.2 and documented on the project control plan.

Section 8.0: Plan Acceptance

Until signatures from all management with a personal stake are obtained, the project manager's commitment is conditional. The necessary signatures and commitments are documented as described in this book. This approval is essential. The visibility is important for the project manager so that he or she may share the responsibility for the seemingly unproductive efforts of nursing the project plan through to acceptance. Each of the managers supplying resources to the project must sign and date this form. The project manager's commitment, then, cannot really begin until all

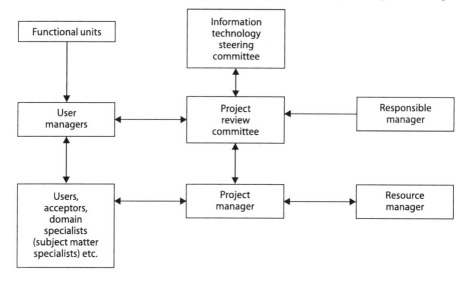

Fig. 7.2 Project control communication channels.

resource managers and the project's responsible manager, have all given their approval.

This section answers the question 'How can it be ensured that the project players agree with and are committed to the plan and that the resources get committed to the project?'.

A plan should be produced for the project as a whole at the stage or major deliverable level (project plan), and for each stage at the deliverable and detailed level (stage plans). In both cases, the following approach should be taken:

- Make sure there is an acceptor. If the plan is completed without an acceptor, then this whole process must be reviewed again with the acceptor when he or she joins the team to ensure the proper commitment to the plan. The remainder of this text assumes that the acceptor is 'on board' and working with the project manager in drafting the particulars of the planning kit.
- Work with the acceptor to complete the deliverable acceptance matrix, making sure that *all* deliverables are accounted for.
- Select those documents or deliverables that should have a deliverable acceptance form and identify them in the acceptance sign-off required column.
- Prepare a deliverable acceptance form for those selected with the name of the individual who will be assigned as the respective deliverable acceptor. This must be used by the project acceptor to solicit (during the planning phase) the commitments for ultimate acceptance responsibility. Recognizing acceptance activities here may lead to adding more deliverables and tasks to the planning and estimating work sheets.
- Identify with the acceptor, where possible, the standard to which objective deliverables will be produced, and the individuals who will recommend acceptance.

This will have an impact upon the resource estimates. When this cannot be done, identify the individual who will determine later what standard will be used.

- Complete the project organization form, documenting the essential individuals estimated to be needed.
- Identify with the acceptor the activities that will be required to get the job done. Do not estimate the duration yet.
- With the acceptor, use the activity resource estimates form to match required resources to activities.
- Schedule the resource allocations on the resource schedule work plan. Re-examine and revise, if necessary.
- Schedule the activities on the activity planning schedule form.
- Identify all avenues for sharing responsibility during the project and the tools for keeping them open on the project control plan form.
- Complete the plan acceptance form, filling in all names, and submit it for approval.

The project manager should prepare a draft outline of the plan but not attempt to resolve all the questions or fill in all the blanks at this time. The draft should be used to facilitate a dialogue between the project manager, the acceptor, the responsible manager and the resource manager(s). This dialogue is integral to the successful completion of the plan. On completion of the draft, a copy should be sent to everyone involved in the project. After they have had time to review it, the project manager should meet them (individually or in a group) to update the draft and prepare the final plan.

To minimize the effort required to complete this docum-ent there are some basic 'don't's. *Don't*:

- make the first draft too detailed. The detail will come from interaction with others.
- prepare this document in isolation. It may be hard selling the ideas, so be prepared to make changes.
- go too far with the detailed work plan. Only plan in detail up to the point where you stop feeling comfortable with your predictions. Allow time in each phase to do the detailed planning for subsequent phases. Current information may then be used for planning.
- make the duration of activities too long. To achieve this, break them down into the smallest component possible. Long time frames become impossible to control.
- have activities where the completion cannot be identified by a clearly recognizable deliverable. It must be obvious when an activity is complete or control of the project status will be lost.
- have any stages without a formal acceptance at the end of it. Formal acceptance at the end of each stage will minimize the work involved in the final acceptance.
- get caught up in debates over resource commitments. If the problem cannot be solved with realistic changes to the project schedule, then the manager or the responsible manager is much more likely to be able to resolve this type of problem.

- expect to complete the plan in one draft. It will probably be necessary to go through several iterations, especially to the resource estimation and scheduling sections.

- forget that, as project manager, you are the one with the primary personal stake in the plan's acceptance and you will have to push for its acceptance.

As can be seen, completion and approval of the plan, therefore, may be difficult. It will take time. It will cause conflicts. It will definitely force serious consideration of responsibilities and resource commitments.

A plan acceptance form (Fig. 7.3) is an integral component of the systems project management methodology. It answers the question: 'How do I, the project manager, ensure that the project players agree with and are committed to my plan, and that resources get committed to the project?'. It also ensures that the answer to this question is made known. It is the project manager's responsibility to complete the form and ensure that everyone signs and dates it. All individuals named on the form should respond promptly upon receipt of the document.

The names and positions of all people required to sign should be entered by the project manager before circulation of the plan. Individuals' signatures on this document indicate that they have read the plan and agree to its approach and, furthermore, that they agree to commit to the responsibilities and provide the resources specified. If there are some items that they find irrelevant, or some facet to which they are unable to commit, then it should be highlighted under 'Comments'.

The responsible manager first approves this plan by signing this document. The project manager should then obtain the signature of the acceptor. This document, along with the project plan, should then be forwarded to all resource managers for their commitment to the project.

Project name:	Project number:	Project manager:	
Plan proposed by:	Signature:	Date:	
We, the undersigned, have reviewed the plan, accept the described activities and agree to commit to the responsibilities; and provide the necessary resources.			
Name	Position	Signature	Date
Observations – comments:			

Fig. 7.3 Plan acceptance form.

Project name:	Project number:	Project manager:	

Project deliverable: Yes _____   No: _____

Stage deliverable(s) as specified:

All the work for this project or stage has been completed to my satisfaction. I therefore recommend that the results be accepted:

Name	Position	Signature	Date

I accept full responsibility for this project or stage and recognize it as complete:

Name	Position	Signature	Date

Comments:

Fig. 7.4 Project or stage completion form.

Until all the required signatures are obtained, the project is in limbo. However, let common sense prevail, because to be realistic, it is unlikely that all signatures to the project will be obtained before it starts. However, the project manager's commitment should be conditional until the resource commitments are approved.

A project or stage completion form (Fig. 7.4) is an indispensable systems project management methodology document. The form answers the question: 'How will I know when the project or stage is completed?'. It provides a formal mechanism to make the completion of each project or sub-project or stage and acceptance of responsibility for the results by the acceptor visible.

It is the responsibility of the project manager to obtain the acceptor's signature on this document, as well as the signature of all those who will recommend acceptance. However, it is the acceptor's responsibility to sign the document once he or she is confident enough to accept responsibility for the project's results, and to inform the appropriate managers. Is this a rigid process? Yes, it is rigid, but it enforces a discipline that should be agreed to at the beginning of a project, i.e. a ground rule that sign-off will be an acceptance to payment and also a transfer of responsibility to the client. Some projects go on and on because there is no clear delineation of completion. Is it practical? Of course, but it is not easy to implement because there is a resistance to taking responsibility for a finished deliverable by line managers. Many excuses can be found not to sign off, but they are not reasons (for example, 'I don't have time to read the requirements document'). Of course, the result will be dependent on the attitude of the client and it will be up to the project manager whether it is necessary for any one deliverable. For example, it may only be necessary to minute, at a steering committee meeting, that the deliverable can be accepted.

This form should be contained in the stage completion report at the end of the stage, as well as in the project plan. In order for the project manager to obtain the acceptor's signature on this document, the two of them must work closely together from the time that the unsigned document is first displayed in the project plan through to the project's completion, as signified by the confident acceptance of responsibility for the project's results by the acceptor.

Throughout the project, the project manager should strive to ensure that the acceptor has all the information required to accept the end product when it is fully developed. This is a process of managing expectations. It can be described as a strategy of 'no surprises'. The objective is for the acceptor to get what has been expected.

7.3 Testing

There are many components to testing and appropriate references should be reviewed. In Chapter 3 we explained quality management and testing. Testing verifies that the deliverable meets specifications. It is a subset of quality management.

A full-scale test effort would include:

- A test strategy, i.e. what is to be tested (source code, integration, manuals, system), how and by whom.
- A plan and schedule.
- A process for correction of errors found or changes desired.
- Having determined a strategy and plan, it is the obligation of an independent test team to execute the plan and prepare a test report.
- Transition to production from test.

As the systems development life cycle (Fig. 7.5) is an outline of what is to be delivered, it follows that testing should test the deliverables in the cycle, i.e. requirements, design, development and production. These are each taken and expanded upon in the following sections.

7.3.1 Requirements

This function is part of a project initiation and is one of the most important aspects to be tested. The traditional approach to verification is with the aid of checklists of attributes, such as:

- Each requirement should be noted as being mandatory, secondary or tertiary.
- The client should have signed off that the requirements are sufficient.
- Each requirement should be testable in the developed system.

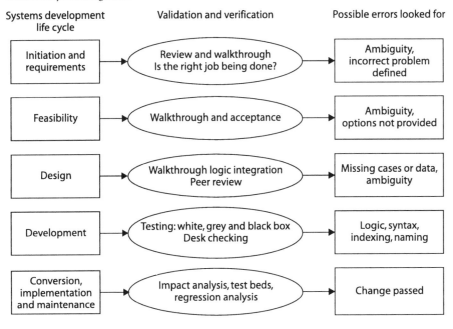

Fig. 7.5

7.3.2 Design

Elements of design can be evaluated by checklists similar to those used in requirements. One important aspect to be verified would be algorithms. Several analytic methods are available to analyze design properties, such as each logical path confirming that the control logic corresponds to the different classes of data and algorithms being verified by functional analysis.

7.3.3 Development

At the first level of testing is the program code, i.e. unit module testing. This is usually done by the programmer, although analysts will regularly verify that good programming practices etc. are followed. This is followed by sub-program testing, i.e. integration of modules, by development staff in conjunction with the test team. At this time, the system is tested against the requirements. On satisfactory completion of this step all modules are tested in an integrated mode with equipment and other systems, and interfaces and functionality are demonstrated. Finally, comprehensive testing of an operational system is done; when accepted, this constitutes acceptance of the system.

Subsequently code reviews should be undertaken, using manual or automated techniques, to detect violations. Validation analysis can be either static or dynamic. Static validation does not require execution of the program; it involves clarifying the internal logic structure, detecting dangerous constructs and validating algorithms. Dynamic validation determines the behaviour of source code during execution.

7.3.4 Operations

Errors will always be found in production systems, although a good quality management programme will obviously minimize them. After the error has been corrected, the software should be retested, i.e. regression testing should be performed.

A deliverable acceptance matrix (Fig. 7.6), is an essential systems project management methodology document. The matrix, when completed, answers the question 'Who is going to help decide what is required to complete the project or stage?'. The completed form does this by identifying the deliverables, who will accept each one, who will deliver each one, and who will recommend that acceptance takes place.

Completing the acceptance matrix therefore accomplishes the following:

- It indicates that each deliverable has an individual responsible person delegated for delivery and another for acceptance, thus establishing a sub-project circle for every deliverable. Therefore there should be no problem with interpretation at completion, because of the visible singular responsibility for each deliverable.

- During the process of completing the matrix, the acceptor will begin to understand his or her commitment and involvement in the project. For instance, the acceptor will realize that the outline of documents must be approved before the activities for their completion, since he or she must be prepared to accept ultimate responsibility for them. In some projects (particularly smaller ones), the acceptor alone will accept all deliverables. In others (particularly the larger ones or those with multiple user interests), the acceptor will realize that an acceptance team must be established, which in some cases might be more involved than the delivery team. In any case, the acceptor will begin planning for acceptance *now*!

It is the project manager's responsibility to complete this form in consultation with the acceptor and also to put it in the project plan for acceptance of commitment by all individuals named for delivery, acceptance and recommendation.

The project manager should identify with the acceptor or the team, in a joint application development session for example, all deliverables that will have to be produced as a part of the overall project completion, as well as the standard to which they will be produced. Commitments for the delivery of the deliverables should be solicited from members of the team at the time that their delivery responsibilities are assigned. Likewise, the acceptor must solicit commitments for the acceptance of each deliverable if he or she is not going to perform the acceptance task. However, it is unrealistic for an acceptor to be able to understand everything that needs to be accepted. Therefore, to reiterate: an acceptance team can be established consisting of specialists who can give unbiased recommendations to the acceptor.

Deliverables requiring signatures on deliverable acceptance forms must also be identified at this time and documented on the form. If there is to be a separate recommendation from other individuals reviewing the format and level of detail (standard) and/or the content, they must also be identified by the deliverable acceptor at this point. The early drafts of this form may, therefore, have many blanks or question marks until suitable deliverers and acceptors are found.

Project name:	Project number	Project manager:	
Deliverable	**Individual responsible for:**		
	Deliverable delivery	**Recommending acceptance sign-off**	**Acceptance sign-off**
Project initiation			
Functional requirements – preliminary analysis			
Feasibility study			
User detailed requirements			
Business system design			
Concurrent data model			
Logical data model			
Detail/comp/sys/req			
Conversion plan			
Implementation plan			
Comp/sys/des/ov			
Computer system design			
Database schema			
Application data dictionary			
Application user manual			
Training manual			
Integration test plan			
Acceptance test plan			
Beta test plan			
Integration test			
Quality assurance			
Training schedule			
Test report			
Sign-off			
Operations manual			
System manual			
Program manual			
Beta test report			
Post-implementation report			

Fig. 7.6 Deliverable acceptance matrix.

In some projects, it may be advisable to create one or more 'deliverables' to cover certain responsibilities that may not be directly associated with a particular task. An example of this might be 'user readiness'. The deliverable for this responsibility could be stated on the deliverable acceptance form as: 'I accept responsibility for the user's readiness to operate the system'.

Although common deliverables may be specified, such as user manuals and training programs, there might still be some 'cracks'. Even with all the deliverables completed, the users might still be unable to use the system for some reason or other. Establishing an individual responsible for cracks will ensure that they will discover them before they become gaps.

Completion of the deliverable acceptance matrix is an integral component in identifying progress towards completion during project control, and in identifying the activities, time frames, and resource requirements for the project.

Having completed a list of deliverables, the challenge is to arrange them into a logical order of dependent tasks. There are two basic ways to schedule chronologically tasks: sequential and concurrent. It is useful to define a task (activity) as 'one of a group of assigned pieces of work, the sum of which completes an event in the project'. For example, an event can be to install plumbing in a building. The tasks that enable this event to get completed are (to name a few):

- Detail pipe paths
- Determine type of pipe
- Decide on lengths required
- Determine diameters
- Determine number of bends and junctions needed

This is an important concept, because some managers (clients) are only interested in events, whereas supervisors and project managers are generally interested in the tasks (activities) that are required to produce the deliverable (event).

Sequential tasks (Fig. 7.7(a)), follow one after the other, i.e. one must be completed before the next can commence. However, the plan can be changed (Fig. 7.7(b)) to illustrate that concurrent tasks can occur simultaneously, as illustrated. It is shown that:

1 You cannot review documentation until it is written, and you should review it before it is typeset, i.e. these tasks are sequential.
2 The task 'Arrange for printing' can be done concurrently with reviewing the documentation.

A more detailed network diagram is illustrated in Fig. 7.8. To develop a network such as that in Fig. 7.8 a critical path methodology is used, and the path is delineated as a solid line. This line can be defined as the longest one through a project plan and determines the project completion date. One problem commonly encountered is where the plan keeps identifying that the project is not going to be completed until some time in the distant future, when reasonableness indicates that the anticipated workload could be handled by the assigned resources within a shorter period.

This problem is common, and it has nothing to do with the project management system being used. It arises because the planner is unaware not only that applying a

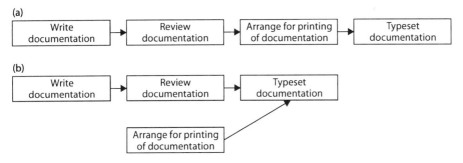

Fig. 7.7 (a) Sequential and (b) concurrent tasks.

critical path method (CPM) (a process well understood), but also levelling a network can lead to problems. Levelling is, however, a crucial step in project planning and it is this aspect that is not always understood. This is compounded when we think of the automated tools that have been relegated to a very narrow group of individuals and are not used by the typical manager.

We will illustrate that the critical path, although necessary, is not as important as resource levelling, and we will also clear up some misconceptions. Resource scheduling is usually the primary goal of planning, so it is more important to understand how resource levelling works in the system being used. Otherwise, as will be shown, the project schedule may indicate some surprising results. Understanding this will assist project managers in understanding levelling.

The underlying calculation technique for determining critical path(s) is used by nearly all project management systems to assign dates to events or activities. An event is defined as a set of activities. For example: in building a computer system, there may be nine major events: initiation/requirements, feasibility, analysis, computer and business design, computer and business development, testing and implementation. Each of these events has a number of tasks associated with it.

The critical path method consists of forward and backward passes through the planning network of activities to determine early and late start dates for each task based upon its connected dependent activities. The earliest date possible is that on which a task can start (or finish), and the latest date is that on which a task can start (or finish) and allow the project to finish in the shortest possible time. 'Float', i.e. spare time, is the difference between these two dates.

An activity with zero float is said to be critical. The collection of all these zero-float critical activities in a project will always form one or more critical paths throughout the network. That is, any delay on a critical path will delay the project if no corrective action is taken. It is apparent that the sum of the times to complete the project along any critical path will also be the shortest possible time in which the project can be completed. Any delay to an activity on the path will delay the project by the same amount of time. Of course, overtime and other compensatory methods may make up this lost time.

A critical path method uses only the project start date and the duration of each task to arrive at dates; it does not consider resource constraints. This leads to a common problem, i.e. equating critical path calculations with project scheduling. They are two entirely different things.

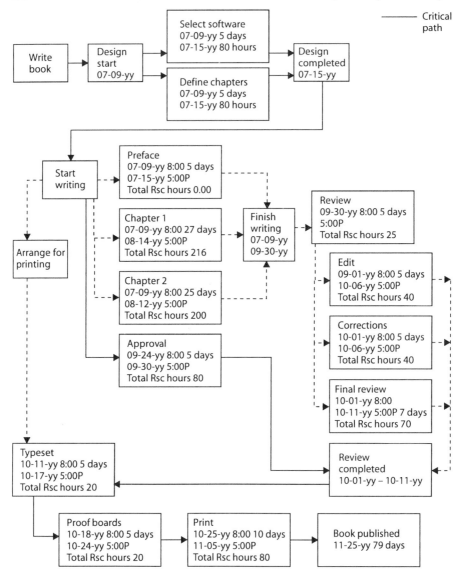

Fig. 7.8 A network diagram.

A common mistake made by some project managers and planners is the assumption that the critical path represents an attainable schedule. It does if one has an unlimited amount of resources. For most projects, this is simply not the case. This is where the second half of the planning process comes into play, i.e. levelling or equivalency scheduling.

One interesting thing about levelling is the disappearance of the critical path. The concept of float or criticality no longer has any meaning, since once the plan is levelled a delay in any activity or task can, in principle, delay the finish date of the project. In a sense, every task becomes critical and has zero float. There are, however, some exceptions to this generalization.

The scheduling or levelling process is certainly a difficult part of planning, but this is where the computer can be of most assistance. All computer project management systems can perform critical path calculations and also levelling, with various degrees of effectiveness. However, bear in mind that, from a theoretical computing perspective, levelling is a very difficult and computationally intense process. For this reason, levelling algorithms can vary greatly in speed and intelligence.

Levelling refers to the process of examining how resources are being used and arranging tasks to ensure that each resource's utilization does not exceed its availability. In simpler terms, levelling means ensuring that the project staff are working full-time (utilized) at no more than seven or so hours a day (their availability). In almost all cases, the levelling process will result in a longer plan. Consider Figs. 7.9–7.11, which outline the same project with the same tasks. Except for Task 50, which was automatically changed by the computer program and its levelling process the projects are exact duplicates. Project plan CPM-A (Fig. 7.9) has no levelling and no split resourcing and indicates a completion time of 225 days; CPM-B (Fig. 7.10) has full levelling and no split resourcing, but shows 257 days to complete; and the third plan, CPM-C (Fig. 7.11) with full levelling and split resourcing indicates a duration of 235 days. How can this be?

Misconceptions about what levelling is and how it can be used often lead to these scheduling differences. A typical misconception might be described as assuming that the system will understand how the work is really going to be performed. If levelling is carried out, there are certain concessions that must be made in the planning and estimating process to ensure that a satisfactory result is obtained. Bear in mind that when we talk of resources they may be equipment. To illustrate:

> Assume you have assigned Clive Burnett, a senior analyst, to work for 200 days on the project. You utilize these completely by allocating them in the plan to Task 50. In the middle of the project, however, Clive is going on vacation for 10 days. In most project management systems this would be handled by allocating a 10-day task (Task 40) for the vacation that uses Clive full time thus making him unavailable for other tasks. This vacation task would normally have a fixed date associated with it because levelling can schedule the vacation. Without levelling CPM-A, the plan shows that the project can be completed in 225 days. This is misleading. Therefore, after the fixed date has been allocated the project would be levelled. The result with most systems would be to push Clive's Project X task out into the future until it starts on his return from vacation, i.e. CMP-B, where we now show a project completion time of 257 days. This was the problem mentioned above, i.e. reasonableness indicated that the project could be completed sooner. The reason is simple. The system cannot move the vacation because it has a fixed date, so it must move one of the tasks, because otherwise during the vacation Clive would be working double time. On the other hand, if we split resources, as in CPM-C, this has the effect of making the time to complete reasonable, i.e. 235 days. Note that Task 50 has been automatically increased to 210 days to accomodate this.

In Fig. 7.9, the sum of the tasks on the critical path = 225 days to complete the project. This is not correct because the method used, i.e. no levelling and splitting of resources, does not take into account that Clive will be taking holidays. Of course as mentioned earlier, if we had unlimited resources we would simply replace Clive with another individual (Keith) and the project could be done in 225 days. Assuming we

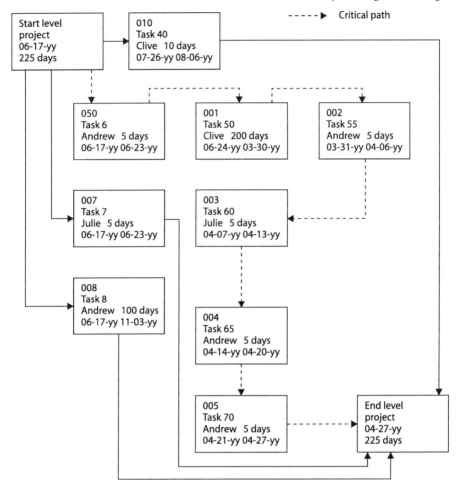

Fig. 7.9 CPM-A: CPM network schematic with no levelling and no split resourcing.

cannot replace Clive, we would either do resource levelling but not split resourcing (CPM-B, Fig. 7.10) or we could level and split resources (CPM-C, Fig. 7.11).

Figure 7.10 shows a completion time of 257 days. How can this be? CPM-A and CPM-C indicate 225 and 235 days, respectively. As explained, this is the result of levelling and splitting resources. Thus project managers should understand this aspect, otherwise they may have different views of a project. A Gantt chart of the 225 days is shown in Fig. 7.12 and can be compared to the Gantt chart for CPM-B (Fig. 7.13) to appreciate the differences.

The Gantt chart for CPM-C would appear as in Fig. 7.14. You can see that the tasks are levelled and add up to 235 days. This contrasts with the other charts, which depict different values for the same project plan.

It should also be realized that by creating task dependencies between projects you are in fact sharing resources. Therefore levelled projects are better for managing

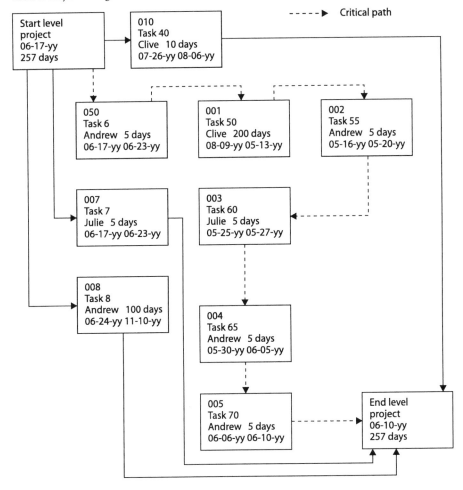

Fig. 7.10 CPM-B: CPM network schematic with full levelling but no split resourcing.

resources. However, it may be necessary to freeze a project to protect the levelling that has been accepted.

Is there a solution to the problem of different values? Here are five possibilities:

1 Stick to a spreadsheet or personnel planning system for this type of high-level modelling. This will be adequate if the number of activities and resources remain small. The major drawbacks are that dates will not be recalculated automatically if the durations of activities change and the data will not integrate with any detailed plans.

2 Use a project management system that supports individual resource calendars. This solves the specific vacation problems described above. It will not work, however, if Clive, rather than going on vacation, is assigned to another project for two weeks.

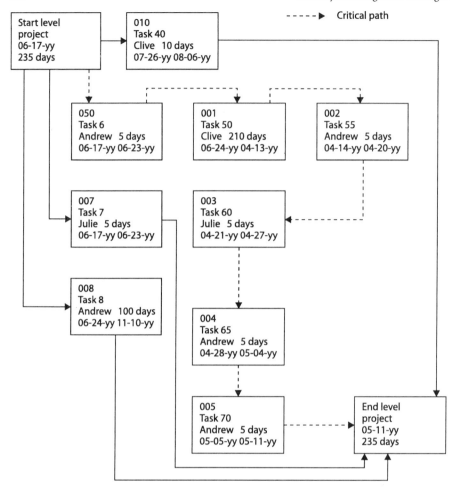

Fig. 7.11 CPM-C: CPM network schematic with full levelling and split resourcing.

3 Use a project management system, such as Microsoft Project 98, that supports activity splitting. Activity splitting allows certain tasks to be flagged as splittable. The computer can then split these activities around other shorter duration tasks to come up with a viable schedule. This is illustrated in CPM-C, which takes 235 days to complete. You will note that Task 50 has been increased by the computer from 200 days to 210 days to take into account the vacation.

4 Recognize that many levelling programs add up how much a resource is being used on a given day and, if necessary, delays one task or another until each resource's utilization is equal to or below its availability. This is not too useful for high-level planning, and because of this the reader should be prepared to split large tasks artificially and level the project manually. In other words, it would be better to avoid computer levelling programs altogether if they do not facilitate resource splitting.

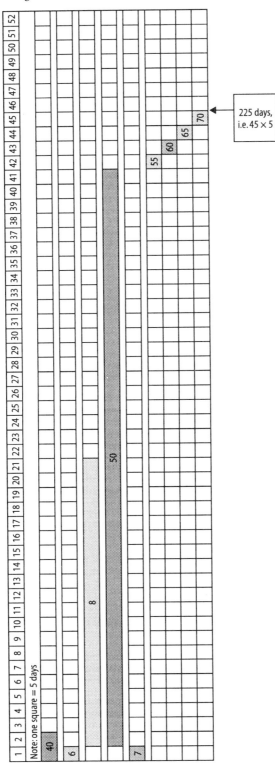

Fig. 7.12 Gantt chart: CPM-A.

	1	2	3	4	5	6	7	8	9	10	11	12	13	14	15	16	17	18	19	20	21	22	23	24	25	26	27	28	29	30	31	32	33	34	35	36	37	38	39	40	41	42	43	44	45	46	47	48	49	50	51	52
6																																																				
						8																																														
7																																																				
						40																																														
7								50																																												
																																																	55			
																																																		60		
																																																			65	
																																																				70
5	22 days						68 days															132 days																									20 days			
5	27 days						105 days															237 days																									257 days			

Fig. 7.13 Gantt chart: CPM-B.

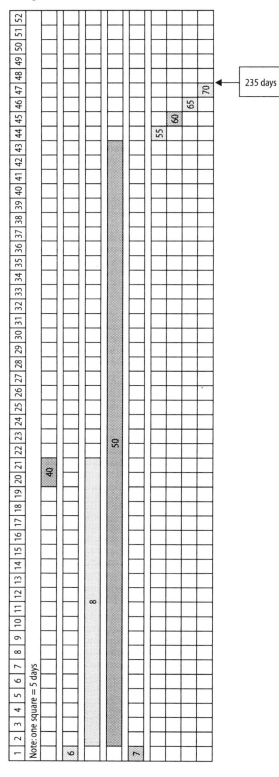

Fig. 7.14 Gantt chart: CPM-C.

5   A preferred approach is to plan projects in as much detail as possible, with a mix of larger and smaller activities with varying utilization of resources. In addition, it is also preferable to apply one resource per task. If the time of individuals is being planned then each estimate for each resource should include total duration and either an hour per day value used or a total effort value. They are equivalent.

Another problem, commonly encountered, is where tasks are performed on a regular basis but require less than one day, i.e. it is necessary to apportion the time over a week. Many situations can be thought of, such as maintaining a piece of equipment that takes x hours per day. This can be modelled in one of three ways, namely:

1   The resource availability could be reduced by one hour per day. However, the project control system will not account for time spent on these tasks. If it were a constant however, this would not present a problem.

2   Allocate one long task at x hours per day.

3   Allocate a series of x hours per day for the task or divide the total time for the week by two and assign two tasks per week. Each should have a not-earlier-than date associated with it that will ensure that it is scheduled in the correct week. This is the most flexible approach but requires a little more data entry and maintenance.

It is generally accepted that automation is not required for a small number of tasks. Where the tasks are many, say more than 100, automation is appropriate if the plan is to have any chance of being kept up-to-date. To keep a project on track, consideration should be given to breaking it down into sub-projects, each with a project leader or project manager. For example, a 24 month project could be broken down into four sub-projects, each of six months duration, thus making the whole project more manageable. In this way, tangible results may be demonstrated quickly so that the project team, users and management can see that the project is working. Take, for example, implementing office automation consisting of email, word processing, scheduling, calendaring and a standard menu. This could be broken down into four project teams: technical configuration; menu and email; calendaring and scheduling; and word processing. However, planning should be done up-front for the whole project.

An activity planning schedule (Fig. 7.15) (automated or manual), is an essential systems project management methodology document. This document, when completed, ensures that the project manager is able to describe the tasks anticipated for the delivery of the project and deliverables, as described in the deliverable acceptance matrix. It is an obligation of the project manager to input the necessary transactions to obtain the printout and include it in the project plan.

These types of report can be produced by project management software packages such as Prima Vera, WebProject, Timeline (Symantec Corp.), Microsoft Project, Project Workbench (Applied Business Technology) and Prestige (Lucas Management Systems). These packages range from simple schedulers to enterprise-wide solutions. PlanView Inc.'s Intelligent Planner is an IS-specific project management package that has integrated function point analysis, automatic correct mechanisms, multi-user accessibility, client–server architecture and record locking, and is GUI-based. Most of the products mentioned can run on MS-DOS, Windows or OS/2 platforms. They help a project manager organize, analyze and report on the project from the natural perspectives of tasks, resources, dates and accounts.

The activity planning schedule should be prepared in conjunction with the activity resource estimates form and the work plan and work plan–resource schedule. These three will most likely go through several iterations before the proper balance between time, resource availability and activity definitions is achieved. This is the important document for communication with management and team members in the control stage of the project. This first schedule in the plan provides the starting point for the continuous replanning for completion exercise that will take place throughout the project until completion.

Now that it is known what has to be done, who is going to do it must be determined, i.e. what resources are required. A resource is someone or something that either performs a task, or is needed for the task to occur. It can be an employee, a consultant, budget, machinery, materials etc. Therefore it is necessary to do some matchmaking – fitting the best resource to the most appropriate task.

Next, it is necessary to estimate the time for each task. This is very difficult and depends on many factors – see Chapter 6 on estimating. Against each task a time should be estimated for it to be completed. The activity resources estimates form (Fig. 7.16) can be used for this component.

The activity resource estimates form is an optional systems project management methodology document. The purpose is to answer the question 'What resources are likely to be required to complete each activity?'. It identifies each resource (individuals, computer costs, other costs etc.) estimated to be required to complete each activity identified on the schedule. It does not attempt to distribute the resources over any time. The results can be included in the activity planning schedule. It is the responsibility of the project manager to complete this form and include it in the project plan.

This form is a worksheet that may be inserted into the main body of the plan, put in an appendix, left out or not used if inappropriate. To estimate the resources and activity schedule, this form should be completed first. It will provide an estimate that can then be distributed over time and, therefore, provide a schedule of resources and time, thus ensuring resource balancing and confident scheduling. The components of the form are:

- *Individual or resource type*: Enter the name of each known individual on the delivery and acceptance teams or, if individuals cannot yet be identified, enter the resource type or skill level (e.g. programmer).
- *Resource estimate by activity*: In the heading row, enter the activity number of each activity. In the space below, enter the estimated person days and/or cost for each person or resource type named in the first column. The bottom rows provide total estimates for the activity.

The work plan and resource schedule (Fig. 7.17) is an optional systems project management methodology document. It answers the question 'How can resources be applied to the project activities to get an estimated schedule?'. It is a simple way of documenting who is going to do what and when. It takes the resource requirements by activity from the activity resource estimates form for all delivery and acceptance

Project name:				Project number:					Page – of –		
Stage or event:				**Responsible individual**							
Project manager:				**Date completed:**							
Resource	Task	February			March		Duration (days)	Task ID	Start	Finish	Priority	Allocation	Hours	Status
		09	16	23	02	09								
JL SH	Initiation	XX	XX	XX			10	1	09/02/yy	20/02/yy	1	100%	150	Crit
KB	Analysis		X	XX	XX		12	2	18/02/yy	03/03/yy	1	75%	90	Crit
MB	Sys Mod				XX	X	7	3	30/02/yy	09/03/yy	1	75%	40	Crit

Fig. 7.15 Activity planning schedule.

Project name:		Date:		Project number:		Project manager:				
Individual or resource type	Resource estimate by activity									
Total person hours										
Cost of person hours										
Other costs										
Total costs										

Fig. 7.16 Activity resource estimates form.

The work plan and resource schedule (Fig. 7.17) is an optional systems project management methodology document. It answers the question 'How can resources be applied to the project activities to get an estimated schedule?'. It is a simple way of documenting who is going to do what and when. It takes the resource requirements by activity from the activity resource estimates form for all delivery and acceptance staff and distributes them over a schedule by month. This provides a monthly resource schedule and a time for each activity to be recorded on the project activity planning schedule. This document is the basis for resource commitment in the plan acceptance. It is the project manager's responsibility to complete the form and to enter it in the project plan.

This form should be completed once the activity resource has been determined in as much detail as accuracy permits. It should account for all activities and ensure the proper sequence for interdependent activities. It must include all activities expected to require any of the team members' time, such as vacations, group meetings and education, since the schedule is built around the available time for each resource. To complete the form, process it as outlined below:

- *Individual or resource type*: Enter the name of each known individual on the delivery and acceptance teams or, if individuals cannot yet be identified, enter the

Project name:		Date:	Project number:			Project manager:		
Individual or resource type		Activity	Activity resource by period					
			Period ending					Total
			Period 1	Period 2	Period 3	Period 4	Period 5	
		Total						

Fig. 7.17 Work plan and resource schedule.

resource type or skill level (e.g. junior programmer). Entries should correspond to those made on the activity resource estimates form.

- *Activity*: Enter all activities by name or number for which time will be required from the indicated individual or resource type.
- *Activity resource by period*: In the heading row, enter the name of the months for which activities will be performed. In the other rows, enter the estimate of resources required in person-days and/or costs for each activity.
- *Total*: When resource estimates have been recorded for all activities, fill in the totals for the activity (row) and month (column) for the individual or resource type. If the total resources for the month exceed the number of available resource days for the month the schedule may have to be revised or the work reassigned to another resource.

The project control plan (Fig. 7.18) is an integral component of the systems project management methodology. It ensures that sufficient project control and adequate communication are maintained throughout the life of the project. It identifies the methods and tools that the project manager will use to control the project. As such, it must describe each avenue for sharing responsibility or communication channel that must be kept open by the project manager to maintain his or her own, as well as others', personal commitment to completion. As a minimum, this must include the following avenues:

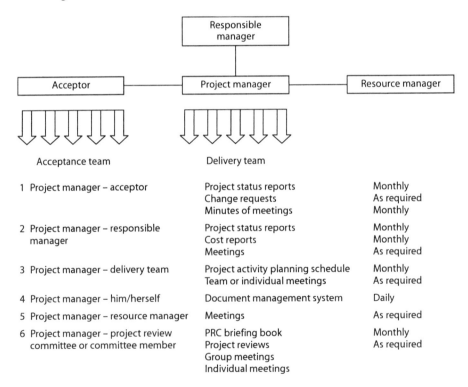

Fig. 7.18 The project control plan.

project manager ↔ responsible manager
project manager ↔ acceptor
project manager ↔ project team members

In addition, the following may be included:

project manager ↔ resources manager
project manager ↔ him- or herself (personal files)
project manager ↔ project review committee member

It is the project manager's responsibility to complete this form and include it in the project plan.

The project control approach to be planned for is fully described in Chapter 8. The following is a brief summary of the project management methodology tools that should be considered for each avenue.

- *Avenue for sharing responsibility*: Others may be added to the pre-printed list.
- *Tools*: List the tools that will be used to keep open each avenue. Standard systems project management methodology tools are described earlier in Chapter 8 on project control.
- *Frequency*: Indicate the frequency of use of each of the tools. This should conform to a calendar cycle (e.g. weekly, biweekly, monthly etc.) or be *ad hoc*.

7.4 Summary

In previous chapters we have covered an approach to project management, the skills needed of project staff and how to motivate them. These aspects were then expanded to illustrate the activities needed to complete a project and the roles and responsibilities of each party that had an interest in the outcome of the project. This chapter has taken the aforementioned components and shown how they should be included in a project plan. The problem with resource levelling was explained and should lead the practitioner to fully appreciate its implications. We have seen the different forms needed to ensure commitment and how they help keep open the channels of communication. If used as a monitoring tool, they help the project manager keep the project on schedule. Having progressed to this point, it is now essential to learn how to control project activities and this is the subject of the next chapter.

8. *Project Control*

8.1 Introduction

Up until now we have covered the organization of a project team; the tools that the project manager uses to ensure communication between the project team and management; the requirements of initiating a project; how to estimate the time and resources required; quality management; and the planning of a project. This chapter leads on from these aspects and explains how to control the development of the deliverable(s). Therefore project control deals with knowing where you are and ensuring you get to where you want to go and, when necessary, sharing the concern with the appropriate authorities.

Controlling projects is all about worrying and dreaming: worrying about what is and is not happening, and dreaming about what might or might not happen.

Poor managers don't make the time to dream. They don't worry enough. Eventually, they slide into a crisis-to-crisis situation, when they don't even have time to worry. Good managers organize their worrying and dreaming and delegate as much of the worrying as possible. This gives them the vital time to dream and allows them to stay a step ahead of problems. How does a project manager delegate some of this worrying and dreaming? Delegation can be passed to others by soliciting personal commitments for deliverables and monitoring them on a regular, cyclical schedule.

It should be pointed out that we have been talking about a project manager. In fact, a project manager cannot meet staff regularly and be expected to do all the other things one expects of such a person if, say, the project consists of more than 10 people. Where the project is large, its component parts should be broken down into smaller projects and managed by project leaders who report to the project manager. In this context, the term project leader is synonymous with project manager, and each leader would complete the forms, such as those illustrated in this book, for his or her sub-project. Thus, using Fig. 8.1 as an illustration, we would have six project leaders reporting to a Senior project manager or project director. Each leader would each have their own plans and schedules albeit linked into one overall plan and schedule.

The project control tools detailed in this chapter assist in the communication process by providing a set of standard forms that, when completed, regularly facilitate communication by the project manager. They also enable the manager, in a structured and disciplined way, to keep on top of the numerous tasks that befall a project manager. In following such a process, it must be realized that the accuracy and completeness of information received varies inversely with the organizational

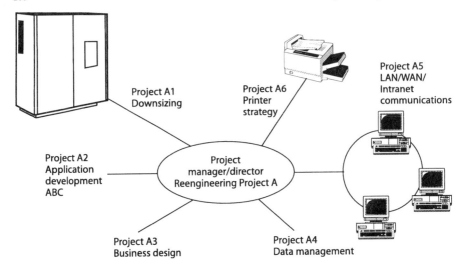

Fig. 8.1 A project with six sub-projects.

position of the receiver. Thus, the boss rarely has the full or correct story. Although the project control process helps, the information received has been filtered and reflects the view of the individual. Therefore, learn to weigh the information received accordingly and walk about among the project team to learn orally and at first hand what is actually happening.

8.2 Project Control Activities

As mentioned earlier, project control is about communication and getting help when needed. Table 8.1 describes the three major communication channels (avenues for sharing responsibility) available to the project manager and shows when and how to use them.

8.2.1 Project Control

To control projects it is essential that reports be available for analysis and to ensure that the project is kept on track when variances to plans are noticed. One such process is to use a project control plan (Fig. 8.2). This is integral to a good systems project management methodology.

   The purpose of this form is to help answer the question 'How will sufficient project control and adequate communication be assured throughout the project?'. In the control stage, the completed form, if used by the project manager, acts as a reminder and makes visible to everyone else where the avenues for sharing responsibilities (communication channels) are, and, therefore, who is going to provide help when needed. It is the project manager's obligation to ensure that all necessary avenues are open and that this form is visible and kept current.

Table 8.1 Communication: minimum guidelines.

Communicate with	Purpose	Regular or on-demand	Written or oral	Individual or group	Frequency
Responsible manager	Share responsibility Ensure proper credit Financial review Inform	Both	Both	Individual	Monthly
Acceptor	Share responsibility Changes Status	Both	Both	Individual	Monthly
Project team	Share responsibility Planning Coordination	Regular	Oral	Individual	Weekly
	Direction Status Morale Motivation	On-demand	Oral	Group	As required

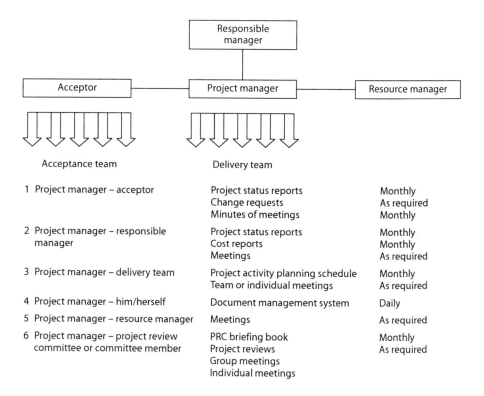

Fig. 8.2 The project control plan.

As soon as any avenue is perceived to be closed the project manager must work with the other project players to open it up again, or find an alternative avenue and display it on a revised project control plan.

8.2.2 Questions

The following questions, when posed by the project manager during the project, enable the verification of personal commitments to complete the deliverables assigned.

- *How can the most help be obtained from project team members?* A project activity planning schedule (automated or manual) can be used as a vehicle to review and plan remaining work. This will elicit participation among members. Outstanding activities that remain to be done are addressed by the individuals responsible for doing them. During the review the members' current respective commitments to completion can be verified. The review is also a vehicle for regular individual meetings with each project team member to solicit their continuing commitment. A by-product will be an accurate statement of the state of the project.

- *How can the most help be obtained from management?* Using a project status report form enables the soliciting of assistance from managers with a personal stake in the project's success. It also continues to confirm to these managers the project manager's personal commitment to completing the project. This report also provides a vehicle for regular meetings with the responsible manager, and facilitates the sharing of responsibility through the project review committee of which the client, i.e. responsible manager, is probably the chairperson.

- *How can the most help be acquired from the users and the acceptor?* Again, by using a completed project status report form, constraints to progress will be highlighted. This acts as a trigger to solicit assistance from the acceptor and the acceptance team. By regularly outlining the state of the project, the acceptor's confidence is cultivated. It also serves as a vehicle for reaffirming the acceptor's commitment to the project. A well-documented status provides a vehicle for regular meetings with the acceptor to share guardianship of the project with the project review committee.

- *How will the project's financial situation be known?* A current completed project cost report form will communicate to all interested parties the costs expended for the current fiscal year and for the total project.

- *How are changes to the user's requirements controlled?* For control, it is essential that a change procedure be in place that requires a change request and authorization form to be completed and approved. This is necessary to document and produce an audit trail of all formal requests and approvals for all changes to the specifications. This ensures that the project manager does not have to 'pay' for the extra workload due to changed specifications.

- *How can all members of the project review committee have access to the information necessary for committee meetings?* Preparing a project review committee members' briefing manual will ensure that each member has all relevant project information and is aware of the state of the project. This information could be put in a common automated directory. Members could be kept informed by simply routing information by email or sending an email notification informing all parties that it had been updated and should be reviewed. This directory could contain timely information pertaining to the project for electronic access and review by any interested and authorized person.

- *How are important decisions taken and key events that take place in project meetings recorded?* After each meeting, a meeting minutes form should be completed. This will:
  - Document decisions and assignment of responsibilities for follow-up action.
  - Make visible relevant issues.
  - Ensure universal understanding of who is committed to do what.
  - Document precisely and detail the preparation of items to be reported to, and decisions to be acquired from, the project review committee. This should also be filed in the PRC briefing manual.
- *How is the crucial information needed to control the project stored and retrieved?* To do this in a disciplined manner a project manager's document management system should be established to store and retrieve information, such as questions and answers, accepted or rejected solutions, and status information. These will provide an audit trail of the project's progress.
- *How can all senior managers concerned with the project be kept informed of, and contribute to, the project?* Establishing project review committee meetings ensures a regular forum for timely, considered and relevant advice from interested senior managers to the responsible manager and project manager. An electronic bulletin board could also be used as an ongoing communication tool.

8.2.3 Project or Stage Control (Checklist)

In enabling project control to be seen as a positive and useful component of project management, it is necessary to monitor progress toward the completion of deliverables on a regular cyclical schedule. This is facilitated by performing the following tasks on a weekly basis:

- *Project manager*: Meet each team member and confirm their current commitment to complete the assigned tasks, i.e. current schedule. If changes are in order, update the current activity planning schedule and inform interested parties. Of course, it may be impossible to do this with a large team. However, one solution may be to use subordinates to verify with individuals who report directly to them.
- *Stage coordinator or team leader*: This action is the same as for the project manager above, except that it applies to the coordinator's team members, stage and deliverables.

The following tasks should be performed monthly:
- *Project manager*: Complete a project status report and send copies to the responsible manager and to the acceptor. Also complete a cost report and send copies to the responsible manager and other interested managers, but especially those with a personal stake.
- *Responsible manager*: Review the project status and cost reports. Subsequently arrange to discuss any points that are unclear or need explanation.
- *Acceptor*: Review the project status report as for the responsible manager.

- *Project manager*: If necessary, meet the responsible manager to discuss the project status and cost reports.

    Prepare for and circulate the agenda for a project review committee meeting.
- *Responsible manager*: Chair a project review committee to review the state of the project, costs and constraints to progress. The purpose is to ensure that the project is still on track (if not, why not?) and to decide on appropriate corrective action.

The following tasks should be performed whenever required:

- *Acceptor*: Request and authorize changes as required using appropriate change request and authorization form. Meet responsible manager.
- *Responsible manager*: Meet project manager, project review committee and acceptor.
- *Project manager*: Keep project control plan current. Ensure that changes are performed only if they are covered by approved change request and authorization forms.

    Ensure that minutes are taken at all significant meetings (especially project review committees) and document on meeting minutes form. For informal meetings write a 'Note to file'.

    Ensure that all relevant documents are filed in the document management system.

    Supply appropriate documents to project review committee members.

    Meet responsible manager, acceptor, resource manager and project team as a group when required for motivation and communication; meet project review committee.

8.2.4 Project Manager's Filing System

To assist the project manager in keeping track of the myriad pieces of information received during the project life cycle a filing system or automated document management system should be established as soon as the project is approved or an individual is assigned to the project. This is a desirable systems project management methodology tool. Its purpose is to answer the question 'How can I, the project manager, record and store the crucial information that may be needed to keep track of the project?'. It provides the project manager with a simple, organized collection of information pertinent to the project. It can be used by the project manager to store and retrieve the questions, solutions and status information required to control the project. Once the project is complete, it serves as an audit trail of the project's progress. This could also be included in the automated directory mentioned earlier, with subdirectories for different components, e.g. status, user manual and test results.

The accountability for establishing the system is the project manager's, as it also is to ensure that the files are kept up-to-date. Each individual involved in the project should ensure that the project manager receives a copy of each document that has any relevance to the project.

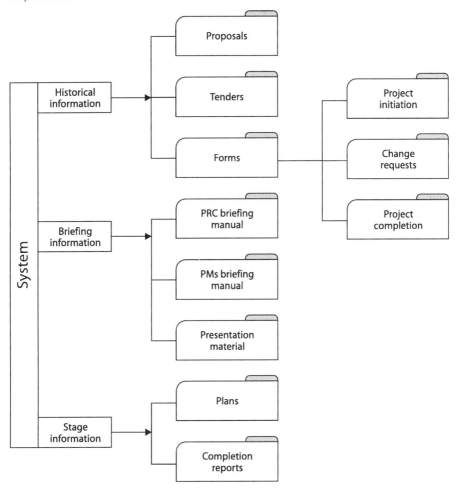

Fig. 8.3 A document management system.

The format (Fig. 8.3) is a simplified example of a filing document management system.

8.2.5 Stage Information

For each of the SDLC stages (initiation, feasibility, analysis, business design, computer system design, computer system development, business system development, acceptance testing, conversion and implementation, and post-implementation evaluation) the following items are stored:

● Stage plan
● Systems project management methodology deliverables
● Acceptance form for each SDLC deliverable in the stage

- Initial or updated project plan (as required)
- Stage completion report
- Stage project completion form

In approaching the filing system, the project manager should use it to smooth out some of the worrying about the project. These files should, therefore, document and assist in the management of the project. Deliverables should be filed separately from, but in proximity to, the other files.

8.2.6 Project Review Committee Members' Briefing Manual

Similar to the project manager's filing system is the project review committee members' briefing manual. This is integral to good systems project management. Its purpose is to answer the question: 'How can I, the project manager, ensure that all members of the PRC have access to the information necessary for committee meetings?'. It assures the project manager that all members are prepared for the meetings and are aware of the status of the project.

The project manager should provide each project review committee member with a binder separated by appropriate divisions. Experience has shown that when PRC members are asked to maintain their own briefing manuals they tend to become out-of-date and incomplete because of the incorrect filing of documents by PRC members or failure to file documents. Of course, if the project manager, the PRC and team are established as an automated workgroup, the distribution of paper and the destruction of trees could be minimized. At a PRC meeting, for example, information could be displayed from a computer on a screen and discussed dynamically. Alternatively, everybody could be informed electronically when something is of interest or needs action, e.g. by email or using the WebProject package.

The process to be followed should be determined between committee members and the project manager. One practice is for a project administrator to collect the PRC manuals at the end of each PRC meeting; update them systematically as the project progresses; and return them to the PRC members a few days before the next PRC meeting. The agenda for the next PRC meeting may be clipped to the cover of the manual and should list the new documents to be reviewed before the meeting. This is also a candidate for email or workflow software.

The following is a suggested format for this manual, or automated directory, using an appropriate binder:

- Project status reports
- Project costs – reports
- Correspondence
- PRC meetings

and a section for each of the applicable SDLC stages containing:

- Stage plan
- Systems project management methodology deliverables (e.g. request for changes)
- Acceptance form for each SDLC deliverable in the stage

- Updated project plan (as required)
- Stage completion report or stage acceptance form
- Agenda and minutes

One of the first major steps in project control is planning. Here a project activity planning schedule (automated) can be very useful. Its purpose is to answer the question 'How can the most help be obtained from my project team members?'. Systems projects are distinctive and need to be managed carefully. They are labour intensive and team members need to be service-orientated as they are delivering a product to a client that can span a period of many years, e.g. the Channel Tunnel or the 'Star Wars' defence systems.

In the control stage, a planning schedule provides the project manager with a vehicle for communicating with each member of his project team to determine the situation (or current commitment to completion) of the tasks required to achieve project completion. It also ensures a common understanding by the team members of what will be done in the future. It is, therefore, an invaluable tool for project control. A schedule allows the project manager to show to the acceptor and responsible manager the up-to-date status. An automated capability allows easy and rapid updating of such reports.

To help manage projects, another essential ingredient (in addition to scheduling) is the ability to track what is happening. We have seen in the previous chapter how to plan projects. We now concentrate on the control aspects. Tasks and the resulting deliverables should be measurable and the responsibility for completing them clearly delineated.

To accomplish this, a process to supply consistent and frequent reports should be implemented. Such reports track progress and signal an early warning if the project is getting off-track. They also provide information about the quality of plans, estimates and project staff. Regardless of the project size, the project manager should have a weekly status report to keep control. For large projects, say greater than 100 activities, a good automated system will help in scheduling and tracking.

The project manager should meet each project team member individually on a periodic basis (weekly or biweekly) to determine the member's personal commitment towards completing the assigned tasks. By doing so, the project manager will be in a position of confidence regarding what has to be done to achieve project completion. Team members during the meeting with the project manager should be able to confirm that the current estimates to complete their tasks are still valid or need to be changed. Again, you may have a problem with a large team, so the meetings may be infrequent.

After the meetings, it is the project manager's obligation to inform the responsible manager and acceptor of any resulting changes in schedule or of any new requirements for resources.

8.2.7 Reports

The format of the types of report that follow can be produced by most project management software packages, although users need a good grounding in project management concepts to use them. The reports reflect the way an organization does business. Therefore, apart from the PERT, CPM and bar (Gantt) charts, which are standard, reports are usually custom tailored. Some software packages, such as Super Project, Prima Vera, Timeline and Harvard Project Manager, provide, among others, two reports that display the activities (tasks) and corresponding situation, budget information and schedule information for a project: a detailed status report (Fig. 8.4) and a bar chart (Fig. 8.5).

The contents of these reports and other associated reports should be described in the user documentation.

The schedule is a simple list of each task. It is used by the project manager to *plan* the resource's work and to set objectives for the current planning period. This report is invaluable when used at meetings held with individual members of the project team. Such meetings should be held weekly or bi-weekly. They should concentrate on the personal commitments to completion and not be a justification of how each person spent their time. Together the project manager and the individual agree on the individual's current commitment for completing all of his or her activities. The

Compare scheduled, actual dates, person days and budget: page 1 of 3

Organization:	Date:	Project No.:	Project name:	
Client:	Department:			
Heading/task	Status	Scheduled start	Scheduled finish	Actual finish
Development: bibliographic		01-01-92	06-03-92	
Specifications	Schd/crit	01-01-92	02-13-92	02-13-92
Architecture layout	Schd/crit	01-01-92	02-04-92	02-04-92
Functional specifications	Schd/crit	02-05-92	02-13-92	02-13-92
Build prototype	Schd/crit	02-14-92	03-12-92	03-12-92
Kernel structure	Schd/crit	02-14-92	03-03-92	03-03-92
Test	Schd	03-13-92	04-29-92	
Preliminary test	Schd/crit	03-13-92	03-19-92	03-19-92
Advanced test	Schd/crit	03-20-92	03-26-92	03-26-92
Simulation	Schd/crit	04-14-92	03-29-92	
Final sign-off	Schd	04-29-92	04-29-92	
Documentation	Schd/crit	03-27-92	06-03-92	
Outline	Schd/crit	03-27-92	06-30-92	
First draft	Schd/crit	03-31-92	04-13-92	
Second draft	Schd/crit	04-14-92	05-04-92	
Printer	Schd/crit	05-05-92	06-03-92	
Training	Schd	05-05-92	05-05-92	
Management	Schd	05-05-92	05-05-92	
Staff	Schd	05-05-92	05-05-92	
Marketing	Schd	05-06-92	05-26-92	
Marketing plan	Schd	05-06-92	05-08-92	
Assignments	Schd	05-11-92	05-26-92	

Fig. 8.4 Detailed status report (page 1).

Compare person-days: page 2 of 3

Heading/task	Person-days budgeted	Person-days used	Variation (less than budget)
Development – bibliographic	1024	475	(549)
Specifications	52	65	13
Architecture layout	20	25	5
Functional specifications	32	40	8
Build prototype	60	50	(10)
Kernel structure	15	15	0
Test	70	70	0
Preliminary test	40	35	(5)
Advanced test	20	20	0
Simulation	10	10	0
Final sign-off	5	5	0
Documentation	100	80	(20)
Outline	20	20	0
First draft	20	20	0
Second draft	20	20	0
Printer	40	0	(40)
Training	100	0	(100)
Management	20	0	(20)
Staff	80	0	(80)
Marketing	150	0	(150)
Marketing plan	75	0	(75)
Assignments	75	0	(75)

Fig. 8.4 *(continued)* Detailed status report (page 2).

report is adjusted to reflect this plan. At the same time, new activities may be assigned and/or old ones may be shifted or removed. During this individual meeting, the project manager through interaction with the individual confirms commitment to the recorded completion date for each activity. Larger projects will need this automated bar chart system because it is easier to maintain. For simpler projects, a manual schedule should suffice.

The project manager should receive the total project report and individuals should keep a copy of their reports for their own activities.

8.2.8 Project Activity Planning Schedule (Manual)

For small projects, say fewer than 100 activities, it was usually not appropriate to develop a computerized schedule. However, with the PC being ubiquitous, it is easy to computerize any size project plan. However, the purpose and responsibilities of a manual approach are the same as for the automated schedule described above.

Compare budget: page 3 of 3

Heading/task	Budgeted	Budget variance (negative)	Comments
Development – bibliographic			
Specifications	100	(20)	Caused by overtime
Architecture layout	30	(10)	Underestimated
Functional specifications	90	(10)	Specification change
Build prototype	250	0	
Kernel structure	50	0	
Test	600	100	
Preliminary test	150	50	
Advanced test	150	50	
Simulation	200	0	
Final sign-off	0	0	
Documentation	400	(50)	Specification change
Outline	25	(5)	Resource sick
First draft	25	(5)	Resource change
Second draft	50	(10)	
Printer	300	(30)	Overtime
Training	600	0	Specification change
Management	100	0	
Staff	500	0	
Marketing	500	0	
Marketing plan	300	0	
Assignments	200	0	

Fig. 8.4 *(continued)* Detailed status report (page 3).

The activity planning schedule (Fig. 8.6) could be used for small projects in the same manner as indicated for the automated schedule. It will, however, have to be redrawn each time a meeting is held with a team member and an activity changed. For larger projects, the automated schedule is preferable due to ease in updating.

8.2.9 Project Status

Knowing the channels of communication it is now necessary to keep all interested parties up-to-date on the state of the project deliverables. To do this, a project status report form (Fig. 8.7) is completed and distributed regularly (monthly). This form is an essential systems project management methodology document. Its purpose is to answer the question 'How do I make sure I get the most help from my management and my acceptor?'. Monthly, it reaffirms acceptance of the project responsibility by the project manager and to confirms the project manager's commitment to deliver the end product. Only with this primary purpose to guide its preparation can recipients be assured of its accuracy in reporting the state of the project. This report

Activity	Resource	Jan	Feb	Mar	Apr	May	Jun	Jul	Aug	Sep	Oct	Nov	Dec
Define specifications													
Architecture layout	WT												
Functional specifications	RM												
Build prototype													
Kernel structure	KB												
I/O system	WT												
Test	LM												
Prelim test	JP												
Advanced test	KB												
Simulation													
Documentation	WM												
Guide	WM												
First draft	WM												
Second draft	KB												
Review meeting	FP												
Printer													
Marketing	CL												
Marketing plan	CL												
Press meeting													

Fig. 8.5 Bar chart (Gantt) schedule.

Project name:	Project number:	Project manager:	
Stage/event	Responsible person:	Date completed:	Page of
	Assigned to:	Activity:	Period ending date:

Fig. 8.6 Activity planning schedule.

should be addressed to the responsible manager, i.e. the person accountable to senior management for the project with a copy going to the acceptor. As such, the report must answer the following questions:

- When will the project be completed?
- What is the current cost estimate to completion?
- Do I (the responsible manager) have to worry about it or are you (the project manager) still looking after it?
- Is any help needed?
- Are there any obstacles to progress that the project manager cannot solve?
- Have there been any changes to the objectives or schedule?

It is the project manager's obligation to prepare this report monthly, or more frequently if specified in the project plan. The responsible manager should review the report and take any appropriate action that is deemed necessary.

8.2.10 Financial Commitment

This is a statement of the current commitment of financial requirements for the total project, as described in an attached cost report. See Fig. 8.8 for an example.

8.2.11 Schedule (Commitment) for Completion

This is a concise statement of the current commitment to the project completion date (by stage and deliverable where appropriate). If there are any changes to the objectives or schedule they must be documented in this section, which may refer to an attached current schedule or report.

Project name:	Project number:	Project manager:	
Report period:	To:	Responsible manager:	

(A) Financial commitment: see cost report

(B) Schedule (commitment) for completion

Stage or milestone	Planned completion date	Stage or milestone	Planned completion date

Accomplishments this period:

Constraints on progress:

Objectives next period:

Fig. 8.7 Project status report.

8.2.12 Accomplishments This Period

This includes milestones met or major accomplishments during the past period. These must be quantifiable items. Items that are almost (say 90%) completed, or about to be completed, should not be included. Specific reference to those objectives accomplished during this period that are outlined in the previous report should be included. State 'Nil' on the report when nothing visible has been accomplished in the project in the past month. There should be no discussion of how or why the time was spent or how much time was spent.

8.2.13 Constraints to Progress

This is the section where the project manager can share the project responsibility with management and other principal characters. Here should be mentioned all the issues, problems and opportunities with which help is needed. Problems already solved or those that are no longer obstacles should not be mentioned. When problems are highlighted, it is a call for help that is saying, 'If you don't help me with these problems, I may not be able to make the commitment', or more subtly, 'If you don't solve this problem, you can have your project back'. All stated problems should be accompanied by a recommended solution. If there is not a recommended solution, then state so but explain why.

When a status report says 'Nil' in this section, the project manager is saying, 'Don't worry about this project, everything is under control – I am handling it'.

8.2.14 Objectives Next Period

The planned accomplishments for the next period that are of interest to the readers of the report should be listed:

- Milestones that fall next month
- Problems that should be resolved. Some of these could be stated in the 'obstacles to progress', so the project manager is saying: 'You should help me with this issue this month'.

The project manager should stick to visible objectives and avoid listing how the project team members are going to spend their time.

A project manager should not have to spend more than one to three hours preparing this report. If it takes longer, there are problems managing the project. However, the extra time would be worthwhile if it helped in getting the project back on-track.

The report should not be cluttered with discussion of how or why time was spent on different activities. It should be concise and factual. There will be an opportunity for discussion at a review meeting with the responsible manager. Problems should not be hidden because the project manager hopes they will go away or thinks that people are too busy to help. They should be brought into the open to give people a chance to help. The report should be submitted to the responsible manager monthly, together with the information or project resource usage. It is important that, as a minimum, both the responsible manager and the project manager review the report in a scheduled meeting and decide upon any action to be taken.

8.2.15 Project Resource Usage

In addition to wanting to know the state of the project deliverables, management are always keen to know the resource expenditure against the deliverables so that they may determine the project's continuing viability. Therefore a cost/person-year (P-Y) report form (Fig. 8.8) is an important systems project management methodology document. In most organizations such a form will already have been designed, possibly as a by-product of a financial cost system. Its purpose is to answer the question for anybody who wishes to ask: 'What is the project's financial or P-Y status?'.

The project manager should analyze this report and use it to communicate monthly to the responsible manager for the project. It highlights the project's financial and person-year status, and encourages the project manager to perform

Project name:		Project number:			From (project manager):	
Report period from:		**To (responsible manager):**				
Note:	1. For chargeback, break down each stage into contract staff, travel, internal staff, equipment and software. 2. For organizational staff, provide a total by stage for each organizational entity.					
Check one:	Cost report: ☐		Person-year report: ☐			
	Current fiscal year 19___/19___					
	(A)	(B)	(C)	Current FY budget	(D)	(E)	(C+D+E)
Deliverable or stage	Actual costs – current month (budget)	Actual costs – year to date (budget)	Estimated remaining costs	Total A+B	Previous years expenditures	Future years estimated expenditures	Estimated project total
Total							
Comments:							

Fig. 8.8 Cost/person-year report.

periodically an accurate review of its financial health. Separate forms should be completed for costs and internal person-years.

The project manager would complete this form or obtain it from finance and ensure that it is circulated monthly to the responsible manager for review. For an example of a typical format, refer to Fig. 8.8. An explanation of how to complete the form follows.

- Check the 'Cost report' box if the report is to be used to record costs attributed to the project. If it is to record internal person-years, check the 'Person year report' box.
- *Current fiscal year 19___/19___*
  Enter the fiscal year for which this portion of the report applies.
- *Actual costs – current month*
  Enter the costs or P-Ys expended in the month for this project (by sub-project or stage). The budgeted amount can be put in brackets underneath the actual.
- *Actual costs – year to date (A)*
  Enter the costs or P-Ys expended to date in the current fiscal year, including the current month amounts (by sub-project or stage).
  The budgeted amount can be put in brackets underneath the actual.
- *Estimated remaining costs (B)*
  Enter the current cost estimate or P-Ys for the work that is yet to be performed on the project in the current fiscal year (by sub-project or stage).
- *Total A+B (C)*
  Enter the estimate of costs or P-Ys for the total work to be performed in the current fiscal year (by sub-project or stage). Add columns A and B to get this total.
- *Current FY budget*
  Enter the current fiscal year approved budget moneys or P-Ys for the project (by sub-project or stage).
- *Previous years expenditures (D)*
  Enter the costs or P-Ys expended for all work performed before the current fiscal year (by sub-project or stage). Current fiscal year amounts must be excluded. This value should only change yearly.
- *Future years estimated expenditures (E)*
  Enter the costs or P-Ys anticipated for all work in future fiscal years (by subject or stage). Current fiscal year amounts must be excluded.
- *Estimated project total (C+D+E)*
  Enter the cost estimate or P-Ys for the total work to be performed in all fiscal years of the project (by sub-project or stage). Add columns C, D and E to get this total.
- *Totals*
  Sum the sub-projects and/or stages for each of the columns.

It should be noted that the current month and the accumulated year to date columns should reflect the actual costs to date. The 'Estimated remaining costs' column, however, is the current best estimate of what is left to do. This should not be determined by starting with an old or original estimate and working backwards.

8.2.16 Change Management

No project is completed without changes being requested. Therefore, to control them a process for initiating a change request and authorization form should be implemented. For good management it is an essential project management methodology document. Its purpose is to answer the question 'How can changes to the users' requirements be managed?'. The objective of such a process is to ensure that changes are made with minimal disruption to the client.

The process of change management provides a formal mechanism for handling changes to deliverables during the project. It ensures that these changes are properly documented and communicated to the relevant people (i.e. visible), and that the end-product description and schedules are modified appropriately. It also provides the justification for amendments to the budget.

The obligation to request a change rests with anybody who perceives a need or problem. The individual would request a change through the acceptor whenever a modification to the end-product description (e.g. specifications) is appropriate.

The project manager would initiate a change request whenever it is observed that modifications are being, or should be, made at the project working level.

The acceptor's responsibility is to decide whether this change is desirable and to discuss its impact on the schedule with the project manager. The project manager would assess the impact of the change on the project schedule and the resources, and update the schedule accordingly.

Both the project manager and the acceptor must agree and authorise the change. If there is any disagreement, it is the responsibility of the Responsible Mana-ger to be the final arbiter.

The acceptor would ensure that the change request and authorization form is completed properly and a copy forwarded to the originator of the request and to the project manager.

It is the project manager's obligation to keep track of all change requests to ensure that proper sign-offs are obtained; to ensure proper flow from individual to individual; and *not* to start any change until an authorization form is obtained. This applies to user requests. Numerous technical changes occur throughout any project, and these should also be documented with a change form for audit and control purposes. In the latter cases, the authorizer can be one of a number of different individuals, depending on what the change will have an impact on. Figures 8.9(a) and (b) provide a format for a change request.

The process uses a two-pronged approach, as described below.

Page 1 – Step 1: Request

The requester should fill in the description of the request and the reason for it, discuss it with the acceptor and then sign and date the form. The acceptor should then authorize the request.

When this is done, the analyst assigned to work on the change should analyze the risk, impact, lead time, documentation, and training required to action the changes, review it with the project manager and, when agreed upon, return the analysis to the acceptor.

(a)

Project name:	Project number:	Project manager:
Title of change request:		**Request number:**
Description of requested change:		
Expected benefits/reason for change:		
Request originated by:	**Signature:**	**Date:**
Estimate of time and cost to analyze this request:		
Project manager:	**Signature:**	**Date:**
Further analysis authorized: Yes ___ **Further analysis rejected:** Yes ___		
Name:	**Signature:**	**Date:**

Fig. 8.9(a) Change request and authorization form. Step 1: request.

Analysis

The analysis should stress impact assessment as a mandatory component. This ensures that the technical completeness and feasibility of the changes are considered. This, as a minimum, should cover:

- Determining the technical risk and impact that will probably occur during and after the changes are implemented. This would cover the probability of success and the difficulty of backing out of the change. Also determined are the effects on the number of users and criticality.
- Determining the levels of testing required.
- Assessing back-out and recovery plans.
- Validating that all technical dependencies and impacts have been identified.
- Evaluating the composite effect of all the changes. The estimated time to apply the change, the level of effort required and the skill set required to effect the change should be covered.

(b)

Proposed solution (anticipated impact on system):

Estimated impact on project (plan, schedule, resources etc.):
The summary results of an analysis should be written in this area and the full analysis attached.

Stage deliverable activity	Elapsed days	Revised completion date	Estimated costs
Total			

Analyzed by:	Signature:		Date:

Project manager:	Signature:		Date:

Change authorized: Yes _____   No _____

If no, explain:

Fig. 8.9(b) Change request and authorization form. Step 2: authorization.

- Determining the amount of documentation that will need to be disseminated to those affected by the change.

When the change has been analyzed, it should be categorized by its characteristics, i.e.:

- *Category 1*
  There is a possibility of a major impact and the change would be visible to all users. It will take a long time to action and backing out once started will be virtually impossible. Because of its size, a high level of resourcing will be required
  Some examples of this type of change are new releases of system and network software and applications; installation of new hardware and upgrades; and environmental changes to electrical and cooling systems and buildings.

- *Category 2*
  A significant impact will be made and visibility is apparent to many users. Further backing out will be an intricate process and time to action the changes will be significant.
  In addition to the examples illustrated in *Category 1*, but to a lesser degree, examples are system generators, JCL changes, hardware moves and recabling, and microcode change.

- *Category 3*
  The change in this category will be visible only to a few, and backing out will be easy. In addition to the examples in Categories 1 and 2, others that belong in Category 3 are enhancements; fixes during maintenance and tuning of the software system; functional enhancements and database changes to the application systems; and engineering changes to hardware.

- *Category 4*
  To fit into this category, the impact will be minimal and changes are a regular day-to-day event. They are the same as for Category 3 except for functional enhancements; specified fixes during maintenance to the software system; and engineering changes. These would automatically put the change in Category 3.

- *Category 5*
  This is an emergency change and is required to fix an existing problem immediately.

Categories 1 and 2 will need a more in-depth analysis and automatically need senior management approval to proceed. However, the other three categories can be handled within a routine procedure. If the acceptor has the authority, and decides the change is desirable and justifiable in time and cost, the request can be authorized. If not, the 'Further analysis rejected' section is completed, giving reasons for rejecting the change. A copy of the form is forwarded to the appropriate people, principally the originator of the request. If the originator does not have the authority, such as in Categories 1 and 2, then it should be passed to senior management for approval. This could be a project review committee.

Page 2 – Step 2: Authorization

After approval of the analysis, the project manager completes the proposed solution (anticipated impact on system) and the 'Estimated impact on project' sections after discussing them with the acceptor. They will jointly decide whether to accept or reject the change.

The acceptor completes the 'Authorized/rejected' section and fills in any comments.

Once the relevant signatures have been obtained, the project manager sends a copy of the form to the acceptor.

8.2.17 Project Review Committee Meetings

In addition to meeting project team members, it is essential that the project manager keeps management informed of the status and financial health of the project. One way to do this is to establish a project review committee and hold regular (monthly) meetings. These meetings are considered essential for managing successful systems development projects. The purpose of these meetings is to answer the question: 'How can I, the project manager, ensure that all senior managers concerned with the project are kept informed about, and are participating in, the project?'. Such meetings ensure a regular forum for the consideration of timely and relevant advice from interested senior managers (PRC members) to the responsible manager (PRC chairperson) and to the project manager on the subject of project progress and problems.

These meetings are not intended to be a forum for reviewing in detail all project deliverables. That is the responsibility of the respective deliverable acceptors, not of the PRC, although a PRC member may also be an acceptor. PRC members will, however, accept the deliverables after assuring themselves that the contents meet specifications, either through verification or, if they so choose, a review, but this is secondary to their main purpose of giving advice to the chairperson and project manager. Note: a project manager is not a member of the committee but reports to it about progress etc.

The responsible manager (project review committee chairperson) is responsible for calling and running the meetings. At the first meeting a regular date for the next 12 months could be agreed upon and recorded in managers' schedules. This will ensure that time is allocated well before other commitments can usurp the meeting. An automated calendaring and scheduling system would help in blocking out the dates for a whole period of time. It is the responsibility of the project manager, on behalf of the responsible manager, to ensure that agendas are prepared and circulated in time for members to review inclusions in the PRC members' briefing manual; to prepare project status presentation materials; and to arrange for meeting minutes to be taken and distributed.

It is the duty of all meeting participants to review all briefing materials for the meeting and to be prepared for serious discussions of agenda items.

PRC meetings should follow a format and be run by the chairperson according to Fig. 8.10, a suggested meeting agenda.

Before the meeting, all documents mentioned in the agenda should be circulated. At the outset of the project, a standard time in each month should be established for the monthly PRC meeting. This time should be close to the beginning of the month so that the project manager's status report to the executive responsible, as of the previous month's end, can form the basis of the presentation to the PRC members at the meeting. If the presentation at the meeting covers a different period to that covered by the status report, confusion will arise over what has been completed and, more importantly, over what is planned for the next period. The meeting should be held each month regardless of whether there are perceived problems or not, so that the project manager can build the confidence of the members towards successful project completion and to avoid the sense that PRC meetings only deal with 'bad news'.

The approach to following the agenda, as structured above, is to gain from the members any advice and assistance in resolving project problems and conflicts. It also serves to remind them of forthcoming project deliverables, major review points and other activities that may make additional demands on their time or on their staff's time. In turn, the members have an opportunity to learn of the state of the

Project name:	
Project review committee meeting number:	
Date, time and place:	
Agenda	**Prime reporter**
1 Approval of previous meeting minutes	Chairperson
2 Progress since previous meeting (planned as of previous meeting and others) 2.1 Completed activities 2.2 Successful activities	Project manager
3 Request for changes impacting schedule and/or cost	Chairperson or project manager
4 Current schedule for remaining work 4.1 Stage level of detail for remainder of project 4.2 Deliverable and sub-deliverable level of detail for remainder of stage	Chairperson or project manager
5 Current cost estimates and budgets	Project manager and others
6 Unresolved issues and obstacles to progress 6.1 Issues outstanding from previous meeting and plans for resolution 6.2 New problems since previous meeting	Chairperson or others
7 Planned progress for next period 7.1 Deliverables to be completed 7.2 Activities to be finalized	Project manager
8 Other business	Others
9 Confirmation of next meeting	Chairperson

Fig. 8.10 A suggested meeting agenda.

project in terms of completion, plans and problems, and they have a chance to raise questions or obtain clarification from the responsible manager or project manager about any aspect of the project. It also provides them with an opportunity to inform the responsible manager and project manager of any upcoming activities, especially within the user organizations, which may have an impact on the progress of the project.

The following is a list to follow of recommended steps for the project manager (or other designated person) on behalf of the PRC chairperson to prepare for and run successfully PRC meetings:

● Prepare monthly status and cost reports and send to responsible manager.
● Discuss status and cost reports with the responsible manager.
● Confirm the time of the meeting and the list of participants with the responsible manager and confirm the room booking. Ensure that any necessary equipment, refreshments and a secretary are arranged. (It is a good idea to check equipment etc. well before the meeting, so that if anything needs changing there is time for it to be done).

- Contact participants for agenda items.
- Confirm agenda with responsible manager.
- Draw up and distribute agenda to participants at least three days before meeting.
- Ensure that all materials for the members' briefing manual are received at least three days before the meeting.
- Prepare presentation materials for items 2–7 on the agenda (flip chart or overhead transparencies suggested).
- Arrange equipment and supplies for meeting.
- Run meeting according to agenda.
- Ensure that minutes of meeting are taken.
- Draft minutes.
- Review minutes with responsible manager and get approval.
- Distribute minutes to attendees and absentees by two days after meeting.

It should be noted that many of the booking and arranging functions might be delegated to a project support officer or a meeting secretary. Items 3, 4, 6, 7, 9, 11, 12, 13 and 14 lend themselves naturally to such delegation.

During the meeting, the following points should be kept in mind by all meeting participants:

- *Agenda item 2*: Progress since previous meeting
  There is only one measure for completion, and that is 100%, with *no more work to be performed*. If it is a deliverable, it is *not* completed until it is *accepted*.
- *Agenda item 3*: Requests for changes impacting schedule and/or costs
  This includes all 'official' change requests documented, as well as unofficial requests made verbally.
- *Agenda item 4*: Current schedule
  This schedule is the current one committed for the work yet to be done. As such, it is the project manager's best estimate of how to get to project completion from the current point in the project, *regardless* of how the current point was reached. This will also discuss significant deviations from the previous month's estimates.
- *Agenda item 5*: Current cost estimates and budgets
  This should be based on the cost report from the project manager and should emphasize the current estimate to completion for the fiscal year. In addition, total project costs should be compared with the current budget.
- *Agenda item 6*: Unresolved issues and obstacles to progress
  This is the opportunity to get help from the members of the committee. As such, it must address any difficulties that have arisen which may have an impact on the progress or success of the project. For example, delays in obtaining project staff or other resources would affect the project. Delays may also be caused by users in providing information or assistance to the project; disagreements on assistance to the project; disagreements among participants about the scope, objectives or other aspects of project; etc.

  For each of these perceived problems, a solution should also be provided. If you cannot think of one, say so and ask for direction.

- *Agenda item 7*: Planned progress
  The planned progress should be related to completion (again 100% *only*), and should highlight planned acceptance of deliverables. It should correspond to the project manager's status report.
- *Agenda note*: Documents to be reviewed prior to meetings
  These should have been made available with sufficient lead time to ensure a healthy, meaningful, responsible discussion at the meeting.

Minutes should be recorded for audit and record purposes. A useful format is the meeting minutes form. This is an optional systems project management methodology document whose purpose is to answer the question: 'How can important decisions taken and key events that take place in project meetings be recorded?'.

Minutes record the decisions taken during project meetings and the responsibilities assigned for follow-up action. This will ensure that all relevant issues are 'made visible' to all concerned and that all individuals involved have a common understanding of what took place and who is responsible for what.

It is the obligation of the project manager to identify the situation in which minutes should be recorded and to ensure that an individual is assigned to this task. Subsequently it is this individual's responsibility to review them with the chairperson of the meeting and get them signed. The individual is obliged to ensure that copies are circulated to all attendees, invitees, project staff and other involved individuals. A suggested format is shown in Fig. 8.11.

The intent of the minutes is only to record the decisions affecting the project and commitments for follow-up results. It is not intended to be a record of each word and point made.

The form should be used as a front page only. Subsequent pages can be blank paper following the format of the bottom half of the form.

It is recommended that each meeting be numbered and that each minute be sequenced within the meeting number, e.g. '5 – 16' indicates meeting number 5, minute 16. This will ensure that each point can be uniquely identified throughout the project.

Project name:	Project number:		Project manager:
Topic of meeting:		Approved:	
Date:		Time:	
Present:			
Absent:			
Minute	Minute narrative		Action responsible person

Fig. 8.11 Meeting minutes form.

We have emphasized the fact that good communication is one of the essential ingredients of successful implementation of projects. It has also been pointed out that there is a paradigm developing in the management of projects. To reiterate what was said in the Preface: 'An example of how a global project was managed is one in which Malaysia's International Shipping Corporation (MISC) implemented MISC*Net, a networking project to link online all of its shipping agents worldwide to its HQ in Malaysia. Project management was a key component in the solution prior to awarding the contract. IBM and MISC worked on the International Project Management System. Project specialists got feedback daily, and if a partner from the other side of the world did something, all that was required was to update the work status on one terminal for all to be aware of it being actioned'.

Two products, Microsoft Project 98 and the Java-based WebProject, allow use of the Internet. Project 98 allows the communication of project information to every team member through the use of any MAPI-compliant email system. Assignments can be given to team members and they can report as required on the status of their tasks and automatically update the project plan. It is also easy to publish schedule information and, using hyperlinks, obtain information from sources other than Project 98. For more information go to `http://www.microsoft.com/project/learn/whatsnew/`.

WebProject is a Java thin client application that uses a three-tier client–server model to utilize the Internet effectively (Fig. 8.12). We will provide a simple overview to illustrate its main functionality. Simply stated, it is a project management tool that empowers distributed teams to collaborate on projects, share job know-how and synchronize the actions of the project team. The planning and managing of projects with their strict deadlines and constraints is simple and easy. Of course, this is only

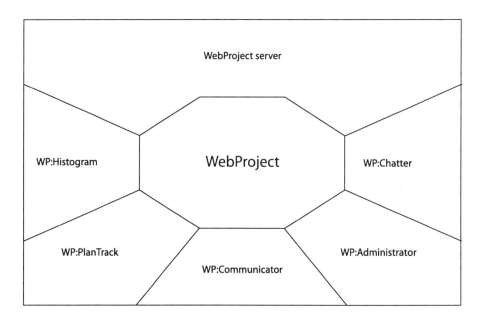

Fig. 8.12 WebProject.

Please enter your User Name and Password:

Name: [   ]   Password: [   ]

and click a button below to start:

| PlanTrack | Communicator | Histogram | Chatter | Administrator |

Not connected to WebProject:Server.

Fig. 8.13

simple and easy if one knows how to plan and manage; the software cannot do these for you.

The sign-on is simple and access to the five major components is illustrated in Fig. 8.13. As can be seen, the interface is clean and requires minimal machine-user interaction.

New projects can be defined and resources assigned to tasks over the Web (Fig. 8.14). Using 'Tracker', you can track your projects from anywhere in the world. From the screen shown in Fig. 8.14, you can quickly see that the planned estimate of 32.0h for 'Requirements' is verified, i.e. 8.0h has actually been used with 24h remaining. It is simple to view which projects and tasks team members are assigned to and how much time they are to spend working on tasks, even across multiple projects. Actual hours spent on tasks are recorded in an intuitive bar chart–spreadsheet combination. These are submitted to a database to be approved or rejected by a manager, i.e. this a paperless environment.

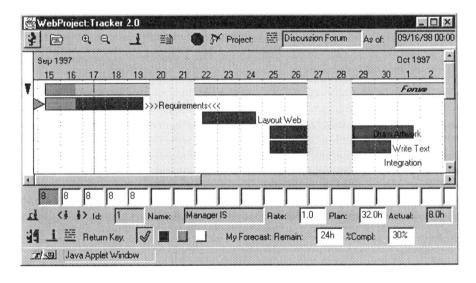

Fig. 8.14

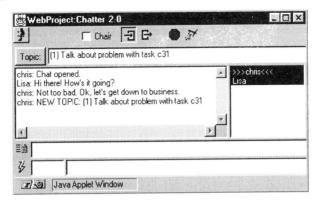

Fig. 8.15

Whereas it used to be necessary to congregate in a project room or hold conference calls to learn about the status or issues of a project, it is now easy to hold a virtual project status meeting through WebProject Chatter (Fig. 8.15). Essential team members can participate in discussions on task-related problems and issues on a task-by-task basis. You can create a virtual 24-hour day, with efficient communication independent of geographic location.

A project pinboard (Fig. 8.16), lets project team members post important notes for all to see and discuss. For example, a pinboard could be used to post an agenda for project status charts.

Another important feature is the ability to view resource availability and usage in intuitive histograms (Fig. 8.17). You can view the planned and actual workload and the availability of your resources with a click of the mouse. You will know whether you have the capacity to take on that extra project. Using simple project and resource filters, you can select exactly the data you want to see.

It is simple to integrate with other project management software, such as Scitor Project Scheduler or Microsoft Project Scheduler, and WebProject can connect to any major database server through JDBC (Fig. 8.18). In addition, it is possible to export and import project data to and from MPX format files and Microsoft Project database tables. As can be below, the screen is a simple view of active and MPX projects.

Project Pinboard and Task Discussion for: Layout Web

Pinboard: Delete | Vote | Add

chris (1) Discuss problem with TS54
Lisa (1) Text needs for more links to www
chris (1) Another pin board topic

08/25/97 (chris): We'll have to change page 32
08/25/97 (chris): That's right, but don't forget image 23b
08/25/97 (Lisa): I need more images!

Message: Delete | Read | Answer | Add   Close

Fig. 8.16

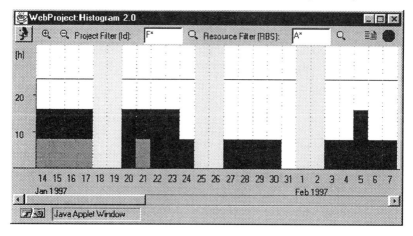

Fig. 8.17

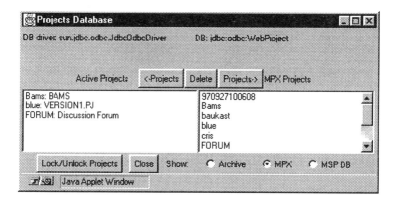

Fig. 8.18

As the Web becomes ubiquitous, so will its use by managers. Moreover, *as the paradigm of technology is evolving, so is the paradigm of project management.*

8.3 Summary

Although this chapter has gone into specifics about the completion of forms (automated and manual) it should be understood that the intent is to enunciate the requirements of a good methodology. The cookbook approach can be developed by any organization to suit its environment and culture. Blindly following and applying the principles outlined can court disaster. As all managers control and approach their jobs differently, so they should evolve their own workable controls. The methodology in this chapter will not infringe upon this prerogative of management. However, using the forms as a checklist and as a method of communication can prove to be invaluable. Further, automating the forms and reports can be a very effective method of storage and retrieval.

We have introduced the concept of change using the Web. It can easily be seen how this can save on travel time, and creatively used, how it can help everybody view information at a time and place convenient to themselves.

The next chapter will cover the completion activities that are necessary to ensure that the project loop is closed. It too follows a cookbook approach, and the comments above will apply.

9. *Project and Stage Completion Activities*

9.1 Introduction

In previous chapters we have explored how to initiate a project; how to control its progress; how quality management and testing subscribe to quality deliverables; and how a project team should be organized. Thus we were exposed to *how* to manage a project, and by linking this to the systems development life cycle we learned *what* is managed in a systematic way.

By using experience and instinct, together with methodologies, a project manager will know when a project or stage is complete. However, it is appropriate to ensure that all interested parties in the outcome are cognizant that the project or a stage completion has been accomplished. In addition to these parties being aware of completion, it is also an integral part of any process to ensure that they approve of what has been delivered.

Getting the project completed is the whole thing. Any project management process must provide guidelines for management of product acceptance and project sign-off. Therefore it is important to communicate the project goal and to cultivate the necessary acceptor confidence. It is not sufficient to indicate progress by giving a 'percentage complete' figure.

There are several valid reasons why the completion phase of a systems implementation project is reputed to be the hardest. Here are some of them:

- Often both user and implementation team personnel spend excessive time in the completion phase because they are not sure how to recognize when the job is done.
- Since the final acceptance is crucial, all the mistakes or uncontrolled activities throughout the project become part of a 'clean-up' job.
- Too often the project time and effort required to progress from 80% completion to 100% completion turns out to be 100% or 200%, and even then there is no time for documentation.
- Some development projects never get finished – because the development team, or part of it, is required to keep the system operational.

Other than legitimate reasons for delay in completing a project, a review of the above points will reveal that the completion phase is only difficult if the project manager has been deficient in:

- project identification
- project planning
- project control

The importance of planning stands out particularly in this analysis. Obviously, the first and most important project step is to *plan for project completion*, i.e.

1 How will it be recognized that the project is finished?
2 What is the objective?

The next most obvious planning requirement is *documentation*. What information do we need, and in what format, to recognize that the job is complete? This section outlines some standards and procedures to practice to ensure that the product will be accepted and also that acceptance is visible and understood to be the completion of any contractual commitment. On a continuing basis it is also important that progress towards completion is visible and that the acceptor gains confidence in the product through the completion phase.

9.2 The Activities

9.2.1 Visible Goal

First, the goal must be made visible. The signature of the acceptor on the acceptance document first shown in the project plan is the visible product. There may be several concrete items or various documents (as identified in the SDLC accompanying this acceptance as part of the product), such as:

- Acceptance test documentation
- Systems test documentation
- Systems documentation
- Program documentation
- Operations documentation
- User manuals
- Training manuals

These must be identified in the project plan in the deliverable acceptance matrix (Figs. 9.1(a) and (b)). The acceptor's signature, nevertheless, is the completion event. If the acceptance document is not signed, the job is not done.

9.2.2 Visible Progress Towards Goal

If the unsigned acceptance document is made visible, signifying that completion has not taken place, how do we answer the question 'How close is completion?'. If we do not visibly communicate the answers to this question, we will fail in two ways.

First, we will miss the opportunity to cultivate a feeling of confidence in the acceptor. If the acceptor is continually exposed to visible progress towards the goal in

(a)

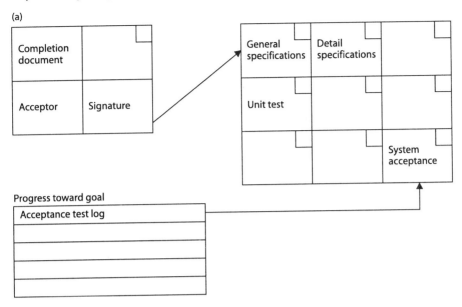

Progress toward goal

Acceptance test log

(b)

Project name:		Project number:		Project manager:	
Deliverable	Planned completion date	Acceptor	Signature	Date	
Acceptance test documentation					
Systems test documentation					
Systems documentation					
Program documentation					
Operations documentation					
User manuals					
Training manuals					

Fig. 9.1

the finishing stages, then increasingly confidence will mount and the exercising of acceptance will be easier to accomplish.

Second, the project team must all see the goal; their ability to work towards the goal will be enhanced by witnessing the progress towards its end.

The project manager therefore communicates the progress towards the goal of completion. One way is to establish a deliverable acceptance matrix/completion grid, i.e. a list of deliverables representing completion. Each of the items on this list can be further broken down into sub-deliverables. The completion of each sub-deliverable shows the progress towards the deliverable. The status information of this grid is represented only in yes or no terms by a signature. That is, a deliverable is either completed or not completed. The level of nesting should be such as to provide the necessary visibility of progress to build confidence for the acceptor and direction for the project team. The project completion forms in this chapter, when completed, ensure this by providing a standard that enables the project manager to answer the questions below. These must be asked at the completion stage of the project in order for the project manager to complete his or her commitment and to be relieved of the project responsibility:

- *Is the project or stage completed?*
  The project or stage completion form, when signed first by the acceptor and then completed by other interested parties, will signify *yes*.
- *Is the deliverable complete?*
  The deliverable acceptance form will signify *yes* if it is completed and signed by the acceptor or a member of the acceptance team.
- *How can the results of the project or stage be summarized and communicated?*
  By completing a stage summary report the visibility of what has been completed in the stage will be raised. This helps build acceptor confidence to get project or stage acceptance.
- *How can the resource managers be informed of the performance of team members?*
  A completed performance review memorandum will provide input to the employee appraisal process. It also completes the project manager's responsibilities to resource managers for this project.

9.2.3 Project Stage Deliverable Completion (Checklist)

This is concerned with completing deliverables, project stages or the entire project and turning it over to the client. It provides guidelines for ensuring that product acceptance and project or stage completion steps are visible and acknowledged by all involved.

The project manager may delegate some responsibilities to the stage coordinator or other members of the team. Figure 9.2 outlines the tasks that should be performed for each deliverable.

The tasks (Fig. 9.3), should be performed for each stage, and for the project as a whole:

Responsibility	Action	Form
Project manager or delegate	Asks for recommendation for deliverable acceptance from deliverable recommenders	Deliverable acceptance form
Deliverable recommenders	Recommends deliverable acceptance to deliverable acceptor	
Project manager or delegate	Asks for deliverable acceptance from deliverable acceptor	
Deliverable acceptor	Accepts deliverable by signing deliverable acceptance form	

Fig. 9.2 Project or stage deliverable completion checklist.

Responsibility	Action	Form
Project manager or delegate	Prepares a project or stage completion report	Project or stage completion report
	Asks for recommendation of project or stage completion from project review committee members	
Project review committee member	Recommends project or stage completion by signing the project or stage completion form	
Project manager	Asks for acceptance of project or stage completion form from acceptor	
	Accepts project or stage completion by signing project or stage completion form	
Project manager	Completes team member performance review with team member and documents it in a memorandum	Performance review memorandum
	Sends performance review memorandum to team member's resource manager	

Fig. 9.3 Project or stage deliverable completion checklist.

9.2.4 Project or Stage Completion

The process to be followed to ensure that all parties accept that the end has occurred is for a project stage completion form to be completed. The *purpose* of this form is to answer the question 'Is the project or stage completed?'. It provides a formal mechanism to communicate to all participants the completion of each project, sub-project or stage, and acceptance of responsibility for the results by the acceptor.

It is the responsibility of the project manager to obtain the acceptor's signature on this document as well as the signatures of those who will recommend acceptance. The acceptor signs the document once he or she is confident enough to accept responsibility for the project's results and to inform the appropriate user staff that the project stage is complete. Figure 9.4 is a suggested format.

The *approach* for the project manager to obtain the acceptor's signature on this document is to work closely together. This should be from the time that the unsigned document is first displayed in the project plan through to project completion, which is signified by acceptance of responsibility for the project's results by the acceptor.

Throughout the project, the project manager should strive to ensure that the acceptor has all the information required to accept the end product when it is fully developed. This is a process of managing expectations. It can be described as a strategy of 'no surprises'. The objective is for the acceptor to get what has been expected.

In practice, a formal presentation by the acceptor, or project manager, of the results to an acceptance team and/or the project review committee may be necessary to satisfy other users who may be affected by the deliverables of the project before the acceptor is in a confident position to sign. This document should be circulated with the project or stage completion report.

Project name:	Project number:	Project manager:	
All work for this project/stage has been completed to my satisfaction. I therefore recommend that the results of this stage be accepted.			
Name	Position	Signature	Date
I accept full responsibility for this project/stage, and recognize it as complete.			
Observations/comments:			
Name	Position	Signature	Date

Fig. 9.4 Project or stage completion report.

9.2.5 Deliverable Completion

In addition to project or stage completion there are innumerable deliverables that get completed. Therefore ensuring that a deliverable acceptance form is completed will answer the question 'Is the deliverable complete?'. It provides a formal mechanism to communicate the completion of a project product and the transfer of the responsibility for the product from the project manager to the deliverable acceptor. Another benefit is that it shows the progress towards project completion and cultivates acceptor confidence through the acceptance of regular deliverables throughout the project. The acceptor's responsibility is to sign this document or to delegate it to a member of the acceptance team.

The project manager's responsibility is to ensure that the form is signed by the deliverable acceptor, as well as by those who will recommend acceptance, or to delegate that responsibility to a member of the project delivery team. The project manager must also provide any assistance or information that the acceptor requires to accept responsibility for the product. When satisfied with the product, the acceptor would inform the appropriate functional units that the product has been completed.

In order for the project manager or delegate to obtain the acceptor's or delegate's signature on this document, they must work closely together. This participation starts from the time that the deliverable is first identified in the deliverable acceptance matrix through to successful product completion, which is signified by acceptance of responsibility for the deliverable by the acceptor.

A suggested format for deliverable acceptance is illustrated in Fig. 9.5.

Project name:	Project number:	Project manager:			
Description of deliverable or product:					
I have reviewed the deliverable (product) and accept that it satisfies my requirements according to the specifications. I therefore recommend that it be accepted.					
Format and level of detail:					
Name	Position	Signature	Date	Comments attached: yes or no	
Content:					
Name	Position	Signature	Date	Comments attached: yes or no	
I accept responsibility for this deliverable:					
Name	Position	Signature	Date	Comments attached: yes or no	

Fig. 9.5 Deliverable acceptance.

9.2.6 Stage Completion Report

In addition to completing a stage completion form it is integral to good communications that a report be written on completion of a stage. Its *purpose* is to answer the question: 'How can the results of the project or stage be made known to all interested parties?'. Such a report will help build acceptor and management confidence in getting project or stage acceptance.

The project manager has the *responsibility* to produce this report and circulate it to the members of the project review committee.

PRC members review the report before their next meeting so that they are in a confident position to recommend project or stage completion acceptance to the chairperson. The chairperson also reviews the report as the responsible manager and decides whether to accept the project or stage completion based on the report's contents and input from the PRC members.

Figure 9.6 is a suggested format for the report.

Section 1.0: Purpose of report
Provide information to obtain stage completion acceptance.
Release project managers of all delivery responsibilities for the stage.
Ask for sign-off of project or stage completion form (attached to report).

Section 2.0: Summary
A statement of what happened during the stage, including:
- startup and completion activities
- who did what and when
- a summary of significant findings and analyses
- a description of problems encountered and resolved

Section 3.0: Deliverables summary
A description of deliverables, who accepted them, who recommended acceptance, and the acceptance dates for all stage deliverables.

Section 4.0: Costs
These should be compared with the budgeted amount.

Section 4.1: Person years
A recording by skill type (job classification) of individual staff, both internal and contract personnel, including both delivery and acceptance team and project review committee staff members.

Section 4.2: Operating moneys
A recording by expenditure type (contract costs, computer cost, testing, training, travel and living expenses, others) of all moneys spent on the stage by fiscal year.

Section 5.0: Updated project plan
This consists of a revised plan for the major deliverable or stage level for the remainder of the project.

Section 6.0: Recommendations
Ask the acceptor to accept the stage as being completed.

Fig. 9.6 Stage completion report.

In approaching the writing of this report it is well to remember that the contents should be a surprise to absolutely *no one*, since the contents should continually be made visible throughout the stage. It should summarize the stage and instill confidence in the acceptor to accept responsibility for the stage's results and therefore allow the project to proceed to the next stage. The project or stage completion form should be included in the report.

9.2.7 Performance Review

At the conclusion of a stage or deliverable a performance review memorandum may be in order. This memorandum is an optional systems project management methodology document that may, however, at the discretion of the resource manager, be required. It serves as notice of the culmination of a review process started when a team member was first assigned to the project. To reiterate: the resource manager when assigning a team member should have arranged a contract with the project manager, establishing goals for the employee in quantitative and qualitative terms.

The *purpose* of this memorandum is to answer the question 'How can I let the resource managers know the performance of my team members?'. It provides an essential input of the annual appraisal of staff assigned to the team.

It is the resource manager's responsibility to request a performance review for the team members assigned to the team. Upon such a request, it is the project manager's responsibility to provide a serious appraisal of the team member in conjunction with the team member. Should the memorandum not be requested, the reason for this should be discussed with the appropriate manager.

The review should be documented in the format desired by the resource manager. However, a suggested approach is the preparation of a memorandum covering the following points:

- A description of the employee's responsibilities, goals etc.
- A description of the degree of attainment of each responsibility, including substantiating information. An explanation should be included when unavoidable factors have affected achievement.
- An assessment of overall performance, as well as quality of work and managerial performance (if applicable).
- An assessment of skills, abilities and personal suitability.
- An assessment of the individual's career potential and required training.
- Although this review is done according to the wishes of the resource manager, the team member should participate by reviewing it and commenting on it *before* it goes to the resource manager.

9.3 Summary

Signing off on a project signifies its end, and the project team may be disbanded. Completing the deliverable forms in this chapter concludes the full project management methodology. The components covered have included planning, organizing, quality management and the controlling of projects. The emphasis has been on systems projects, but the principles are useful for consideration in any project.

Summary

In a perfect world there would be only perfect employers who provide the perfect work environment for perfect employees who perform their jobs perfectly. The real world is far from this utopian vision. Therefore this book helps resolve the problems of employees not knowing what to do and employers not knowing what to expect from projects. It therefore shows how to get the job done. The author, an international consultant, uses the book as a tool in developing nations, where, in many cases, training is a low priority.

The book has covered a project management methodology and explained the management of the deliverables as outlined in a systems development life cycle. Linked to these is the quality management function, which is necessary to ensure quality deliverables and that value for money expended is obtained. True improvements in quality will only be realized when automation is applied to test planning, design, execution and management/analysis, with the support of a common test repository. A key to success is to make all automated tool and implementation decisions in relation to an overall testing model.

The book has been constructed logically. The preface assesses why there is a need for methodologies and highlights the fact that considerable changes are taking place that need to be managed through standards. Chapter 1 explains the philosophy of project management and introduces the concept of change and situation analysis. Chapter 2 outlines the elements of the project management methodology, i.e. the skills and commitment of project team members. This is followed by a heavy emphasis on quality management (Chapter 3), especially the different testing approaches. Automated testing and its appropriateness in a complex development environment are also explained. It is explained that it is essential in a client–server and GUI environment. Chapter 4 links the SDLC to the project management methodology, namely initiation, planning, control and deliverables. Having described an infrastructure, the roles and responsibilities of the individuals who would contribute to the success of a project were highlighted in Chapter 5. Subsequently, Chapter 6 described the activities required to initiate a project and to estimate its duration and costing. In Chapter 7 the tools (forms) used in the process were illustrated and their uses explained. It was also explained that understanding resource levelling was especially important because of the fact that different results could be calculated for the same project. The next two chapters, 8 and 9, explain how to control a project and what activities are required to ensure that all interested parties have accepted the deliverable(s).

Undoubtedly the book has been formal (rigid) in many places. This is unfortunately necessary to illustrate the point that administering a process is a procedural approach that is essential if an organization wants users and project staff to reap the gratification of delivering a quality product on time and within budget. Development of any product can only succeed if the process is properly managed. There is no one approach that will guarantee this. Even under the best possible circumstances many things go wrong. However, linking quality management and metrics with the methodologies is integral to reaping the benefits of standards and procedures. The treatment of project team members in a manner similar to that accorded to programmers in 'egoless programming' will assist in getting the best out of the team as a whole. Much of this will rest on the abilities of the project manager, with, of course, management's support.

A project management methodology (PMM) enables a project manager to manage each stage of the systems development life cycle (SDLC) in a natural progression. Henri Fayol's model, developed in 1916, is still a valid statement of the managers' and project team members' roles, as illustrated (slightly modified) in Fig. S.1. The 'deliverables' in the model can represent those produced from following an SDLC. There are numerous methodologies available, with various strengths and weaknesses. Many of them concentrate on one aspect, such as design and development; development in a data sharing environment; requirements specifications; or modelling parts of development.

CASE tools, although automating many of the functions of the systems development life cycle cannot replace the written word in explaining the who, what, why, when and where. We are currently going through a change to development using CASE. This is an integrated toolset that is automating many of the systems development functions. Not all organizations can afford CASE. Irrespective of this, there will always be a need for the written word to explain the principles etc. behind the tool. The use of CASE will entail a technology transfer and it will be important to ensure there is an implementation life cycle that is project managed to ensure success. One component of this life cycle is education. It will be necessary to conduct methodology training using different approaches, e.g. classroom, video, computer-based training, coaching and multimedia to prepare properly for the change.

Project management software does not negate the usefulness of a methodology. In common with construction supervisors and engineers, informatics professionals work on projects. Such software can assist a project manager considerably and complement the methodology.

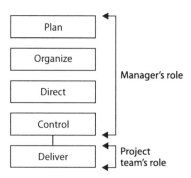

Fig. S.1 Henri Fayol's model of roles.

Much emphasis has been placed on the motivation and commitment of individuals. This is the backbone of any success in delivering quality products on time and within budgets. Managers should experiment with 'worker empowerment' as much as possible. This essentially means spreading decision-making and sharing responsibility. This should give workers a better sense of belonging and of being a participant in what happens. If a project team lacks motivation or commitment, or has structural problems with people, then the project is doomed to failure. Valuing employees will go a long way towards motivating staff. Commitment can be fostered by letting employees know up-front whether the project will require 10%, 20%, 30%, ..., 100% of their time, as well as the priority of the project.

In this book the methodology and the people working with it are given wide visibility. When organizing for a project, compromises must be made, and the personal qualifications and aspirations of the individual play an important part. In making compromises, however, it is desirable that the task shall not be one of making A responsible for the actions of B, C and D, but of linking all the activities that logically should be placed under a unified control. In his book *Managing the Structured Technology*, Ed Yourdon states:

> Something happened to the personality and mentality of the data processing profession as a whole as we moved to the ultrasophisticated on-line, real-time, fourth generation and fifth-generation machines of the 1980s. The profession began to attract people who are clerks. They think like clerks, and they approach computer programming and systems analysis with all the enthusiasm of a sleepy civil service clerk who knows that he is just one year away from retirement. When such programmers and systems analysts are forced to learn structured programming, structured design, top-down implementation and structured analysis, a frightening large number of them are unable to learn them. It is literally all they can do to write programs in a helter-skelter fashion to which they have become accustomed. To suggest that they should introduce some organization, some common sense, some structure into their work is beyond their ken.

This is very harsh on them and applies as well to many other individuals. There are many good clerks and civil (public) servants. However, the message is worth repeating to the extent that there are numerous individuals who lack the appropriate training, skills and aptitude to be in the profession or in the subset that they practice. Even with excellent qualifications, the pretty box may still be empty without experience coupled with commitment and motivation. The message should also be taken to heart, as the problem of inexperience is now becoming worse with the shortage of staff, due in part to the proliferation of personal computers and easy to use software. Thus it can be seen that some of the most important factors for future success will be education and training, coupled with experience. They must go hand in hand. The author believes that a properly motivated workforce will gladly take training and education in its own time if necessary as long as the rewards merit the effort. This can be seen in the highly successful Higher National Certificate programs in the UK and the Work Programs in North America. Therefore, as this book points out, motivating, obtaining commitment and monitoring progress, together with appropriate planning and control, will go a long way towards producing quality deliverables. The paradigm of development with no-touch code or automated testing will also help in this regard. However, this must be approached with caution because of the problem of what or who verifies the output (i.e. proves that the resulting deliverable is correct). A classic court case in Britain emphasizes the point. The Viper (Verifiable Integrated Processor for Enhanced Reliability) project claimed that its microprocessor design was mathematically provable. Although no bugs have ever been found, and for all practical purposes it has been considered to be bug-free, it could not be proven.

There is a need to approach projects in a systematic way. The effort of this book is to unify technical and managerial methods, i.e. to form a methodology. The purpose is to provide a coherent methodology that covers the whole development life cycle. CASE is being touted as the new way to develop systems. However, other components are also becoming important, such as object-oriented programming, super smart cards with biometrics and multimedia. As these unfold, there will still be many businesses who are not large enough or where new technology is inappropriate to warrant the investment. They will continue using old and tried methods, whereas the larger companies who can afford it will adopt the new paradigm of marrying old methodologies into an automated environment.

We are seeing paradigm shifts to electronic government, electronic commerce, biometrics, telemedicine, smart cards, reengineering, client–server architectures, multimedia, multidimensional databases, downsizing–rightsizing, outsourcing, enterprise-wide networking, asynchronous transfer mode (ATM), cell relay, frame relay, groupware, office automation and so on. All of these need project managing and standards. The paradigm change of using the Net to control a project, e.g. via WebPRoject, is a major advance from having captive project teams. It may be concluded that a project is easy to manage, i.e. all that need to happen is to produce the specified requirements within the planned time frame and budget. John Shelton, a senior project manager with DEC in the UK is quoted as saying: 'The universal truth of project management is that it's difficult, and anyone who tells you otherwise is a liar'. This statement should not negate the positive point that many projects are successful, and it is perhaps the large ones that get the press when in trouble. However, the many issues that arise during any project can be minimized by:

- Ensuring that the project is initiated properly with appropriate attention to functional specification and commitment of management.
- Spending time planning and then doing more planning before starting a project and breaking its deliverables down into the smallest component parts, or even into smaller projects.
- Assigning a senior executive with some power to be the champion of the project and chairperson of a review committee.
- Finding a project manager with a mix of technical, interpersonal and conceptual skills, with a bias toward the conceptual skills. Don't give a mission-critical system project to a junior staff member on a sink-or-swim basis.
- Assigning members to the team because the project is a challenge to them and obtains their commitment. Make sure the team is balanced and qualified.
- Ensuring that a project management methodology and systems development life cycle are followed rigorously, using the principles of communication, quality control, participation, discrete deliverables and sign-offs.
- Following the principles of a joint application development (JAD) or joint application requirements approach in getting user participation.

- Testing the system fully and thoroughly, and not trying to implement prematurely because it will look bad to go over the deadline. Ensure that a change control procedure is in place.
- Letting professionals (educational technologists) develop training packages using good documentation as the basis. Consider training in-house staff as trainers so that ongoing training can be given at minimal cost and on an as-required or regular basis.
- Keeping informatics staff trained in the use of up-to-date tools by providing appropriate training.

If an organization does not have standards, then this book can be used as the basis for developing some. In the future, many existing methodologies will be modified or supplanted by those based upon different concepts. As better ones emerge, probably in the CASE arena, they should lead to a small set yielding standardized forms of work products.

There are numerous other methodologies, such as Hoskyn's prism, than the ones illustrated in this book. However, if a different model is already being used in an organization, then this book can be used for comparative purposes. If an organization does not have standards, then this book can be used as the basis for developing some. The process of creating deliverables through a structured methodology can sometimes be a waste of time. Rapid prototyping and following an evolutionary path can be a quick way to show results. This can be a satisfactory process if the changes can be kept in balance through procedures that ensure that like changes are grouped for action at the same time. Such an approach depends upon speed, getting started and keeping rolling and being flexible enough to change at will. Large cumbersome methodologies fit only a certain size of project. However, projects must still be initiated, planned, created, evaluated and improved. This book illustrates a middle of the road methodology. Masses of paperwork are not generated, and functions that are unnecessary are discouraged. Although a methodology does not give new insight, if it comes from outside an organization there is no bias relative to the viewer and therefore can be considered objective. The results of using the principles and guidelines in this book should therefore go a long way towards successful project management and the production of quality deliverables. Also it should stimulate thought on other aspects that may have been touched on lightly.

This book has depicted how to get the job done by working hard and smart, by being flexible and practical, and by working together as a dedicated loyal team for the good of the whole, i.e. shooting for effectiveness. The approach to emphasize is that teams are becoming a reality, with the shift from tackling a solution from a project management point of view (i.e. inward-looking) to one of forming teams, consortia and alliances to ensure that a best solution is provided, as opposed to the best management. The critical success factors in a systems development project are a good project management methodology that is used to manage the stages of a systems development life cycle; quality management; commitment; and empowerment of the individuals.

If you have any comments or suggested improvements, the author may be reached at burnett-ken@usa.net.

References

Abdel-Hamid, T.K. and Madnick, S.E. (1990) *Software Project Management.* Englewood Cliffs NJ: Prentice Hall.

American Society for Quality Control – Cost Effectiveness Committee (1971) *Quality Costs – What & How,* 2nd edn. Milwaukee.

American Society for Quality Control – Cost Effectiveness Committee (1977). *Guide for Reducing Quality Costs.* Milwaukee.

Asner, M. (1990) *Up Your Computer.* Reston VA: Reston Publishing.

Association for Systems Management (1976) *Peopleware in Systems.* Cleveland OH.

Barnett, A. *Effective Data Systems Development.* Maryland: Barnett Data Systems.

Bennis, W.G. (1966) *Changing Organizations.* New York: McGraw-Hill.

Boehm, B.W. (1981) *Software Engineering Economics.* Englewood Cliffs NJ: Prentice Hall.

Boehm, B.W., McClean, R.K. and Urfrig, D.B. (1975) Some experience with automated aids to design of large-scale reliable software. *IEEE Transactions on Software Engineering,* SE-1, 125–33.

Burrill, C.W. and Ellsworth, L.W. (1983) *Quality Data Processing: The Profit Potential.* Tenafly NJ: Burrill-Ellsworth Associates.

Cotter, R.D. (1984) *Quality Control in Systems Development.* Pennsauken NJ: Auerbach Publishers.

Crosby, P.B. (1979) *Quality is Free.* New York: New American Library.

Crouse, R.L. (1984) The information center is the productivity center. *Technical Report TR 19.90204.* Essex Junction VT: IBM.

Crouse, R.L. (1985) Staffing the information center. *Information Center* 1(1), 42–6.

Date, C.J. (1981) *An Introduction to Database Systems.* New York: Addison-Wesley, p. 214.

Date, C.J. (1984) *INFO IMS,* second quarter, p. 27.

De Marco, T. *Controlling Software Projects. Management Measurement & Estimation.* New York NY: Yourdon Press.

Desanctis, G. and Courtney, J. (1983) Towards friendly user MIS implementation. *Communications of the ACM,* October.

GUIDE International. *Estimating Using Function Points.* GUIDE Publication GPP-134, Chicago IL.

Fayol, H. (1949) *Industrial and General Administration* (transl. C. Storrs). New York: Pitman.

Freedman, D.P. and Weinberg, G.M. (1982) *Handbook of Walkthroughs, Inspections and Technical Reviews.* Boston MA: Little, Brown.

Fujii, M.S. (1977) Independent verification of highly reliable programs. *Proceedings of COMPSAC 77.* Chicago: IEEE, pp. 38–44.

Hall, D.M. *Management of Human Systems.* Association for Systems Management.

Hall, E. (1989) Project control. *Direct Access,* 1 September.

Harvard Business Review *Performance Appraisal.* Cambridge MA: Harvard Business Review.

Hinton, B.L. An empirical investigation of the Herzberg methodology and two factor theory. *Organizational Behaviour and Human Performance.*

Howden, W.E. (1978) A survey of static analysis methods, in *Software Testing and Validation Techniques* (eds W.E. Howden and E. Miller). New York: IEEE Computer Society, pp. 82–96.

Howell and Teichroew *Mathematical Analysis for Business Decisions.* Illinois: Richard D. Irwin Inc.

Hughes, C.T. and Clark, J. (1990) Stages of case usage. *Datamation,* 1 February.

IBM (1984) *Managing End-User Computing.* White Plains NY: IBM.

Information Systems Design Methodologies (1983) Proceedings of the IFIPWG8.1 Working Conference on Future Analysis of Information Systems Design Methodologies. York, UK, 5–7 July.

Jones, C. (1991) *Applied Software Measurement: Assuring Productivity and Quality.* New York: McGraw-Hill.

Juran, J.M. (1974) *Quality Control Handbook,* 3rd edn. New York: McGraw-Hill.

Kast, F.E. and Rosenzweig, J.E. (1970) *Organization and Management: A Systems Approach.* New York: McGraw-Hill.

Kerzner, H. (1979) *Project Management: A Systems Approach to Planning, Scheduling and Controlling.* New York: Van Nostrand Reinhold.

Kidder, T. (1981) *The Soul of a New Machine.* Boston: Atlantic Monthly/Little, Brown.

Kouzes, J.M. and Posner, B.Z. (1989) *The Leadership Challenge: How to Get Extraordinary Things Done in Organizations.* San Francisco: Jossey-Bass.

Krauss, L.I. *Administering and Controlling the Company Data Processing Function.* Englewood Cliffs NJ: Prentice Hall.

Kroenke, D.M. *Database Processing: Fundamentals, Design, Implementation,* 2nd edn. Chicago: Science Research Associates.

Laurel, B. (ed.) (1990) *The Art of Human–Computer Interface Design.* New York: Addison-Wesley

Light, H.R. *The Nature of Management.* Liverpool: Pitman.

Lucas, H.C. Jr (1974) *Toward Creative Systems Design.* New York: Columbia University Press.

McGregor, R.D.D. (1985) *Redefining Policies for the Growing Information Center.* Nashville TN: Information Center Conference and Exposition, August.

Marfleet, B. (1991a) Methodologies – making accurate cost estimates. *Computing Canada,* June.

Marfleet, B. (1991b) Incorporating design changes. *Computing Canada,* 15 August

Management, Measurement and Estimation

Miles, R. (1990) Project management. *Computing,* 11 October.

Myers, G.J. (1979) *The Art of Software Testing.* New York: John Wiley & Sons.

Nissen, H.W. The nature of the drive as innate determinant of behaviourial organization.

Olive, A. *Analysis of Conceptual and Logical Models in Information Systems Design Methodologies.* Facultat d'Informatica, Universitat Politecnica de Barcelona.

Quick, T.L. *Inspiring People at Work.* Executive Enterprises Publishing Co.

Scacchi, W. (1984) Managing software engineering projects: a social analysis. *IEEE Transactions on Software Engineering,* January.

Scott, W.G. and Mitchell, T.R. *Organization Theory: A Structural and Behavioural Analysis.* Homewood IL: Richard D. Irwin, Inc.

Shaw, J.C. and Atkins, W. *Managing Computer Systems Projects.* New York: McGraw-Hill.

Sloma, R.S. (1984) *No Nonsense Planning.* New York: Free Press.

Stanley, F.J. (1983) *Establishing a Project Management Methodology.* Pennsauken NJ: Auerbach Publishers Inc.

Stokes Jr and Stewart, L. (1991) Climbing the new IS corporate ladder, Auerbach. *Information Strategy,* Summer.

Taylor, F.W. (1923) *The Principles of Scientific Management.* New York: Harper.

Theodore. *Applied Mathematics, an Introduction.* Homewood IL: Richard D. Irwin Inc.

Walsh, M. (1990) *A Common Sense Way to Introduce Case Technology.* Toronto: NOW.

Whiteside, L.W. *Effective Management Techniques for Getting Things Done.* West Nyack NY: Parker Publishing Company Inc.

Yourdon, E. (1982) *Managing the System Life Cycle: A Software Development Methodology Overview.* New York: Yourdon Press.

Index

DATE DUE